THE REFERENCE SHELF   VOLUME 40 NUMBER 4

CRIME AND
ITS PREVENTION

EDITED BY
STEPHEN LEWIN

Managing Editor, World Week Magazine

THE H. W. WILSON COMPANY
NEW YORK   1968

THE REFERENCE SHELF

The books in this series contain reprints of articles, excerpts from books, and addresses on current issues and social trends in the United States and other countries. There are six separately bound numbers in each volume, all of which are generally published in the same calendar year. One number is a collection of recent speeches; each of the others is devoted to a single subject and gives background information and discussion from various points of view, concluding with a comprehensive bibliography. Books in the series may be purchased individually or on subscription.

CRIME AND ITS PREVENTION

Copyright © 1968
By The H. W. Wilson Company

First Printing 1968

Second Printing 1970

Third Printing 1973

International Standard Book Number 0-8242-0103-5
Library of Congress Catalog Card Number 68-17131

PRINTED IN THE UNITED STATES OF AMERICA

PREFACE

There are no easy explanations for the phenomena collectively called crime. Crime is a deceiving concept because it covers an enormous range of human behavior. Crime may be associated in the public mind with muggings, burglaries, and riots, but crime is also a businessman placing a bribe to win a city contract. It is also a syndicate-controlled loan shark taking over a business from a businessman who couldn't meet the exorbitant repayment schedule. It is a quiet student who suddenly takes a rifle to the top of a university tower and begins shooting at those below. Trying to find a single comprehensive answer to "the crime problem" is, as the President's Crime Commission has noted, like trying to lump together measles and schizophrenia, or lung cancer and a broken leg.

Crime is often mistakenly thought of as the vice of the few. It is not. About 40 per cent of all U.S. males will be arrested for a nontraffic offense during their lifetimes. A recent poll found that 91 per cent of a representative sample of Americans admitted that they had at one time committed acts for which they might have been imprisoned.

Clearly, then, crime is not just the responsibility of the police, the courts, and the prisons. Crime cannot be controlled without the active support of individual private citizens, schools, businesses, and labor unions. This is so because crime has its effect on everyone—not just the criminal and his victim. The fear of crime has affected basic patterns of life for many Americans. A recent study in two large American cities, quoted by the President's Crime Commission, found that 43 per cent said they stayed off streets at night. About 35 per cent said they do not speak to strangers any more because of their fear of crime. This pervasive fear of crime appears to have eroded the quality of life for many Americans.

This book is an attempt to tie together the various strands of "the crime problem" and to explain problems in law enforcement, punishment, and crime prevention. The first two sections are devoted to a discussion of crime itself: first, individual, unorganized crime or "crime in the streets," as many Americans think of it; next, organized crime. The third section discusses the lot of the policeman; the fourth, the role of the courts. The last section examines various suggestions for halting the steadily increasing crime rate.

The editor would like to thank the various authors, editors, and publishers who granted permission for the use of material included in this book. He also wants to add his special appreciation to his wife, Deirdre, who assisted greatly in the preparation of this manuscript.

STEPHEN LEWIN

August 1968

CONTENTS

I. CRIME IN THE STREETS

EDITOR'S INTRODUCTION

The apparent spread of crime throughout the United States poses a crucial problem to society. In many U.S. cities crime rates are rising, and fear is rising at a faster rate. "Crime in the streets" has become a major political issue. People have moved out of their old homes into "safer" neighborhoods; facilities open at night find participation down because people are afraid to come out at night.

Broadly, "crime in the streets" may be said to include any unorganized crime. It covers a broad spectrum, ranging from mugging and robbery to juvenile delinquency, spontaneous crimes of violence, and car theft.

The first article in this section explains just how broad a field "crime" is. It is an excerpt from the report of the President's Commission on Law Enforcement and the Administration of Justice. The report is an indispensable source of information for anyone who wishes to study crime in the United States. The second selection, "Crime and Lawlessness" is excerpted from an article in *Senior Scholastic*. It examines the growing public climate of fear that is one of the most striking results of the increasing crime rates.

Most city dwellers will be well aware of the type of crime discussed in the third selection. Free-lance writer John Bowers, writing in *Harper's Magazine*, examines the soaring rate of burglary in the nation's cities. The next selection is excerpted from an interview with Professor Sheldon Glueck and his wife Eleanor, both of them eminent criminologists on the faculty of the Harvard Law School. This is followed by an article on drug addiction and crime by Dr. Charles Winick, director of the American Social Health Association's Program in Drug Dependence and Abuse. The next selection, a *Time* magazine essay, addresses itself to the question: Is the United States a violent society? The final selection, from the New York *Times*, presents the text of President Johnson's statement to the members of his newly appointed commission to investigate violence in the United States.

THE CHALLENGE OF CRIME IN A FREE SOCIETY [1]

There is much crime in America, more than ever is reported, far more than ever is solved, far too much for the health of the nation. Every American knows that. Every American is, in a sense, a victim of crime. Violence and theft have not only injured, often irreparably, hundreds of thousands of citizens, but have directly affected everyone. Some people have been impelled to uproot themselves and find new homes. Some have been made afraid to use public streets and parks. Some have come to doubt the worth of a society in which so many people behave so badly. Some have become distrustful of the government's ability, or even desire, to protect them. Some have lapsed into the attitude that criminal behavior is normal human behavior and consequently have become indifferent to it, or have adopted it as a good way to get ahead in life. Some have become suspicious of those they conceive to be responsible for crime: adolescents or Negroes or drug addicts or college students or demonstrators; policemen who fail to solve crimes; judges who pass lenient sentences or write decisions restricting the activities of the police; parole boards that release prisoners who resume their criminal activities.

The most understandable mood into which many Americans have been plunged by crime is one of frustration and bewilderment. For "crime" is not a single simple phenomenon that can be examined, analyzed, and described in one piece. It occurs in every part of the country and in every

[1] From the report of the President's Commission on Law Enforcement and Administration of Justice. *The Challenge of Crime in a Free Society*. Supt. of Docs. Washington, D.C. 20402. '67. p 1-15.

stratum of society. Its practitioners and its victims are people of all ages, incomes and backgrounds. Its trends are difficult to ascertain. Its causes are legion. Its cures are speculative and controversial. An examination of any single kind of crime, let alone of "crime in America," raises a myriad of issues of the utmost complexity.

Consider the crime of robbery, which, since it involves both stealing and violence or the threat of it, is an especially hurtful and frightening one. In 1965 in America there were 118,916 robberies known to the police: 326 robberies a day; a robbery for every 1,630 Americans. Robbery takes dozens of forms, but suppose it took only four: forcible or violent purse-snatching by boys, muggings by drug addicts, store stickups by people with a sudden desperate need for money, and bank robberies by skillful professional criminals. The technical, organizational, legal, behavioral, economic and social problems that must be addressed if America is to deal with any degree of success with just those four kinds of events and those four kinds of persons are innumerable and refractory.

The underlying problems are ones that the criminal justice system can do little about. The unruliness of young people, widespread drug addiction, the existence of much poverty in a wealthy society, the pursuit of the dollar by any available means are phenomena the police, the courts, and the correctional apparatus, which must deal with crimes and criminals one by one, cannot confront directly. They are strands that can be disentangled from the fabric of American life only by the concerted action of all of society. They concern the Commission [President's Commission on Law Enforcement and Administration of Justice] deeply, for unless society does take concerted action to change the general conditions and attitudes that are associated with crime, no improvement in law enforcement and administration of justice, the subjects this Commission was specifically asked to study, will be of much avail.

No Cure-All

Of the everyday problems of the criminal justice system itself, certainly the most delicate and probably the most difficult concern the proper ways of dealing individually with individuals. Arrest and prosecution are likely to have quite different effects on delinquent boys and on hardened professional criminals. Sentencing occasional robbers and habitual robbers by the same standards is clearly inappropriate. Rehabilitating a drug addict is a procedure that has little in common with rehabilitating a holdup man. In short, there are no general prescriptions for dealing with "robbers." There are no general prescriptions for dealing with "robbery" either. Keeping streets and parks safe is not the same problem as keeping banks secure. Investigating a mugging and tracking down a band of prudent and well-organized bank robbers are two entirely distinct police procedures. The kind of police patrol that will deter boys from street robberies is not likely to deter men with guns from holding up storekeepers. . . .

A skid-row drunk lying in a gutter is crime. So is the killing of an unfaithful wife. A Cosa Nostra conspiracy to bribe public officials is crime. So is a strong-arm robbery by a fifteen-year-old boy. The embezzlement of a corporation's funds by an executive is crime. So is the possession of marihuana cigarettes by a student. These crimes can no more be lumped together for purposes of analysis than can measles and schizophrenia, or lung cancer and a broken ankle. As with disease, so with crime: if causes are to be understood, if risks are to be evaluated, and if preventive or remedial actions are to be taken, each kind must be looked at separately. Thinking of "crime" as a whole is futile.

In any case it is impossible to answer with precision questions about the volume or trends of crime as a whole, or even of any particular kind of crime. Techniques for measuring crime are, and probably always will be imperfect. Successful crime, after all, is secret crime. The best, in fact almost the only, source of statistical information about crime volumes is the *Uniform Crime Reports* of the FBI. The UCR is the product of a nationwide system of crime reporting that the FBI has painstakingly developed over the years. Under this system local police agencies report the offenses they know of to the FBI; the UCR is a compilation of these reports. This compilation can be no better than the underlying information that local agencies supply to the FBI. And because the FBI has induced local agencies to improve their reporting methods year by year, it is important to distinguish better reporting from more crime.

What the UCR shows is a rise in the number of individual crimes over the years at a rate faster than the rise in America's population. It shows an especially rapid rise in crimes against property. Furthermore, Commission surveys of the experience of the public as victims of crime show that there is several times as much crime against both property and persons as is reported to the police. Even in the areas having the highest rates of crime in our large cities, the surveys suggested that citizens are victimized several times as often as official records indicate. As might be expected, crimes the public regards as most serious, particularly those involving violence, are generally better reported than less serious crimes.

While it is impossible to offer absolute statistical proof that every year there are more crimes per American than there were the year before, both available statistics and the facts of social change in America suggest that there are. . . .

Crime and Fear

The most damaging of the effects of violent crime is fear, and that fear must not be belittled. Suddenly becoming the object of a stranger's violent hostility is as frightening as any class of experience. A citizen who hears rapid footsteps behind him as he walks down a dark and otherwise deserted street cannot be expected to calculate that the chance of those footsteps having a sinister meaning is only one in a hundred or in a thousand or, if he does make such a calculation, to be calmed by its results. Any chance at all is frightening. And, in fact, when Commission interviewers asked a sample of citizens what they would do in just such a situation, the majority replied, "Run as fast as I could or call for help." Commission studies in several cities indicate that just this kind of fear has impelled hundreds of thousands of Americans to move their homes or change their habits. . . .

Two striking facts that the UCR and every other examination of American crime disclose are that most crimes, wherever they are committed, are committed by boys and young men, and that most crimes, by whomever they are committed, are committed in cities. Three quarters of the 1965 arrests for Index crimes, plus petty larceny and negligent manslaughter, were of people less than twenty-five years old. [Index crimes—murder, nonnegligent manslaughter, forcible rape, robbery, aggravated assault, burglary, larceny ($50 or more), and auto theft—are the offenses which make up the FBI crime index.—Ed.] More fifteen-year-olds were arrested for those crimes than people of any other age, and sixteen-year-olds were a close second. Of 2,780,015 "offenses known to the police" in 1965—these were Index crimes—some 2 million occurred in cities, more than half a million occurred in the suburbs, and about 170,000 occurred in rural areas. The number of city crimes per hundred thousand residents was over 1,800, the suburban rate was almost 1,200, and the rural rate was 616.9. In short, crime is evidently associated with two powerful social trends: the increasing urbanization of America and the increasing numerousness, restlessness, and restiveness of American youth. The two trends are not separate and distinct, of course. They are entangled with each other in many ways, and both are entangled with another trend, increasing affluence, that also appears to be intimately associated with crime. An abundance of material goods provides an abundance of motives and opportunities for stealing, and stealing is the fastest growing kind of crime.

For as long as crime statistics of any kind have been compiled, they have shown that males between the ages of fifteen and twenty-four are the most crime-prone group in the population. For the last five years, as the result of the "baby boom" that took place after the Second World War, the fifteen—twenty-four age group has been the fastest growing group in the population.

The fact that young people make up a larger part of the population than they did ten years ago accounts for some of the recent increase in crime. This group will continue to grow disproportionately for at least fifteen years more. And so it is probable that crime will continue to increase during this period, unless there are drastic changes in general social and economic conditions and in the effectiveness of the criminal justice system. However, population changes cannot be shown to account for all of the increase that is reported in juvenile and youth crime, nor can the probability that police reporting is more complete every year account for the increase. Moreover, there have been marked improvements in police efficiency and correctional resourcefulness in many localities in recent years, which, all other things being equal, might have reduced crime. It may be that young people are not only more numerous than ever, but more crime prone; it is impossible to be sure.

What appears to be happening throughout the country, in the cities and in the suburbs, among the poor and among the well-to-do, is that parental, and especially paternal, authority over young people is becoming weaker. The community is accustomed to rely upon this force as one guarantee that children will learn to fit themselves into society in an orderly and peaceable manner, that the natural and valuable rebelliousness of young people will not express itself in the form of warring violently on society or any of its members. The programs and activities of almost every kind of social institution with which children come in contact—schools, churches, social-service agencies, youth organizations—are predicated on the assumption that children acquire their fundamental attitudes toward life, their moral standards, in their homes. The social institutions provide children with many opportunities: to learn, to worship, to play, to socialize, to secure expert help in solving a variety of problems.

However, offering opportunities is not the same thing as providing moral standards. The community's social institutions have so far not found ways to give young people the motivation to live moral lives; some of them have not even recognized their duty to seek for such ways. Young people who have not received strong and loving parental guidance, or whose experience leads them to believe that all of society is callous at best, or a racket at worst, tend to be unmotivated people, and therefore people with whom the community is most unprepared to cope. Much more to the point, they are people who are unprepared to cope with the many ambiguities and lacks that they find in the community. Boredom corrodes ambition and cynicism corrupts those with ethical sensitivity.

Gap Between Ideals and Achievements

That there are all too many ambiguities and lacks in the community scarcely needs prolonged demonstration. Poverty and racial discrimination, bad housing and commercial exploitation, the enormous gap between American ideals and American achievements, and the many distressing consequences and implications of these conditions are national failings that are widely recognized. Their effects on young people have been greatly aggravated by the technological revolution of the last two decades, which has greatly reduced the market for unskilled labor. A job, earning one's own living, is probably the most important factor in making a person independent and making him responsible. Today, education is a prerequisite for all but the most menial jobs; a great deal of education is a prerequisite for really promising ones.

And so there are two continually growing groups of discontented young people: those whose capacity or desire for becoming educated has not been developed by their homes or schools (or both), and who therefore are unemployed or even unemployable; and those whose entry into the adult working world has been delayed by the necessity of continuing their studies long past the point at which they have become physically and psychologically adult. Young people today are sorely discontented in the suburbs and on the campuses as well as in the slums.

However, there is no doubt that they more often express this discontent criminally in the slums. So do older people. It is not hard to understand why. The conditions of life there, economic and social, conspire to make crime not only easy to engage in but easy to invent justifications for. A man who lives in the country or in a small town is likely to be conspicuous, under surveillance by his community so to speak, and therefore under its control. A city man is often almost invisible, socially isolated from his neighborhood and therefore incapable of being controlled by it. He has more opportunities for crime. At the same time in a city, much more than in a small community, he rubs constantly, abrasively, and impersonally against other people; he is likely to live his life unnoticed and unrespected, his hopes unfulfilled. He can fall easily into resentment against his neighbors and against society, into a feeling that he is in a jungle where force and cunning are the only means of survival. There have always been slums in the cities, and they have always been places where there was the most crime. What has made this condition even more menacing in recent years is that the slums, with all their squalor and turbulence, have more and more become ghettos, neighborhoods in which racial minorities are sequestered with little chance of escape. People who, though declared by the law to be equal, are prevented by society from improving their circumstances, even when they have the ability and the desire to do so, are people with extraordinary strains on their respect for the law and society.

It is with the young people and the slum dwellers who have been embittered by these painful social and economic pressures that the criminal justice system preponderantly deals. Society insists that individuals are responsible for their actions, and the criminal process operates on that assumption. However, society has not devised ways for ensuring that all its members have the ability to assume responsibility. It has let too many of them grow up untaught, unmotivated, unwanted. The criminal justice system has a great potential for dealing with individual instances of crime, but it was not designed to eliminate the conditions in which most crime breeds. It needs help. Warring on poverty, inadequate housing and unemployment, is warring on crime. A civil rights law is a law against crime. Money for schools is money against crime. Medical, psychiatric, and family-counseling services are services against crime. More broadly and most importantly, every effort to improve life in America's "inner cities" is an effort against crime. A community's most enduring protection against crime is to right the wrongs and cure the illnesses that tempt men to harm their neighbors.

Finally, no system, however well-staffed or organized, no level of material well-being for all, will rid a society of crime if there is not a widespread ethical motivation, and a widespread belief that by and large the government and the social order deserve credence, respect and loyalty.

CRIME AND LAWLESSNESS: WHOSE RESPONSIBILITY? [2]

The man works as a building guard. And he certainly doesn't look anything like a ninety-seven-pound weakling. Yet the words he used to describe his neighborhood on Manhattan's West Side in New York City were words of fear.

"Everybody in the neighborhood is scared to death to go out at night. . . . I live over on Amsterdam Avenue. . . . I wouldn't go out after eight. . . . I'm not a kid, but I've been

[2] From "Crime and Lawlessness: Who's to Blame, the Police or the Public? *Senior Scholastic*. 92:4-9. F. 15, '68. Reprinted by permission from *Senior Scholastic*, © 1968 by Scholastic Magazines, Inc.

mugged already." Whereupon he flipped over his arm to show an ugly knife scar on his arm.

One man describing one neighborhood in one city? Yes—and no. For similar words have been used to describe similar conditions in other neighborhoods in other communities—in cities, in suburbs, or in small towns.

In a recent nationwide survey conducted for a presidential crime study commission, for example, one third of a representative sampling of Americans stated that it was not safe to walk alone at night in their own neighborhoods. In a related, more detailed study of four specific police precincts in Boston and Chicago, 43 per cent of those polled said they stayed off the streets at night, 35 per cent said they do not speak to strangers any more, 20 per cent said they would like to move to another neighborhood—all because of their fear of crime and violence.

Recent statements by public officials at all levels of government have begun to reflect a mounting public uneasiness over crime.

Fear haunts . . . too many American communities [observed President Johnson during ceremonies in 1967 to swear in Ramsey Clark as United States Attorney General]. It assails us all, no matter where we live, no matter how little we own. We fear for our person, we fear for our property, and we fear for our privacy.

America cannot tolerate enduringly this climate of fear. . . . Our streets, our parks, our businesses, and our homes ought to be, should be, and must be made safe. We should be able to greet a stranger as a friend, not as a threat.

The President hit on this theme again . . . [in January 1968] during his State of the Union Message to Congress. "Now we at every level of government—state, local, and Federal—know that the American people have had enough of rising crime and lawlessness in this country," he said.

And in this national election year, when partisan spirits run high, it was probably significant that both Democrats and Republicans in the congressional audience joined in shouts of approval at this point in the President's speech.

"Crime in the streets" is sure to be a prime issue in this year's [1968] campaign, just as it was in 1964 when Republican presidential candidate Barry Goldwater struck hard on the issue.

Clearly, then, Americans have crime on their minds, and the public appears to be getting desperate for answers. But *is* there really a rise in crime and lawlessness in the United States? *Is* the "moral climate" in America declining, as many have charged? Are we more prone toward violence, more disrespectful toward the law than ever before? Has our system of criminal justice become so entangled in obscure points of law as to endanger the safety of the public?

Or, on the other hand, is the public caught up in some kind of mass hysteria fanned by lurid headlines about isolated incidents or by sweeping generalizations about "crime waves"? Is there any truth in a charge that "election-year oratory is preying on the public's fear of crime for political gains"? Is it possible that we may "over-react" to the crime problem and, in the process, set new limits on our own freedom while trying to control the criminal element in U.S. society? . . .

[The President's Crime Commission] noted that when most Americans think about crime, they are concerned primarily with those which most directly threaten their personal safety and property: the danger of being attacked or robbed while going about their ordinary daily rounds, the risk of burglars breaking into their home, or robbers holding up banks and shopkeepers, or car thieves snatching the family auto, or the fear of being caught up in riots and other civil disturbances. All of these are sometimes conveniently grouped under a general—though not especially accurate—heading of "crime in the streets."

Are America's "streets" turning into a crime-ridden jungle? Practically the only available crime statistics on a national basis are the *Uniform Crime Reports* (UCR) issued each August by the Federal Bureau of Investigation. The UCR, however, concentrate on only seven types of serious crimes that the FBI regards as general indicators of the U.S. crime situation. These seven: murder and nonnegligent manslaughter (a homicide that is neither intended nor attributed to negligence; for example, if a night watchman catches a safe cracker and the watchman is killed in an ensuing scuffle, the safe cracker has committed nonnegligent manslaughter—in addition to burglary, of course), forcible rape, robbery, aggravated assault, burglary, larceny of $50 or more, and motor vehicle theft.

If the UCR figures are to be taken at face value, then those who are concerned about crime in America *do* have plenty to worry about. The most recent edition of the UCR, issued last summer and covering the year 1966, listed a total of 3,243,400 reported crimes in the seven categories—a rise of 11.4 per cent over the total for the preceding year. The number of crimes reported went up by 10 per cent over the previous year in the cities and in rural areas. In the suburbs the increase was 13 per cent.

Between 1960 and 1966, observed FBI Director J. Edgar Hoover, the U.S. population grew 9 per cent while the number of reported crimes increased by 62 per cent. Does this mean that the crime rate in the United States is going up almost seven times faster than the population?

Maybe. Then again, maybe not. For many criminologists . . . argue that the UCR figures do not truly reflect the crime situation in the United States. Even the FBI, which stoutly defends the UCR statistics as the best the United States has, readily admits to certain built-in flaws. For the FBI only compiles the UCR totals and must depend on local law enforcement agencies to supply the raw statistics. Despite the Bureau's efforts to set up standards of accuracy in crime reporting, the statistical performance of the local agencies can vary widely from place to place.

Indeed, the FBI admits that a part of the yearly increase in reported crimes, as tabulated in the UCR, is due to generally improving *crime reporting* standards. In 1966, for example, reports of major crimes in New York City went up a

whopping 72 per cent—statistically—over the previous year.
But the city's Police Commissioner, Howard Leary, has ex-
plained that the real rise was 6.5 per cent, and that most of
the statistical jump was due to a change in police recording
procedures. In the past, it was alleged, police precinct com-
manders fudged figures to make their own precincts look
better policed on paper. New York's police commissioner has
put a stop to this practice and has installed a standardized
recording system.

But if the UCR tends to *overstate* any rise in the crime
rate, it also has a tendency to *understate* the total volume of
crimes committed. This is because the UCR lists only crimes
reported to the police. And there is strong evidence to suggest
that many crimes are never reported to the police.

In surveys of high and medium crime areas in three large
cities conducted for the Presidential Crime Commission, researchers found that burglaries were three and a half times
the reported rate. Forcible rapes were three times higher,
aggravated assaults and larcenies more than double, and robberies 50 per cent greater than the reported rate. The reason
most frequently given for not reporting crimes to police was
some variation of "what's done is done, and the police can't
do much about it now." In some cases failure to report crimes
was due to claims that they were "private matters," or for fear
of embarrassing the victims, or a fear of reprisal.

The point is that there is no way yet to prove conclusively
—at least not with available statistics—that the United States
is experiencing a crime wave. Nor does anyone really know
how much crime there is in the United States. Nevertheless,
in the best judgment of the Presidential Crime Commission:
"There *is* much crime in America, more than ever is reported,
far more than ever is solved, far too much for the health of
the nation."

Furthermore, it is of little comfort for the citizen who
must walk the streets to know that, statistically, his chances
of becoming a victim of a serious crime are one in fifty according to the FBI—especially if he feels that he is about to

become that one in fifty. Even those who doubt that there has been a significant rise in the United States crime rate concede that the average person is more jittery than ever about becoming a victim of violence. In part, some believe, this may be due to the many widely publicized incidents of violence in the United States in recent years—from the assassination of a President to a whole series of particularly senseless mass killings. Some are shaken by the violence and sadism portrayed in many of today's most popular books and movies. Some also attribute the growing public awareness of violence in the United States to the impact of TV reporting, which can bring all the anger and gory violence of recent city riots into every living room—and in "living color" yet. . . .

Does this fear of crime restrict the activities of great numbers of Americans? A survey team from the University of Michigan found that library use is decreasing because book borrowers are afraid to come out at night. School officials report that some parents dare not attend PTA meetings in the evening, and park officials point sadly to unused public recreational facilities.

Moreover, some sociologists believe that the mutual distrust fostered by fear of crime may be breeding a curious type of individual detachment toward crime, particularly in the larger United States cities. Numerous news reports in recent years have told of bystanders refusing to heed cries for help from crime victims, or of witnesses failing to go to the aid of policemen being assaulted, or even refusing to call the police while a crime is being committed. All too often the individuals explain their backturning with such words as "I was afraid" or "it was none of my business." . . . The upshot is that, as the level of concern for one another declines, streets and public places can become more dangerous than ever. . . .

Protector or Oppressor?

Which brings us to the other side of the coin: what are the public attitudes toward law enforcement and especially toward its most obvious symbol—the policeman? Volumes have been written on the psychological "love-hate" attitudes of the public toward the police. On the one hand, the policeman is the great protector, the man who stops criminals from giving us a rap on the head or worse. On the other hand, he's the great oppressor, the cop who hands out the ticket when we are caught speeding ("Who, me, officer?").

In addition, there is no way to judge the competence of the police on a national basis. In some areas police departments are models of efficiency while in other areas police protection is admitted to be woefully inadequate. That police effectiveness, equipment, and morale can vary all over the lot is not surprising in a country where police protection is traditionally regarded as a local responsibility. All movements toward a national police force have generally been opposed as steps toward a police state.

Confidence in the ability of the police to control crime seems to depend a lot on whether the person being asked is a member of the white majority or of a racial minority group. A National Opinion Research poll conducted for the Crime Commission showed that 23 per cent of the whites polled believe the police do an "excellent" job in law enforcement, while 7 per cent said the police do a "poor" job. Among non-whites polled, 15 per cent gave the police an "excellent" rating while 16 per cent said "poor." (All the rest expressed some opinion between these two extremes or no opinion.) On the question of police conduct, 63 per cent of the whites polled said they believe the police are "almost all honest" and only 1 per cent said the police are "almost all corrupt." Comparable figures among the nonwhites polled were 30 per cent and 10 per cent. This striking division of opinions, of course, reflects the complexities of race relations in the United States. . . .

More widespread, perhaps, is a belief that the core of the U.S. crime problem lies not so much in any police ineptness as in legal shackles that often prevent the police from acting as effectively as they might. "When you call the police, they come fast," a shopkeeper in New York City told a reporter recently. But then try prosecuting a wrongdoer, he went on. "The whole trouble is that they took the power away from the police. The people know this and the muggers know this. Can you blame people for getting discouraged and frightened?"

The "they" who allegedly took the power away from the police, according to this view, are the courts in general and the United States Supreme Court in particular. In recent years, the Supreme Court has handed down a series of controversial rulings, many of them in close 5-to-4 decisions. These rulings have dealt with proper police arrest procedures and with what evidence may be admitted at trials. . . . They sought to guarantee fair trials under the principle that the accused is innocent until proven guilty.

While hardly anyone suggests that the United States Bill of Rights be scrapped, many have charged that liberal judges have leaned so far over to protect the rights of accused individuals that the safety of the general public has been jeopardized. "In court cases," says District Attorney Michael F. Dillon of Erie County (New York), the whole proceeding has come "to be directed to how the police conducted themselves rather than whether the defendant committed the crime for which he is charged." In turn, this has left an impression in the minds of many that criminals are escaping justice through legal technicalities and finagling.

Others, however, say that pinning the blame on the courts is just a convenient way to skirt the whole crime issue. "Changes in court decisions and prosecution procedures have about the same effect on crime rates as an aspirin would have on a brain tumor," asserts David Acheson, former United States Attorney for the District of Columbia. Attorney General Clark agrees. "Court rules do not cause crimes. People do not commit crimes . . . because they feel they will not be convicted. We as a people commit crimes because we . . . *choose* to commit crimes."

If nothing else, this debate shows that "combating crime" is a great deal more complicated than simply being "against crime.". . .

At issue are some thoroughly sticky questions: How much police power is necessary to control crime and to maintain an orderly—yet free—society? At what point do police powers seriously encroach on the civil rights of the very citizens that such powers are supposed to be protecting?

These questions pop into just about every phase of the crime debate—whether it involves the right of law enforcement agencies to engage in wiretapping, or gun-control laws, or the rights of citizens to express dissent through protest. . . .

On the one hand, there are those calling on the police to take tougher action against lawlessness in the streets. "There is a war in the streets between the lawless and the law-abiding citizens," said Miami (Florida) Police Chief Walter Headley in announcing that his department would have little inhibition against using shotguns and police dogs against rioters. "My men are getting tired of felons being bailed out of jail so quickly that they beat the arresting officer back to his zone. Felons are going to learn that they can't be bonded out of a morgue."

On the other hand, there are those who contend that police toughness, particularly in ghetto areas, will only breed counterviolence. Attorney General Clark argues that crime is mainly caused by social and economic conditions and that harsh police measures may actually increase lawlessness by angering minority groups. Many civil rights leaders, indeed, view talk of tough police crackdowns as a thinly disguised threat to stifle Negro protest against social injustices.

While most people recognize that the police stand at the front line of the fight against crime, some doubt that the basic crime problem can be solved simply through more policing. "The responsibility of crime is not exclusively a police matter," says New York's Police Commissioner Leary. "The police are neither guarantors nor insurers of social behavior.

. . . We can offer no panacea. To look to the police for a miracle cure for the twisted criminal mind is to flirt with fantasy and ignore reality," for the "causes" of crime are deeply rooted in all social problems—and just as varied. . . .

In the end, control of crime remains with the public. The victim of all crime, ultimately, is society. The public and society? Those are just other names for us—all of us together.

BIG CITY THIEVES [3]

On a recent afternoon a secretary employed at the United Nations returned to her top-floor, brownstone apartment to find that it had been burglarized—or burgled, as they say in New York. Missing were her TV, a quantity of jewelry, a fur coat, her good dresses, her best suitcase, and a colorful bedspread. A psychologist in a brownstone down the block had also had his apartment ransacked. Clothes, books, and kitchen spices were strewn over the floor in someone's frantic search for cash. Even the ice-cube trays from the refrigerator had been emptied. Entry in both cases had been by way of a jimmy applied to the front door.

The police were polite, sympathetic, and said, "Probably junkies." They asked some routine questions, pointed out that drop-bolt locks should be installed, and took down the missing items. To date, the thief or thieves have not been caught nor the stolen property recovered.

Since 1960 burglary in New York has increased by 40 per cent to a high in 1965 of 50,106 cases. In the first quarter of 1966 the average rose to more than 5,000 a month, or roughly one every 10 minutes, 24 hours a day. Of more than $33 million taken in 1965, police were able to return only $699,000. Rates for theft insurance have become practically prohibitive, and if a New Yorker hasn't been robbed himself, he has several friends and neighbors who have. . . .

[3] From an article by free-lance writer John Bowers. *Harper's Magazine*. 234: 50-4. F. '67. Copyright © 1967 by Harper's Magazine, Inc. Reprinted from the February, 1967 issue of *Harper's Magazine* by permission of the author.

At 400 Broome Street, on the seventh floor, are the old, musty offices of the Safe, Loft, and Burglary Squad. Detective Robert McDermott, a polite, crew-cut man with a gun on his hip, has been on the Squad more than ten years, and is an expert on burglars. He described to me the different types of housebreakers. The "door shaker" merely enters an apartment house or hotel and begins turning door knobs until he finds one that is unlocked. A "punch-and-grab" man uses a jimmy to force open weak locks, although he may sometimes punch out the lock cylinder or unscrew it with vise-grip pliers. A "loid" expert wiggles a celluloid or piece of Venetian blind strip in a door crack to open a spring lock. Those who sneak in through fire-escape windows, swing down from ropes to get in top-floor windows, or jump from one balcony to another are called "aerialists" and are nimble and usually slight men. If the aerialist is exceptionally agile and brave, he may become a "step-over" thief, one who steps from a fire escape or ledge to a nearby open window. Many New Yorkers have illegally locked metal gates over their fire-escape windows, only to return home one evening to find that a step-over thief has come in through an adjoining and unlocked window.

These types of burglars are nearly always young drug addicts, and account for the bulk of break-ins in New York. An addict usually begins stealing from relatives and friends, and then progresses to the outside world. A door shaker, the most unskilled of apartment burglars, may learn from another addict how to loid a door or use a jimmy. And a novice may be recruited as an aerialist or step-over thief. But no known addict in New York has ever gone on to become what the police call a professional....

The addict burglar looks for cash first thing in an apartment, frequently in whirlwind style. Finding none, he takes items that can be quickly sold through fences—good clothing, radio, TV. If the apartment has a doorman, he takes the items out through a basement exit. Otherwise, he strides with a confident air out the front door. Recently a woman coming in her West Side apartment house held the front door open for a young man going out with a TV set that looked familiar and a pillowcase full of clothing. He smiled, thanked her, and caught a cab. He had just burgled her apartment.

Most apartment burglaries are committed during daylight hours when the tenants are at work. A skilled burglar tries to make absolutely sure no one is inside before he breaks in. He calls from a corner phone booth, rings the doorbell several times, and has an alibi handy if challenged. Occasionally he gets tips from the neighbors about people on vacation. Some burglars follow obituaries and wedding announcements for tip-offs as to when apartments will be deserted. Not long ago a well-to-do couple unexpectedly got tickets through the mail for a hit musical. Thinking it a gift from friends, they went and enjoyed it, but returned to find that their apartment had been burglarized.

Thieves become accustomed to working certain areas, to using particular methods, and develop what the police call an "M.O." (*modus operandi*). One New York addict has been keeping a $40-a-day habit going by stealing nothing but paintbrushes. He has a good fence who gives him 75 cents a brush, and he can steal around a hundred a day. A pocketbook thief works around Times Square from 10:00 A.M. until 2:00 P.M. every day, clearing an average of $30 to $35. "He doesn't know why he chose those hours or the area," a social worker, who has dealt with him, says. "And he can't say why he steals. He claims he doesn't really like to, and wants to quit." (Purse snatchers often return purses after removing the valuables by dropping them in mailboxes or leaving them in apartment lobbies or on stairways. Youths who siphon gas from parked cars sometimes will leave enough for the owner to drive to a filling station. In both cases it could be consideration or it could be not wanting the victim to complain too hotly to the police.)

Women thieves idle through department stores, leaning over in split-second timing to drop merchandise down into outsized slacks. Male boosters shove suits inside their trench coats while an accomplice distracts the salesman's eye. At night panel trucks sweep through the streets—with a man in the rear who lifts parked scooters inside. In the garment center thieves scurry through the lofts, cutting half-dollar-sized holes in protective tarpaulins and using coat hangers to extract dresses from them. A "seat tipper" in a theater dislodges a purse from the seat in front of him with a tap of his toe, extracts the money, and then nudges the purse back in place. Sneak thieves in the guise of delivery boys or tradesmen dart through offices during lunch hours, on the outlook for purses and watches. . . .

"Rip" Man, "Burn" Man

The Safe, Loft, and Burglary Squad keeps folders on all known burglars, past and present. There is a picture of the man, usually a police photograph, and miscellaneous facts about him. One broad-faced man with thick lips was described as a burglar of safes. His method varied from peeling back the protective shield (a "rip" man) to going in via an acetylene torch ("burn" man). His police dossier included his favorite bars, his barbershop, his associates, girl friends, and general way of life ("lives in West Side rooming houses and reads detective magazines"). "If there's a safe burglary that looks like the work of this man," said Detective McDermott, "then we put a tail on him. Most of our work begins as surveillance. Once we bring them in, we have to have evidence."

Another folder showed a smiling, dark-haired man in an outdoor summertime pose (a nonpolice photo), and had much information on him.

This guy is a very successful businessman out in Queens. Owns a couple of dry-cleaning places. But, you know, every so often he gets together with some buddies and they go out of town to pull these big jewel heists. They'll fly to L.A. or Miami one morning, make their score in the afternoon or evening, and jet back home by bedtime. That's his M.O. But don't use his name, please. We got a tail on him right now.

A "pick" man is one who can open locks with wire and a tiny metal tool that has a hook on the end. He is highly skilled, having learned his trade from another burglar or from a locksmith school. A famed burglar named William MacLaren broke into business establishments by drilling a minute hole in the door lock. He covered the spot later with a gold-colored substance that was impossible to detect by the naked eye.

That was his M.O. [said Detective McDermott]. Once inside he could open a safe with the touch of his fingers. Well, a few years back we got a rash of safe burglaries we couldn't explain. Not all the money was taken, no marks were on the safe, and it looked like cases of embezzlement. Then under very close examination we found these tiny drill holes on the outside door locks. That was MacLaren's M.O., and he was currently on parole. We put a tail on him, caught him in the act, and he confessed to all the other burglaries. Funny thing, we caught him in the very same store on Fifth Avenue that we had caught him in before. . . .

Since skilled professional thieves are more than a handful for the Safe, Loft, and Burglary Squad, who takes care of the drug-addicted thieves, whose number has been estimated at anywhere from 23,000 to 100,000 in New York? Unless rich (some are), a male addict must steal to keep his habit going and a female must turn to prostitution. Detectives assigned to precinct squads try to keep burglaries by drug addicts under control, but most admit guardedly that it's too big a problem for them to handle.

"Look, I had three homicides in my area over the weekend," a West Side detective told me. "I have to check them out before I start after the guy stealing TV sets and pocket change."

"Back in the old days," an East Side detective told me wistfully, "we could pick up a guy on suspicion. Now, under the search-and-seizure law we have to have airtight evidence, and it's pretty hard for us to operate."

P——is a New Yorker in his early thirties who has been using heroin since the age of fourteen and has never held a job in his life. He has burglarized untold apartments, boosted countless merchandise from department stores, and once held up a filling station in New Jersey. One recent evening I talked to him in a Greenwich Village apartment. He wore T-shirt, tight khaki trousers, and high-top basketball shoes. Beside him sat his girl friend—a languid and very pretty redhead—whom he called Baby.

I always like to have a key when I *geese* [burglarize] a place, [said P——] and you'd be surprised at all the ways you can come by that key. The other day a guy sold me the key to this model's apartment and told me the hours she would be away. You see, he'd been living with her a while back and hadn't returned the key. So I slip in there, steal furs, wigs, and money, and then I break a back window to make her think someone had broken in that way. But that guy who sold me the key! Man, you'd be surprised at the larceny in people's hearts. I got a habit. I got an excuse.

A few people had paid him to burglarize their apartments and then had split the insurance money with him. . . .

One of the most lucrative dodges today, P—— said, is stealing credit cards. He also told about carting off telephones from apartments. "They can bring about twenty-five dollars in the market. You can't overlook anything that'll bring money." (One junkie he knows in the suburbs specializes in stealing bicycles, even while youngsters are pedaling away on them.) P—— never keeps much money ahead, although surprisingly he has been able to go to Paris twice. Not so surprisingly, he has also been to the Tombs, the City Prison of Manhattan for Men, twice.

"Both times I took Article Nine," P—— said. "That's when the bulls have you on a burglary rap, and you sign to go to a hospital to be cured of addiction. Most addicts take Article Nine, and then go right back to drugs when they get out."

WHY YOUNG PEOPLE GO BAD [4]

Q. Professor and Mrs. Glueck, is poverty at the root of juvenile crime in America today?

A. In some cases, yes. Poverty is involved, for instance, in the case of the mother who has to work outside the home in order to support her family.

But poverty, by itself, doesn't make a delinquent. There are working mothers who somehow manage to give their children a good upbringing.

We do not mean to say that the "war on poverty" is not desirable. What we are saying is that, by itself, it will not bring a substantial decrease in delinquency. You cannot make good parents out of bad ones simply by raising their income or moving them into a new house.

You know, some of the most important individuals in America today came out of the slums. In the old days, we often spoke of "the respectable poor."

In Boston, our research investigators could often tell just as soon as a tenement door opened up whether they were entering the home of a delinquent or of a nondelinquent. All the families in the neighborhood would be poor, but there would be enormous variation in the under-the-roof atmosphere from one household to the next.

On the other hand, it is probable that, in a suburban neighborhood of middle income, you could find similar variations.

Q. Even in affluent families?

A. Oh, yes. You can find low standards of behavior and neglected children in well-to-do families. In fact, delinquency seems to be rising in suburban areas, and the causes for it, we think, are basically the same that you find in the slum areas.

There are mothers of ample income who neglect their children just as much as tenement mothers do, and there are

[4] From interview with Professor and Mrs. Sheldon Glueck (Eleanor T. Glueck), eminent criminologists of the Harvard Law School. Reprinted from *U.S. News & World Report*. 58:56-60+. Ap. 26, '65.

fathers who might as well not be there, for all the time they spend with their children. You see the things that count the most in raising children do not depend so much on dollars and cents as they do on the parents' affection. Parental love is not purchasable. And you don't express this love through overindulgence, or by bribing a child with presents to make up for the lack of that parental love and concern day by day.

Q. Could affluence actually cause delinquency?

A. Sometimes it could, where it builds up a never-ending thirst for material things, such as high-powered cars.

One problem of our affluent society is that it has not yet defined a meaningful role for adolescents. Once there were chores around the house to make a child feel important and useful. Adventuresome youngsters could join a sailing ship or head west. There were many outlets for energy and adventure.

Today, the tendency is to hand everything on a platter to the adolescent. Very little effort is required on his part, so he has really become bored with life, in a sense.

Back of all this, however, is the problem of the inadequate parents. Their children, like those in the slums, grow up with a sense of neglect and insecurity—and this is what lays the foundation for delinquency.

Q. At what age does this tendency become evident in the child?

A. That would vary a great deal. Our basic research shows that about 50 per cent of the delinquents we studied began to show clear signs of maladjusted behavior at the age of eight or under. Virtually 90 per cent showed these signs at the age of ten or under.

Now we have found it possible to arrive at some idea of the child's delinquency potential even before those years by identifying certain pathologic aspects of his family life. The studies we have carried out show that this can be done at the school-entering age—between five and a half years and six and a half. At the present time we are working at and, we hope, succeeding in studies to identify predelinquents at an even earlier age, by combining parental factors and certain childhood traits.

Q. Will parents be able to recognize these traits in their preschool youngsters?

A. Perhaps. But a trained observer is needed. A pediatrician, for example, would recognize them if he had some briefing in the relationship of these traits to later delinquency.

Q. What are some of the traits that point to delinquency?

A. Stubbornness, emotional instability, destructiveness, defiance, for example.

Q. Couldn't some of these be found in healthy youngsters?

A. Indeed, they could. However, it is a question of how these characteristics combine in an unfavorable home atmosphere. If a child has only one or two and there is parental affection and understanding, you wouldn't worry. But suppose he has a combination of them together with neglectful and hostile or unconcerned parents. Then you would have a piling up which might lead to aggressive behavior in the years ahead.

Q. Is there a constitutional factor in juvenile misbehavior?

A. In terms of general health, no. Our studies indicate no significant differences in the bodily health of delinquents and nondelinquents.

Nor, we might add, do there seem to be significant differences in basic intelligence, except that delinquents appear to have less capacity in dealing with abstractions and symbols and more "manipulative" capacity—in doing things with their hands—for instance.

The troubles that delinquents often have in their school work stem more from emotional causes than from a lack of intelligence.

What we do find in our studies of delinquents and non-delinquents is some indirect relationship between a child's body structure and predelinquent behavior.

You see, William Sheldon and other authorities in physical anthropology have noted that people can be classified into roughly four types of body structure:

One is the mesomorph. He is the compact, adventurous, energetic type. Shakespeare's shrew-tamer, Petruchio, might be an illustration.

Then there is the ectomorph, who is linear, fragile and rather inclined to be sensitive and reflective. Hamlet might be considered an example of this type.

The third type is the endomorph, who is inclined to be soft and fat and easygoing, like Sir John Falstaff.

Finally, you have a fourth type who combines, in about equal measure, the qualities of the other three.

Now we have found, in comparing 500 persistent delinquents with 500 true nondelinquents, that almost two thirds of the delinquents were mesomorphic, while less than one third of the control sample of nondelinquents had this kind of build.

We might add that the youngsters we studied were first matched in terms of age, intelligence, ethnic or racial derivation, and residence in the extreme slums of the Greater Boston area.

Q. Why are there more mesomorphs than other types among troublemakers? Do delinquents tend to be athletic?

A. The mesomorph is energetic. He is more assertive and less submissive to authority. He is less sensitive than other types. He isn't nearly as inclined as the ectomorph or endomorph to internalize his emotions. Rather, he is uninhibited in his responses.

The mesomorph tends to have fewer emotional conflicts than the other types do.

Q. Would you call such youngsters inherently bad?

A. No, not at all. A large proportion of law-abiding people in the general population are mesomorphs.

What our studies do point to is this: Mesomorphic predelinquents are more energetic than others and, unless this drive is diverted into acceptable channels by parents and teachers, such children are going to seek outlets elsewhere. Rather than accept strictly supervised recreation, they're likely to seek their adventures in railway yards, wharves and junk yards. In classrooms, they are going to rebel if held too tightly in line for long periods of time. They can't sit through an hour without a change.

Actually, however, body structure is only one signpost in the direction of identifying a child's traits that could lead to trouble.

And his likelihood of getting into trouble or staying out of it rests finally with the parents. It is when we look at them that we get our real look at a child's destination.

Q. In what way?

A. When we set out to see if there was a way to predict the likelihood of delinquency in a child or not, we evolved a table based on five factors, as follows:

Affection of the mother for the child
Affection of the father for the child
Supervision of the child by the mother
Discipline by the father
Cohesiveness of the family

By evaluating the performance of the parents in each of these aspects, we could arrive at a total score which would indicate whether or not the youngster was headed for delinquency.

Now, we had to change this table a little more than ten years ago for a study that the New York City Youth Board wanted to make of a selected group of boys, aged five and a half to six and a half. The reason was that the study involved so many families in which the father was absent.

After some experimenting, we found that we could get just as good predictive results by eliminating the factors of the father's affection and discipline. You know, of course, that this does not mean that the father is not important in child rearing.

Well, this study went on for ten years, and just a few months ago it was announced that 84.6 per cent of the youngsters considered, under our predictive table, likely to become delinquent actually did so. And 97 per cent of those thought unlikely to become delinquents did not.

There was a small group of boys whose chances of delinquency were considered about 50-50. In that group, nine actually did become delinquent.

Q. Are you saying, "This child is sure to become delinquent," or "That child will not become delinquent?"

A. Indeed not. We predict the likelihood of delinquency on the assumption that conditions in the home will remain relatively unchanged. Over the years, our position has always been that we are not predicting a child's destiny, but his destination—and his destination can be changed by effective action.

Q. What seems to be causing delinquency to grow so fast nowadays?

A. There are many causes for this. For the most part, however, what we are seeing now is a process that has been going on since the second World War.

First, you have had more and more mothers going to work. Many have left their children more or less unattended, at home or in the streets. This has deprived children of the constant guidance and sense of security they need from their mothers in their early years.

Along with that change, parental attitudes toward disciplining their young have changed quite rapidly. In the home and outside, the trend has been steadily toward more permissiveness—that is, placing fewer restraints and limits on behavior.

Q. Is this permissive trend new?

A. It's not a new trend, really. Today's parents themselves are the products of somewhat permissive parents of the time before the second World War. There was much support for the philosophy of child rearing which said that, since a child is "creative," it should be permitted to experiment more or less at will, and so on.

Well, just how much that philosophy had to do with permissive parenthood can be argued, but many people feel that it started the whole trend toward permissiveness.

Q. How has that philosophy worked out in practice?

A. Not very well, it seems. Life requires a certain amount of discipline. You need it in the classroom, you need it in the home, you need it in society at large. After all, the Ten Commandments impose a discipline. Unless general restraints are built into the character of children, you can arrive eventually at social chaos.

Q. Are you saying that moral values are crumbling?

A. This is part of the picture. Not only parents but others are uncertain in many cases as to what is morally right or wrong, and that makes discipline harder to enforce.

For instance, children today are being exposed to all kinds of motion pictures and books. It is difficult to decide what motion pictures and books should be censored.

In a broad sense, actually, you might feel that censorship in general is undesirable. Yet you also know that restraint must be imposed at some point—especially where children are involved. But in trying to decide at what point restraint should be imposed, it very often turns out that no restraint at all results. And it is this lack of restraint in the home and on the outside that is back of so much of our delinquency.

Q. Is it bad parents, then, who make bad children?

A. In large measure. It is the affection and discipline the child gets in the home that shape his attitudes and ideals as child and adult.

Q. Does that mean that more discipline is needed?

A. Discipline is always needed. Fifty years ago, much more than now, there was discipline. Children knew the limits on their behavior. They lived in smaller neighborhoods where they were under the eye of parents and neighbors—and what the neighbors thought was important. Religion, too, seemed to have a greater influence on personal behavior.

Also, the home setting itself encouraged parental control. Children were taught by example that each had his or her work to do without question: The father worked out in the field, the mother cleaned the house and cooked the family's food, and the children carried in the wood and helped out.

Today, in our urban centers, the situation is totally different. There are all kinds of distractions for children. Mothers are either working outside the home or preoccupied with all the problems of day-to-day running of the home. Fathers, too, spend more time away from home.

There is less work for children to do around the house, and the parents can't think of other ways to fill up the void, so they leave it to the child himself to work out the problem. In that situation, parental authority is not likely to be strong.

Q. With what result?

A. With the result that the child considers it his right to do as he pleases and to ignore parental wishes. . . .

Q. Is a spanking, or some other form of corporal punishment, an answer to the problem?

A. We do not rule out corporal punishment, provided it is clearly related in the child's mind to the misdeed he has committed. But more use should be made of deprivation of privileges—sending a child to bed earlier if he misbehaves, or not letting him see his favorite television program—as a means of discipline. What is really required is great firmness administered with love.

You see, love is the essential element. We think that it is even possible for a parent to be overstrict at times or too lenient at other times, yet be an effective parent if he really loves the child—because the child then will accept these variations. But if a parent is overstrict or vacillating or lax, and doesn't really love the child, the child very quickly senses this and either takes advantage or rebels.

Now, the earlier in the child's life he senses parental love and guidance, the sooner he will acquire self-discipline—and the less of a disciplinary problem he's going to be as he grows up.

Q. Why do Chinese-Americans, for instance, seem to have few youngsters in trouble, while some other ethnic groups seem to have a high ratio of delinquency?

A. In any group, the incidence of delinquency derives from the strength of the family life. Years ago, we thought of doing a study of Chinese-American delinquents. But we found in our preliminary survey that there were simply not enough Chinese delinquent boys in New York or San Francisco to give us an adequate sample.

Why was this? We think it is because of the strong sense of family, the respect for parents and elders, that exists among the Chinese.

On the other hand, in the ethnic groups where the delinquency rate is high, you tend to find a great deal of desertion by fathers, and much illegitimacy. Even when a mother does show affection for her children, often her efforts to administer discipline are not supported by a strong sense that family reputation is at stake.

Q. What kind of action is needed? Is social work the answer?

A. Actually, we have not seen that the treatment usually given to predelinquent or delinquent children does a great deal of good.

We know of two studies—one in Washington, D.C., and another in the Cambridge-Somerville area of Massachusetts —where treatment was given one group of delinquent children and not to another. In both of these studies, the children had the benefit of some clinical treatment, friendly supervision, recreational activities, neighborhood meetings, health examinations, counseling, and so on. But unfortunately the kind of aid that was given seemed to make little difference in their delinquency rate compared with those children who didn't get treatment.

Q. How would you explain that?

A. As we see it, too much attention or therapy is being directed at the children, and not at the family condition that made them delinquent. This is the sort of social work that delinquent children so often get. In other words, it is the parents who need reeducation more than the child.

Q. How can that be accomplished?

A. By teaching the parents the importance of affection and discipline in their relationship to the child.

Many parents also have emotional problems of their own which need to be worked out if they're going to become effective parents. Clinics for the reeducation of ineffective parents are a major need in preventing delinquency.

Actually, we see training for parenthood as a process beginning in childhood—and certainly young couples about to marry should know what is going to be expected of them in the successful raising of a family.

Now, the earlier this understanding and training can be given in the predelinquency period—before the first signs of trouble are developing in a child—the better chance there will be that corrective measures will succeed.

Q. Can all parents be helped through training?

A. Not all—and, in extreme cases, children should be removed from an environment that is likely to lead them into delinquency. Many could benefit from placement in foster homes, which seem to us much preferable to institutional care, at least of the kind now given to neglected children.

But it is our feeling that many more parents could be helped than is generally realized. So much of the emotional damage to children is the result of downright ignorance on the part of parents.

In that connection, we are much interested to learn that a rehabilitation center in a troublesome area of Louisville,

Kentucky, will try not only to rehabilitate delinquent boys but also to provide weekly counseling and other services to parents to try to improve their relationship to the boys.

Q. Can police and courts help reduce juvenile crime?

A. By the time a child walks into juvenile court, much of the damage to his character has been done, and it is much harder to correct damage than to prevent it.

Q. Do juvenile courts tend to be too soft on youngsters?

A. Sometimes, yes, but more often there is inconsistency because judges have wide discretion, and they may rely on intuition or hunches rather than use of predictive data which their staff could gather for them on each case.

Q. Then is stern punishment a deterrent to further crime?

A. Certainty of punishment is definitely a deterrent. After all, fear is a primary emotion in man. It plays an important part in his training. We have gone rather far in the other direction, in letting the child feel that he isn't going to be punished for misdeeds.

Of course, it is wrong to rely exclusively on fear of punishment to restrain the child. But it is equally wrong to do away with this deterrent.

Q. Can schools help in keeping children from developing into troublemakers?

A. They certainly can. As we have said, there are children whose energies are not suited to long periods of sitting still and whose adventuresomeness has to be satisfied in some acceptable way.

We also think that one of the basic needs of schools, along with other elements of society, is a general recognition that rules must be observed—that, without rules, you drift into chaos and into tyranny and into taking the law into your own hands. You see it not only among delinquents but among young college students, in their demand for more and more freedom from restraints and from higher authority.

Q. What else is needed to keep delinquency from growing?

A. It seems to us that business and industry can help a great deal by providing recreational facilities and nurseries for the very young children of working mothers. This would not be aimed at providing mothers with a free baby-sitting service and nothing more. Rather, it would enable the mother to see her child or children occasionally during the day and maintain warm contact with them.

We have seen something like this system in the Israeli *kibbutzim,* or communal settlements, and we are told that some factories in Europe are beginning to provide this sort of service.

Finally, our administration of criminal justice needs a complete revision. We need to get better men and women into this field. There has to be a better training on the part of judges, prosecutors, defense lawyers, probation officers and others in law, psychology, sociology, biology and other disciplines in attacking the increasingly complex problems that are arising in our modern society. As a start in that direction, we have proposed—and Senator Edward M. Kennedy, of Massachusetts, is sponsoring—legislation to create a national academy of criminal justice which might be considered analogous to West Point in this field.

Q. Do you look for crime and delinquency to continue to grow?

A. Probably. Our own feeling is that, unless much is done to check the vicious cycles involved, we are in for a period of violence beyond anything we have yet seen. . . .

We foresee no letup in this trend. A delinquent child often grows up to produce delinquent children—not as a matter of heredity, but of his own unresolved conflicts which make him an ineffective parent.

In our principal study, we found that 45 per cent of the mothers of the delinquents we interviewed had a history of criminality themselves, compared with 15 per cent of the mothers of nondelinquents. Sixty-six per cent of the fathers had a similar history, contrasted with 32 per cent of the fathers of nondelinquents.

Our trouble is that everyone is so busy managing the children who are already delinquents that they don't have time to think of how to break the vicious cycle that is building up delinquency. We are not doing the main thing that must be done to prevent the predelinquent from becoming a full-fledged delinquent by correcting conditions in the home.

That has been one of our purposes in working for so many years on tracing the roots and the development of delinquency—to provide our authorities with the information they need to act at the earliest possible period in a child's life when trouble signs appear.

DRUG ADDICTION AND CRIME [5]

The interpenetration of heroin addiction and crime is a substantial contributor to the crime rate in the United States. Addiction to opiates, and especially to heroin, is much more likely than any other form of illegal drug use to be related to crime, although several hundred thousand persons use amphetamines and barbiturates outside of medical channels, many persons smoke marihuana, and children as young as eleven and twelve sniff glue. The lack of reliable information and data on the abuse of drugs other than heroin makes it difficult to speak with certainty about the relationship of such drugs to crime.

The Harrison Act, the basic Federal law that regulates opium and its derivatives, was passed in 1914. The laws of our fifty states largely reflect the Act, which does not make it a crime to be an addict but does make possession of narcotic drugs a violation of the law. The severity of the offense and therefore the sentence to which it might lead is related to the

[5] Article by Dr. Charles Winick, director of the American Social Health Association's Program in Drug Dependence and Abuse. *Current History.* 52:349-53+. Je. '67. Reprinted by permission.

quantity of narcotic drugs found in the possession of the offender. Another element in the court's evaluation of the offense is whether the offender was planning to use the drugs for himself or had intended to sell them. The seller, of course, is treated more severely than the user. A person carrying a substantial quantity is presumed to be a seller.

Marihuana is subject to the same legal controls as the opiates, although it is not an addicting substance. Possession of heroin or marihuana for any purpose is illegal and both substances are outlawed in the United States.

The heroin addict contributes to crime in the community because of his urgent and continuous need for substantial amounts of money to buy daily doses of heroin. The typical male heroin addict has no established vocation and lacks an occupation to which he can turn for regular income. As a result, the primary method by which he can get ready cash is engaging in burglary and robbery. The average urban addict needs from $10 to $60 each day in order to maintain his "habit" and, since stolen goods bring only 20 per cent of their value, a representative addict must steal merchandise, each day, that is worth from $50 to $300. The male addict becomes a continuing one-man crime wave and is unlike other criminals in that he *must* "score" every day.

The Illegal Distribution System

In order to supply the growing market for heroin, an elaborate system for smuggling drugs into the country has been developed, along with a network of wholesalers, retailers and "pushers." India and Turkey produce practically all the opium that the world requires for legitimate medicinal purposes and most of the illegal opium reaching the United States comes from Turkey. The farmers who grow the opium poppy in Turkey sell it to the government monopoly at $8 to $12 a kilo (thirty-five ounces). Drugs move into illegal channels through local smugglers, who pay approximately $5 more per kilo than the government price. The smuggler who buys opium from the Turkish farmers is usually armed and extremely well informed on the latest border crossing techniques.

Smugglers usually convert opium to morphine base in order to simplify its illegal transportation because each 10 kilos of opium converts to 1 kilo of morphine base, which also has less of an identifiable and distinctive odor than opium. From Turkey, the opium or the morphine base moves through Syria to Lebanon and then to France or Italy, where a kilo of morphine base may be bought for approximately $20,000. The kilo is only slightly larger than a building brick, and once smuggled across the Atlantic Ocean, can ultimately bring between $800,000 and $950,000 in New York, where it is diluted and sold to the ultimate consumer. The addict in the street who buys a glassine "bag" gets heroin that is from 1 to 5 per cent pure. [Heroin, an addictive narcotic, is derived from morphine.—Ed.]

The Corsicans who appear to dominate the smuggling business have direct relationships with major New York importers; others deal with importers in Montreal who then resell the product in New York. During the 1920's, the organized racketeers who imported and distributed opium operated as a series of small businesses. By the 1930's an understanding was reached among the major gangster groups and developed into a loose confederation that represented a local modification of the Mafia.

It is likely that three or four major importers dominate the New York narcotics distribution system. Even though Federal officials probably know the identity of the key smuggling wholesalers, they may not be able to assemble the evidence needed to convict them in a court of law. They are almost impossible to arrest because they seldom handle or even see the merchandise that their assistants are selling. Only rarely is one of the major wholesalers convicted.

The same considerations make it difficult to crack down on violations of the international machinery for control of opiates, which is exercised through the United Nations' Permanent Opium Control Board in Geneva. The United Nations machinery for enforcement of its national quota system for opium production and use is essentially voluntary in nature and it is unlikely that the machinery for international regulation of opium production can change in the immediate future. Although most countries of the world belong to the United Nations and do cooperate with its efforts to control the legitimate use of opium derivatives, each country must police itself. Thus, even though American authorities might suspect that a particular area in Turkey is providing a substantial amount of drugs for the illegal market and the American government might inform the Turkish authorities, the latter would have to act.

With the opportunity of earning more than one hundred times his investment in a very short time, many a drug wholesaler is willing to undertake the risk involved in the illegal traffic. His courier may receive $5,000 to $10,000 for bringing the drugs across the Atlantic. If the courier is arrested but does not "talk," he knows that his relatives will receive some stipend from the wholesaler. If, however, the arrested smuggler cooperates with the police, it is possible that he or some member of his family may be killed. As a result, the couriers who regularly bring drugs into the country very seldom act as informers against their employers.

One problem in making an effective legal case against the drug wholesalers is that the courier who brings the material across the Atlantic is often the only member of the distribution group who is arrested. The courier seldom knows higher-level members of the syndicate and is likely to be in contact only with other subordinates on either side of the Atlantic. High officials of various governments have sometimes functioned as couriers. In October 1960, United States agents arrested Mauricio Rosal, Guatemala's ambassador to Belgium, and seized 101 kilos of pure heroin. Two other diplomats of ambassadorial rank have been arrested and convicted in recent years.

It has been alleged that Communist China is sending opium to the United States in order to undermine American morals as well as make substantial profits, but there is reason to believe that relatively little heroin comes into the United States from China today, although some does come from the Burma-Laos area. It is possible that Chinese drugs will be coming here in greater quantities in the future, but the wholesale market is already very tightly controlled.

Most of the heroin sold in California comes not from China but from Mexico, where there are a number of relatively small but active opium growers who smuggle drugs over the California border in small quantities, often by automobile. There is reason to suspect that private airplanes are used to fly some heroin into the United States, sometimes dropping the drugs at a prearranged point in the United States and returning to Mexico without even landing here.

The concentration of addiction in a few states and several major cities makes the illegal opiate market compact and easy to serve. Further facilitating distribution, in cities with a high incidence of addiction, addicts tend to cluster in a few neighborhoods. Inasmuch as the typical addict needs heroin every five or six hours in order to avoid withdrawal symptoms, he can be described as being one of the most loyal consumers of any commodity.

The enormous profits deriving from the illegal sale of heroin go into a variety of other smuggling activities. There is reason to believe that a substantial proportion of the other crimes in the United States are financed by profits from the illegal drug traffic. And although such an assertion is difficult to prove, there is every likelihood that considerable legitimate business is financed by profits from illegal opiates.

Does Crime Antedate Addiction?

There has been considerable discussion over whether the drug addict becomes a criminal only or primarily because he needs money for drugs, or whether he was engaging in antisocial activity prior to his addiction. Although the former may have been likely at some time in the past, the latter appears to be true today.

In the 1930's, the typical addict was an indigent white Southerner who was not participating in any subculture of antisocial activities. Since the end of World War II, however, the modal addict has been a Negro, Puerto Rican, or Mexican-American teenager or young adult who was involved in a number of antisocial and frequently criminal activities before he began heroin use. The Federal Bureau of Investigation has analyzed the careers of over 6,000 persons who had been arrested at least twice and had at least one narcotic violation charge. Seventy-three per cent had been arrested on some criminal charge prior to their first arrest for a violation of the narcotics law. The FBI also analyzed 1,000 narcotic offenders who had been identified as addicts by local authorities. For this group also, 73 per cent had been arrested for some other criminal offense before their first arrest on a narcotic charge. In three other follow-up studies of post-World War II addicts in large cities, the majority had criminal records prior to the onset of addiction. Each of the major follow-up studies also concluded that an addict is likely to engage in more criminal behavior after the onset of addiction than before. To some extent, of course, the offenses may be regarded as an extension and continuation of patterns of behavior that antedated addiction.

What kind of crimes do addicts commit? Postaddiction offenses include more income-producing activities than before. The crimes involved are robbery, which is both an offense against the person and a money-producing activity; offenses against property; and drug offenses. Crimes against the person do not increase after addiction, and the increase in robbery is primarily a reflection of its function as a money producer rather than as a crime against a person.

How can the woman addict acquire large sums of money daily? Most women solve the problem by becoming prostitutes. Once they have established themselves as prostitutes, the new vocation offers a continuing opportunity to acquire considerable amounts of cash. The relatively low pay associated with the unskilled work that a former prostitute might find in the legitimate world can hardly compare with the income from streetwalking, being an inmate of a brothel, or working as a prostitute out of a hotel or bar. For all practical purposes, therefore, the female addict will remain a prostitute for much of her adult life.

Jazz musicians and physicians are probably the two occupational groups most frequently found among drug users. Although the incidence of opiate use among these occupations seems to be fairly constant, neither group contributes to crime to any appreciable extent, because the working musician earns enough to buy opiates and the physician has access to the drugs as a result of his professional work.

How much is addiction costing the United States? Let us conservatively assume that the total number of male addicts active in the United States and not currently incarcerated or participating in a treatment program is 45,000. Let us further assume that the typical urban male addict has a minimal "habit" of $10 a day, so that he must steal $50 a day or $350 a week worth of merchandise. These 45,000 men would be stealing a weekly average of $15.75 million or a total of $818 million a year. In addition to such a staggering cost in money, the addict is "tuning out" of the community at an age when most people are making momentous decisions about jobs, marriage and future relationships, and moving into the most productive years of young adulthood. Such human costs are even more disturbing than the losses in money and property that are occasioned by drug use.

Treatment Programs

Effective treatment programs would help to decrease the number of addicts and therefore the incidence of crime. Discussions of addiction usually avoid the word "cure" because to use the word would imply a state of knowledge that we do not at present possess. As a result, any attempt to establish the comparative effectiveness of different programs must be very cautious. One recent experimental program that has had a limited trial but received considerable attention is the methadone maintenance program, set up at the Rockefeller University in New York City. Under this program addicts of long standing are given methadone, a synthetic opiate. They become addicted to methadone, which is a "good" opiate that does not lead either to euphoria or depression when it is used regularly. Methadone appears to block the effect of heroin. The first two years of experience with methadone maintenance, with a sample of 250 voluntary patients, has been comparatively successful. Many patients on methadone have returned to school, obtained jobs, and become reconciled with their families; medical and psychometric tests have disclosed no sign of toxicity.

It is too early to tell whether the methadone program can be extended to large numbers of addicts. It seems to represent the only unequivocal technique for removing addicts from the criminal subculture, short of incarceration. Traditional methods of psychiatry, psychology and social work have been generally unsuccessful in bringing about long-term rehabilitation, with an average rehabilitation rate of 10 to 15 per cent.

Our ability to provide vocational training for former addicts has also been somewhat discouraging, especially when coupled with employers' reluctance to hire a former "dope fiend." The former addict who wants to become a "square" and get a "9 to 5 bag" in a legitimate job may therefore have difficulties in translating his good intentions into action. He may even experience problems in finding a place to live, since a record as an addict is enough to make him ineligible for public housing in most cities.

What is the outlook for the future? The number of drug addicts in the United States has been increasing at the rate of approximately 10 per cent a year. As of the end of 1965, there were 57,199 addicts, according to the Federal Bureau of

Narcotics. For some years to come, we may assume that our addiction problem will remain at least on its present level.

There are, however, some countervailing forces. California and New York, the two states with the largest number of addicts (as of the end of 1965, California had 6,836 and New York had 29,510), have both instituted civil commitment procedures that may ultimately lead to a decline in the number of addicts. The Federal Government is now beginning a similar program. All the civil commitment approaches involve a court which requires an addict to spend some time, often six months, in a treatment facility and to remain under parole supervision for a longer period of time, often two and a half years. The civil commitment programs are rooted in the new official view that regards the drug user as a sick person who needs rehabilitation as well as incarceration but who is unlikely to seek help unless forced to do so.

The civil commitment programs represent a compromise between the punitive and the rehabilitative approach, and reflect our desire to create an atmosphere not hospitable to drug use but receptive to the possibility of rehabilitating the drug user.

If the civil commitment programs are substantially successful over a period of perhaps the next ten years, there should be a decline in the number of addicts. Another factor making for a reduction in addiction is the tendency of perhaps as many as two thirds of addicts to "mature out" and cease using opiates by the time they reach their thirties. We do not know precisely how this comes about; one speculation is that the pressures and decisions that contributed to a teenager's beginning opiate use have become less urgent by his thirties, especially after he has had some experience with the community's law enforcement apparatus.

One additional trend that may work to bring about a decline in the drug problem is the drop in the number of Negro addicts. Negro addicts accounted for 57.8 per cent of all new addicts in 1956 but only 40.2 per cent in 1965. Numerically, this represents a drop from 5,395 to 2,419 new addicts.

Among the reasons for this development are growing racial pride, an increase in the self-esteem of many Negro communities, the effect of education and law enforcement, and the frequency with which Negro slum dwellers have seen many of their relatives and friends destroyed by narcotics. Any status connotation to narcotic use among Negroes has certainly declined, and it is possible that antipoverty programs are providing many Negroes with vehicles of expression that were not previously available and that make addiction less attractive.

A fairly recent development that may contribute to a decrease in addiction is the number of rehabilitation programs that provide employment and create new careers for ex-addicts by making them key figures in the treatment process. Synanon in California is a private program that relies completely on ex-addicts as the whole treatment staff. New York City's Coordinator of Addictive Diseases, Dr. Efren Ramirez, relies heavily on former addicts in his community-based rehabilitation activities. Such new careers may provide work for ex-addicts, may enable them to use their years of opiate use toward a socially constructive activity, and ultimately may help to lead to a decrease in addiction.

Such trends are complicated by the extent to which drug use is now becoming almost endemic among some groups that have previously been fairly immune to it. High school and college students, bohemians, and other young people who are dissatisfied with the quality of the American life are expressing their dissatisfaction and making an ideological statement by taking illegal drugs. Although such drug users are violating the law, they are hardly likely to participate in the kind of crime in which the slum street addict has traditionally been involved.

We are, at the present time, at a crossroad with respect to crime related to drug addiction. Never before has so much crime been traceable to drug use, as the number of addicts has increased to record proportions. But for the first time, massive Federal and state programs are swinging into action.

The next five years will enable us to determine whether such programs, and similar efforts, will lead to a decrease in drug-related crime.

VIOLENCE IN AMERICA [6]

"Man and society are born out of both: violence and gentle cooperation." That is how psychiatrist Bruno Bettelheim defines a paradoxical but inescapable fact touching the whole history of "the children of Cain." How the two forces are balanced in an individual helps determine his behavior, even his sanity. How they are balanced in society helps determine its political organization, the degree and condition of its civilization. In the United States today, it seems to many that violence is in the ascendant over cooperation, disruption over order, and anger over reason.

The greatest single source of this fear lies in the Negro riots that keep tearing at American cities. What is alarming about them is not merely the frustration and bitterness they proclaim, not merely the physical and psychological damage they cause, but also the fact that a few Negro leaders are deliberately trying to justify the riots with a violent and vengeful ideology. This in turn can all too easily be seen as just one aspect of a whole American panorama of violence. The crime rate keeps rising, or seems to, especially in senseless killings and wanton attacks. Fear of the darkened city streets has become a fact of urban life. The memories of bizarre multiple murders linger in the mind—thirteen people dead in Austin from a sniper's rifle, eight nurses in Chicago killed by a demented drifter. The recollection of the Kennedy assassination remains part of the scene. A burgeoning, largely uncontrolled traffic in guns has put firearms into some fifty million American homes, many of their owners insisting that the weapons are needed for self-defense. In the movies and on television, murder and torture seem to be turning

[6] From a Time essay. *Time.* 90:18-19. Jl. 28, '67. Copyright Time Inc. 1967.

Americans into parlor sadists. A recent trend on the stage is the "theater of cruelty," and a growing number of books delve into the pornography of violence. . . .

Violence is so universal and elusive that sociology and psychology can only approximate a complex truth. Comparisons with other countries are illuminating but hardly conclusive. The United States has certainly experienced nothing like the massacre of 400,000 Communists in Indonesia; nor have Watts or Newark approached the lethal fury of an Indian or an Arab mob. But these are countries at vastly different levels of civilization. In the industrialized world, the United States undeniably ranks high in violence. The United States homicide rate stands at around five deaths for 100,000 people. This compares with .7 in England, 1.4 in Canada, 1.5 in France, 1.5 in Japan (but 32 in Mexico). Within the United States, the rate varies widely, from about 11 per 100,000 in Georgia and Alabama to 6.1 in New York and .5 in Vermont. Not that homicide or any other statistics can tell the complete story.

Measuring itself not against others but against its own past, the United States has good reason to believe that the country as a whole is growing less violent. The roots of violence in the American past are obvious: the Revolution, the Indian wars, slavery, the Civil War, that crucial and necessary test between two societies (when Fort Sumter was fired on, Emerson said: "Now we have a country again. Sometimes gunpowder smells good"). Race riots erupted almost as soon as the Negroes were emancipated, the worst being the New York draft riots of 1863. The Ku Klux Klan relied on raw violence to keep the Negroes from exercising the rights they had gained. In its way, frontier violence was also the result of social change: new, transplanted populations, new sources of wealth, new elites struggling for power. The wonder, perhaps, was not that the frontier was violent, but that its people tried so quickly to establish some sort of law.

Changing Pattern

In the cities, each wave of new immigration evoked violent reactions, many of which were instigated in the mid-1800's by the original Know-Nothings and their many later imitators. Immigrant groups themselves battled with one another, caught up in ethnic feuds. Above all, the American labor movement was the most violent in the world. From the 1870's to the 1930's, bloody battles between strikers and company cops or state militia were frequent. Labor leaders often deliberately used violence to dramatize the workers' plight—and, in time, they succeeded. On the fringes of the movement were some odd secret organizations, including the Molly Maguires, a band of Pennsylvania miners who assassinated fellow workers and bosses alike in an attempt to win better pay and working conditions. The Wobblies (Industrial Workers of the World) sang the praises of violence and provided numerous labor saints and martyrs. The great gangs that appeared in Chicago, New York and elsewhere in the 1920's were also social symptoms: not merely the fiefdoms of "little Caesars" bent on money and power, but the expression of a moral vacuum in the United States.

Against this background, violence on the American scene today is still alarming, but it scarcely suggests a disastrous deterioration. Public tolerance of violence seems lower than ever before in United States life, and public respect for law far higher. Above all, there is evidence to show that—some statistics to the contrary—violent crime in the United States is not really growing relative to the population. After massive researches, the President's Crime Commission admits that crime trends cannot be conclusively proven out by available figures. According to FBI reckoning, crimes of violence have risen about 35 per cent so far in the 1960's. But these figures fail to consider two important factors: population growth and changes in crime reporting. Experts believe that part of the apparent increase is caused by the fact that each year the police grow more thorough—and the poor are less reluctant—about reporting crime that previously went unrecorded. Says

sociologist Marvin Wolfgang, president of the American
Society of Criminology: "Contrary to the rise in public fear,
crimes of violence are not significantly increasing."

But their pattern is changing. The incidence of murder
and robbery relative to population has decreased by 30 per
cent in the past three decades. On the other hand, rape has
tripled. Males are seven times more likely to commit violent
crimes than women, but the women are catching up: in five
years, arrests of women for crimes of violence rose 62 per cent
above 1960 versus 18 per cent for men. From the newest
figures, certain other patterns emerge. Despite widespread
fear of strangers, most crimes of violence are committed by a
member of the family or an acquaintance. The arrest rate
for murder among Negroes is ten times that among whites,
but most of the violent crimes committed by Negroes are
against other Negroes. Violence is increasingly an urban phenomenon: twenty-six large cities containing less than one
fifth of the United States population account for more than
half of all major crimes against the person. Poets sometimes
have sociological insights, and Robert Lowell knew what he
was talking about in his lines:

> When Cain beat out his brother Abel's brains
> The Maker laid great cities in his soul.

Innate or Learned?

Violence is not only an urban but overwhelmingly a
lower-class phenomenon. In Atlanta, for example, neighborhoods with family incomes below $3,000 show a violent-crime
rate eight times higher than among $9,000 families. In the
middle class, violence is perhaps sublimated increasingly in
sport or other pursuits. Says sociologist Wolfgang:

> The gun and fist have been substantially replaced by financial
> ability, by the capacity to manipulate others in complex organiza-
> tions, and by intellectual talent. The thoughtful wit, the easy ver-
> balizer, even the striving musician and artist are equivalents of
> male assertiveness, where broad shoulders and fighting fists were
> once the major symbols.

What are the seeds of violence? Freud found "a powerful measure of desire for aggression" in human instincts. He added: "The very emphasis of the commandment 'Thou shalt not kill' makes it certain that we are descended from an endlessly long chain of generations of murderers, whose love of murder was in their blood, as it is perhaps also in ours." Further, Freud held that man possesses a death instinct which, since it cannot be satisfied except in suicide, is instead turned outward as aggression against others. Dr. Fredric Wertham, noted crusader against violence, disagrees sharply and argues that violence is learned behavior, not a product of nature but of society: "The violent man is not the natural but the socially alienated man."

The fact is that if violence is not innate, it is a basic component of human behavior. The German naturalist Konrad Lorenz believes that, unlike other carnivores, man did not at an early stage develop inhibitions against killing members of his own species—because he was too weak. As he developed weapons, he learned to kill, and he also learned moral restraints, but these never penetrated far enough. Writes Lorenz: "The deep emotional layers of our personality simply do not register the fact that the cocking of a forefinger to release a shot tears the entrails of another man.". . .

Violence can be a simple, rational reaching for a goal, in its legal form of war or its illegal form of crime. It can often be irrational, as in a seemingly senseless killing or quarrel. But the distinction between irrational and rational violence is not easily drawn. Even the insane murderer kills to satisfy a need entirely real to him. Violence is often caused by "displaced aggression," when anger is forced to aim at a substitute target. Every psychologist knows that a man might beat his child because he cannot beat his boss. And a man may even murder because he feels rejected or "alienated." But what leads one man in such a situation to kill and another merely to get drunk is a question psychologists have never really answered. . . .

Dealing with violence, the United States faces several tasks, none easy. One is to provide more intelligent, effective law enforcement and, through legislation, to do away with the dangerous unfettered sale of firearms. Another is nothing less than the elimination of the ghetto and what it stands for: an increasingly disaffected population. Though probably there will always be violence—out of anger or greed, love or madness—large-scale, socially significant violence is usually caused by authentic grievances, and the United States should be able to narrow if not eliminate these. But that leaves, finally, the individual flash or explosion of violence; and to deal with this, man must learn more about man—the mystery that can turn creative energy into brute force, a peaceful crowd into a mob, and an ineffectual weakling into a mass murderer.

THE ROOTS OF AMERICAN VIOLENCE [7]

This troubled world will long remember the scar of the past week's violence.

But when the week is remembered, let this be remembered too: That out of anguish came a national resolve to search for the causes—and to find the cures—for the outbursts of violence which have brought so much heartbreak to the nation.

Violence has erupted in many parts of the globe—from the streets of newly emerging nations to the old cobblestones of Paris. But it is the episodes of violence in our own country which must command our attention now.

Our inquiry into that violence brings us together at the White House this afternoon.

You come here from the church, the universities, the Senate and the House, the judiciary, the ranks of the working man, the professions.

[7] "Johnson Statement on Violence," text of statement made at the White House on June 10, 1968, by President Lyndon B. Johnson to the members of his commission investigating violence in the United States. Text from New York *Times.* p 34. Je. 11, '68.

My charge to you is simple and direct. I ask you to undertake a penetrating search for the causes and prevention of violence—a search into our national life, our past as well as our present, our traditions as well as our institutions, our culture, our customs and our laws.

I hope your search will yield:

First, an understanding and insight into the kinds of violent aberrations which have struck down public figures and private citizens alike.

Four Presidents Slain

One out of every five Presidents since 1865 has been assassinated—Lincoln in April 1865, Garfield in July 1881, McKinley in September 1901 and John F. Kennedy in November 1963. In this same period, there have been attempts on the lives of one out of every three Presidents, including Theodore Roosevelt while campaigning in October 1912, President-elect Franklin D. Roosevelt in February 1933 and Harry S. Truman in November 1950. In the attempt on Roosevelt's life, Mayor Anton Cermak of Chicago was killed. In the attack on President Truman, a White House policeman lost his life.

The list of assassinations during the last five years is long and shocking. Here are some:

In 1963: Medgar Evers, ambushed by a sniper; four Negro girls killed in a church bombing; President John F. Kennedy assassinated. Eight thousand five hundred Americans were murdered that year.

In 1964: Three civil rights workers murdered as part of a Ku Klux Klan conspiracy; Lieutenant Colonel Lemuel Penn shot down on a highway. Nine thousand two hundred and fifty Americans were murdered that year.

In 1965: Mrs. Viola Liuzzo. Nine thousand eight hundred and fifty Americans were murdered that year.

In 1966: Malcolm X. Ten thousand nine hundred and twenty Americans were murdered that year.

In 1967: George Lincoln Rockwell. Twelve thousand two hundred and thirty Americans were murdered that year.

In 1968: Martin Luther King, Jr., and Senator Robert F. Kennedy.

Just yesterday, a Jordanian grocer living on Chicago's South Side, was shot to death and police speculate that the killing may have been in revenge for the assassination of Senator Kennedy.

Second, I hope your search will uncover the causes of disrespect for law and order and of violent disruptions of public order by individuals and groups.

Third, I hope your search will lead to sensible and practical actions to control or prevent these outbreaks of violence.

Questions to Consider

Here are some of the questions I hope you will consider:

Is there something in the environment of American society or the structure of our institutions that causes disrespect for the law, contempt for the rights of others, and incidents of violence? If there is, how can we correct it?

Has permissiveness toward extreme behavior in our society encouraged an increase of violence?

Why do some individuals and groups reject the peaceful political and institutional processes of change in favor of violent means?

Are the seeds of violence nurtured through the public's airwaves, the screens of neighborhood theaters, the news media, and other forms of communication that reach the family and our young? I am asking the heads of the radio and television networks and the chairman of the Federal Communications Commission to cooperate wholeheartedly with you.

Is violence a contagious phenomenon? To the extent that it is, are there ways we can reduce the contagion?

What is the relationship between mass disruption of public order and individual acts of violence?

What is the relationship between mental derangement and violence—remembering that half our hospital beds are occupied by the mentally ill?

Practical Steps Sought

Does the democratic process which stresses exchanges of ideas permit less physical contact with masses of people—as a matter of security against the deranged individual and obsessed fanatic?

To the extent we can identify the basic causes of violence and disrespect for the law, what practical steps can and should be taken to eliminate them?

Can our society any longer tolerate the widespread possession of deadly firearms by private citizens?

What—beyond firm and effective Federal and state gun control laws which are so desperately needed—can be done to give further protection to public leaders and private citizens?

How can the government at all levels, the churches, schools and parents help to dispel the forces that lead to violence?

Scope of Inquiry

These are some of the questions that are on the minds of Americans today. But I must leave to you the task of defining precisely the scope and boundaries of your inquiry. For you will be venturing into uncharted ground.

Some of the questions I have asked and the matters you look into may be beyond the frontiers of man's knowledge. Nevertheless, I urge you to go as far as man's knowledge takes you.

Even where basic causes are beyond the knowledge and control of man, you may still be able to propose actions and laws and institutions that can limit the opportunities for violence by individuals and groups. For as I said on Friday:

Two million guns were sold in the United States last year. Far too many were bought by the demented, the deranged, the hardened criminal and the convict, the addict, and the alcoholic. We cannot expect these irresponsible people to be prudent in their protection of us, but we can expect the Congress to protect us from them. . . .

I have spoken before of the terrible toll inflicted on our people by firearms: 750,000 Americans dead since the turn of the century—this is far more than have died at the hands of our enemies in all the wars we have fought. . . .

Each year, in this country, guns are involved in more than 6,500 murders. This compares with 30 in England, 99 in Canada, 68 in West Germany, and 37 in Japan. Forty-four thousand aggravated assaults are committed with guns in America each year. Fifty thousand robberies are committed with guns in America each year.

Search Must Be Made

The truths you seek will yield stubbornly to search. But that search must be made. And it must be started now.

Your work should help us move toward the day when hatred and violence will have no sway in the affairs of men. Since violence is an international phenomenon, your work will be a service not only to your countrymen, but to the world.

The agony of these past days lies heavy on the hearts of the American people.

But let us all now have the will and the purpose to forge our sorrow into a constructive force for public order and progress, justice and compassion. This is the spirit that has sustained the nation in all the years of our history.

It is the spirit, I believe, that can see us emerge from this hour of sorrow—a stronger and a more unified people.

II. ORGANIZED CRIME

EDITOR'S INTRODUCTION

Organized crime on a small scale has long existed in the United States but with the transformation of the country into a modern industrial state, organized crime has developed into a massive operation—larger, indeed, than the largest American corporations. The main sources of income for the crime syndicate (known variously as the Mafia, the Mob, or Cosa Nostra) are gambling, loan-sharking, labor racketeering, and infiltration and takeover of legitimate businesses.

Organized crime today also differs from organized crime of an earlier era in its almost corporate-like structure. When Dillinger was killed, his mob broke up. But when Vito Genovese went to jail, his "family" continued to function normally. The first article in this section, by Mark R. Arnold, staff writer for *The National Observer*, describes the structure and activities of Mafia families in New York City, which he calls "the unofficial capital of organized crime in America." In the second selection, Fred J. Cook, a free-lance writer who has written extensively on organized crime, discusses loan-sharking and its unwitting accomplices—businessmen in need of quick cash. The next article, on criminal infiltration of the securities industry, is by the Attorney General of New York State, Louis J. Lefkowitz. Following this is an article by *Wall Street Journal* staff writer Nicholas Gage which deals with the infiltration by the Mafia into labor unions. The final selection, by University of Pennsylvania professor of law Henry S. Ruth, Jr., examines the reasons why the United States has never succeeded in mounting a sustained effort against organized crime.

HOW ORGANIZED CRIME EXPANDS
AND PROSPERS [1]

A few years ago, Mr. and Mrs. K put their life savings—a few thousand dollars—into a luncheonette business in North Babylon, Long Island. They were just beginning to make a go of it when road-construction crews began tearing up the street next to their front door.

Mr. and Mrs. K have testified about what happened thereafter in appearances before the New York State Investigation Commission. Their story is worth telling because it sheds light on the operations of the most sinister organization in American life—La Cosa Nostra, or the Mafia.

Mr. and Mrs. K testified that they desperately needed cash to tide them over until the construction obstacles were removed, and so they went to a loan shark named Max (Max the Weasel) Lowenstein, who was then one of the few independent, or nonsyndicate, operators in the New York area.

Mafia Family Moves In

What Mr. and Mrs. K didn't know was that Max Lowenstein was having troubles too. Just as they borrowed the money, a Brooklyn-based Mafia family said (by J. Edgar Hoover) to be controlled by Joseph Colombo was making plans to move its loan-sharking and gambling operations into eastern Long Island. One of Colombo's underlings, Felix (Phil) Vizzari, held a series of meetings with Lowenstein. Thereafter, Vizzari emerged with a half-interest in a legitimate concrete business run by Lowenstein and with full control over all of Lowenstein's loan-shark accounts.

Soon, Mr. and Mrs. K were paying interest rates—called "vigorish" in the loan-shark business—of 25 per cent a week. They kept borrowing, and the more they borrowed the more vigorish they paid. Then too, Vizzari began using the

[1] From an article by Mark R. Arnold, staff writer. *National Observer.* p 1. F. 12, '68. Reprinted by permission.

luncheonette as a headquarters for bookmaking and loan-sharking, and the K's—against their will—were forced to handle details of the bookmaking operations. Finally, in desperation, Mrs. K wrote to local authorities.

The syndicate has now moved in and my life is not my own any more [she wrote]. I am willing to take the blame for my errors for doing this, but please get us out of this rat trap we are in. . . . I have been honest and worked almost all of the twenty-five years we are married and we paid our bills somehow or other honestly. I can't help anymore because I am a nervous wreck and live in fear almost every minute. I am turning both my husband and I in. Just give us some peace.

Two Strong-Arm Callers

Several days later, two men forced their way into her house. They took her hand and banged it against a closet door and "kept hitting it up against the closet," she later recalled. "And they said that was only a little bit of what I could expect. My hand the next day was all swollen up, black and blue."

Shortly thereafter, Mr. K ran away and Mrs. K was hospitalized in a state of nervous collapse. They lost the luncheonette and everything else they owned. The couple later was reunited and is now working outside New York State where, at the request of the State Investigation Commission, local police are "keeping a friendly eye out for them."

An isolated incident? Hardly. Loan-sharking in this nation is a $1 billion-a-year business, and most of it is controlled by the syndicate. By La Cosa Nostra. And that's only a part of it. Organized crime is big business, and it's getting bigger all the time.

Increasingly, the chieftains of La Cosa Nostra are moving into what have always been legitimate businesses—real estate, securities, manufacturing, food products, and many more. Another innovation is a relatively new racket known as planned bankruptcy. It gives the chieftains an acceptable "cover" for their illicit activities.

Enormous Income

Just a year ago, the President's Crime Commission reported that while no city in the nation is "completely controlled" by organized crime, "a considerable degree of corruption exists in many." Organized criminal activity exists in 80 per cent of cities with populations of one million or more, it said. And the Justice Department estimates that illegal gambling, the largest single source of underworld funds, yields profits in excess of $7 billion annually. Against that, General Motors earned $1.8 billion in 1966. Loan-sharking, of course, adds another $1 billion, and narcotics produces $350 million.

The people who share the proceeds of this illicit activity are largely known by Federal authorities. The structure and chain of command of the gangs or "families" who compose La Cosa Nostra (there are currently twenty-four) were made a matter of public record as long ago as 1963, in the highly publicized Senate hearings that featured the testimony of former mobster Joe Valachi.

"We know all this and more," says one New York authority, counting up the known basic facts on his fingers, "yet we're powerless." That's an overstatement to be sure. Attorney General Ramsey Clark noted the other day that of the 183 known members of La Cosa Nostra indicted or convicted in the past twelve years, 55 were indicted or convicted during 1967.

Even when allowance is made for the fact that some of the indictments will no doubt be dismissed, it is clear the Government is moving with vigor. Yet, concedes a top Federal prosecutor: "In today's Cosa Nostra operation, no man is indispensable. We're nailing the leaders as never before, but the show goes on."

The Focus of Publicity

What can be done? How dangerous really is La Cosa Nostra? Who runs it and how does it operate? Questions such as these bubble to the top of public consciousness only once in a great while and usually fleetingly. ...

New York is a good place from which to study La Cosa Nostra because its activities here are more closely watched than anywhere else in the country. The New York Police Department's Central Intelligence Bureau, the finest local-police intelligence unit in the nation, has files on the activities and associations of 2,500 individuals in the local syndicates, all cross-indexed and updated continually.

United States Attorney Robert M. Morgenthau, a lean, relentless, and immensely knowledgeable foe of La Cosa Nostra operators, has convicted more members of organized crime than any other prosecutor in the nation. In Queens, Manhattan, and Brooklyn, special racket squads working out of district attorneys' offices and special rackets grand juries devote full time to getting the goods on people behind illicit activities.

A Capital of Crime

It is a good place to study organized crime for another reason too. Of the 24 families in La Cosa Nostra, 9 are important enough to be represented on the decision-making board of directors, called the commission, and 5 of those 9 are head-quartered here. Indeed, half the 5,000 members estimated by the FBI to make up the national crime syndicate operate out of the New York City area, which makes this city something like the unofficial capital of organized crime in America.

The most important of the local family heads is in New York no longer. He is in the Federal penitentiary at Leavenworth on a fifteen-year narcotics conviction. Nonetheless, seventy-one-year-old Vito Genovese, referred to reverently by underlings only as "a certain party," continues to run the rackets by remote control, Federal authorities believe. Genovese lieutenants are extremely active in New Jersey operations from vending machines to night clubs and port facilities, and their influence extends to interests in east-side Mahattan bars and meat dealerships on Long Island.

Another old timer, now in failing health, is sixty-five-year-old Carlo Gambino, who lives in a stately mansion in Massapequa, Long Island, and whose activities, Federal authorities here testified, include almost every known illicit enterprise from labor racketeering to narcotics. Joseph (Joe Bananas) Bonanno, sixty-three, leader of a third New York family, dropped out of sight in 1964 and was believed to have fallen victim of other gangland leaders against whom he was rumored to have plotted. But he reappeared eighteen months later and has since been restored to the front ranks of leadership.

The Youngest Chieftain

Least well-known among the family heads is Brooklyn's Joseph Colombo, at forty-three the youngest La Cosa Nostra chieftain. Colombo (it was his "'family" to whom Mr. and Mrs. K paid vigorish) boasts an almost unblemished police record but his underlings include John (Sonny) Franzese, recently sentenced to fifty years for masterminding a series of bank robberies, more recently on trial for the gangland slaying of Ernest (The Hawk) Rupolo, whose body—hands bound, concrete blocks tied to the legs, one eye shot out—was found in Jamaica Bay in 1964.

The fifth New York family, headed by Thomas (Three Fingers Brown) Lucchese until his death (from natural causes) last July, is now leaderless, owing to the success with which the leading heirs have been prosecuted by authorities in New York.

The non-New York members of the ruling commission, as identified by law-enforcement officials, are Detroit's Joe Zerilli, seventy; Buffalo's Stefano Magaddino, seventy-six; Angelo Bruno of Philadelphia, fifty-seven; and Chicago's Sam Giancana, fifty-nine, who has taken up semipermanent residence in Mexico to avoid an appearance before a Federal grand jury that wants him to testify on organized crime. One more man, a non-Italian, figures prominently in the behind-the-scenes strategy of the nationwide crime syndicate. He is Meyer Lansky, sixty-five, the Miami-based financial wizard and gambling king of the organization. Lansky has been labeled by J. Edgar Hoover as "one of the most powerful racketeers in this country."

Almost all these men are engaged in legitimate enterprises. Joe Bonanno has large real-estate holdings in the Southwest, an interest in some Wisconsin cheeses, and used to have a share in a Brooklyn funeral parlor. Joe Zerilli has important food interests in Detroit and Florida. Carlo Gambino operated for years as a partner in a successful labor-consulting firm. Underlings are involved in everything from mattress making to children's toys. As do other Americans, crime chieftains court respectability. Both Lansky and Lucchese have seen their sons appointed to West Point.

Executive Sessions

These commissioners, or their representatives, meet irregularly to settle "jurisdictional disputes" between families, to target new fields to enter, or elect a successor for a family whose head has died. Since the secret gangland summit at Apalachin, New York, in 1957, for which twenty leaders were convicted of conspiracy (the convictions were later overturned), gangland meetings tend to attract only a few members to reduce the chances of alerting the authorities.

Some families are more active in certain fields than in others, depending on where they think it is to best advantage to "invest" their money. Several Gambino associates have been involved in stock frauds; Lucchese functionaries figured heavily in mob domination of several New York Teamster locals in the late 1950's. Even so, all the major families have a piece of the action in gambling, narcotics, and loan-sharking (the big three money-makers), plus such assorted enterprises as extortion, hijacking, and labor racketeering ("sweetheart" contracts and misuse of pension and welfare funds) .

Often mobsters use loan-sharking as a means of gaining control of legitimate enterprises, which they either continue to run (if they're profitable enough) or bleed into bankruptcy. The Murray Meat Packing Company, a New York City wholesale meat and poultry firm, is a classic example of the "scam," or planned bankruptcy. Involved to differing degrees in this enterprise were two members of the Gambino family. They were Peter Castellana, a cousin of Gambino's who operated a string of supermarkets in New York and supplied them through his own company, a wholesale meat and poultry enterprise, and Carmine Lombardozzi, whose reputation as investment chief or "money man" in the organization earned him the title, "'Wall Street representative of the Mafia."

Limited Capital

The owners of Murray Meat Packing did a $3 million annual business, but their capital amounted to only $125,000. When things went bad, they were unable to obtain a bank loan. A salesman for Castellana's meat company, Joseph Pagano, arranged a loan from an investment firm operated by Lombardozzi and Castellana. Interest was set at 1 per cent a week.

Shortly after arranging the loan, salesman Pagano, who had served seven years on a narcotics charge, bought one-third interest in Murray and signed an agreement with the owners making him company president, with "sole management and control" of the business.

Then the scam began. The idea was to buy as much [as possible] on credit, dispose of it fast, hide the proceeds, and leave creditors in the lurch. . . .

Over a period of months Murray steadily stepped up its purchases from suppliers, selling an increasing share to Castellana's wholesale meat company, often at below cost. All bills were paid promptly at first. Then, according to plan, Murray bought an unprecedented volume of produce, sold most of it to Castellana's outfit, and put the proceeds in the company account. Pagano proceeded to withdraw it systematically, holding off creditors with talk of a "clerical error in the bank."

In the final three months before the company declared bankruptcy, it was looted of $1.3 million. None of it was ever found. At least two creditors were also forced into bankruptcy. The stiffest penalties meted out were five years and $45,000 fines—to Pagano and Castellana. Castellana's meat company was fined $10,000. Argues one Federal prosecutor: "That's what makes scamming so attractive compared to, say, narcotics. You can steal $1.3 million from a company and get five years and a fine that amounts to a small business expense." . . .

How many fixes exist in New York or anywhere else can never be known with any certainty, for organized crime is, of necessity, an invisible empire. It can be dented, but never, on the basis of past experience, destroyed or even crippled.

Consider the experience of United States Attorney Morgenthau in prosecuting members of the Lucchese gang. Lucchese himself is dead. His No. 3 man, Vincent John Rao, received a five-year sentence [in January 1968] for lying to a special rackets grand jury. Half the captains, the day-to-day leaders of the syndicate, are theoretically out of commission. . . .

About 50 members of the 440-member family have been hauled before grand juries in the past three years, some of them two and three times. "We know we're hurting them," says Mr. Morgenthau, but how much? "They move more cautiously now." He adds: "The thing that makes this organized crime is that it is organized. We stop one operator, the next guy in line moves up."

Layers of Intermediaries

One of the problems is that it is hard to connect the leaders with the crimes of their underlings. The leaders are insulated by layers of intermediaries. Indeed, a family boss frequently doesn't know of some of the activities of his people. Another problem is that the law makes no distinction, as to sentencing, between a petty criminal and a hardened syndicate operator. Thus, even important hoodlums frequently don't remain behind bars for long.

"You'd be surprised how often some of these guys get out for good behavior," says one police authority. "The syndicate arranges for them to be offered a 'respectable' job, whereas a petty criminal can't get out early because he has no prospect of employment."

The President's Crime Commission recommended legislation to provide extended prison terms where the evidence indicates a felony was committed as part of a "continuing illegal business" in which the offender occupied a "management position." But there has been no action on the proposal.

Another Commission proposal that prosecutors consider of prime importance would widen the conditions under which Federal grand juries could offer witnesses immunity from prosecution. Brooklyn's district attorney, Aaron E. Koota, has been successful at hauling Cosa Nostra operatives before his grand juries, granting them immunity from prosecution, then asking them how they make their living. Most of them decline to answer, and are then convicted of contempt of court. Several Bonanno and Colombo associates have served thirty-day jail terms for contempt.

Federal Legislation Blocked

One who decided to answer rather than face contempt charges was Gambino lieutenant Carmine Lombardozzi. He has since been indicted for perjury and could get fifteen years, if convicted of lying to the Brooklyn grand jury. New York State's laws make this kind of immunity-granting easy; similar legislation on the Federal level is being blocked in committee by House Judiciary Committee chairman Emanuel Celler, who opposes it as a threat to civil liberties.

Many authorities contend it is futile to think organized crime can be eliminated until court-ordered electronic eavesdropping is permitted on a much larger scale than at present. Contends Professor G. Robert Blakey of Notre Dame Law School: "Only 3 to 8 per cent of the hard-core members of organized crime have been touched by the best" techniques of conventional investigation the nation can offer. This record, measured against the dimensions of the challenge, amounts to a "confession of impotence," he maintains. The only answer, as he sees it, is court-ordered eavesdropping.

Retorts another authority: "Of course electronic eavesdropping would be helpful, but let's not overestimate its role. Most of the big boys carry on as if every message, every phone call, every conversation were being intercepted. In a situation like that, its helpfulness is limited."

The Federal Government is spending roughly $20 million a year to fight organized crime. Some New York loan sharks run through that much money in a month. What are local communities doing? Next to nothing. Says Henry E. Peterson, chief of the Justice Department's organized-crime section:

There has been next to no response on the local or state level to organized crime. What is needed is an extensive prosecutive effort of a continuing nature, backed by an intelligence operation. In New York, Los Angeles, and Chicago you have police intelligence units, which are charged with following the movements of organized crime figures, but only in New York City do you also find special prosecutors whose job it is to follow through on this information and seek indictments.

Why don't more cities follow New York's example? One reason is that it's expensive. Another, experts suggest, is that crime chieftains are often influential in their home communities. They lead ostensibly respectable lives. The attorney for New York's Arthur Tortorello, known to law-enforcement authorities as a particularly violent "enforcer" (he once beat up a messenger because the man didn't bring him enough money), asked for clemency in a stock-fraud case after noting that Tortorello leads a Brooklyn Boy Scout troop for the handicapped.

Basically, organized crime exists because of the protections that democracy permits it to invoke. It flourishes, however, for another reason—because, in the final analysis, it performs a service. A businessman wants to trim labor costs to undercut his competition; a sweetheart contract lets him do it. A housewife dreams of a vacation in the Caribbean; her $2 bet around the corner keeps the dream alive.

Said the President's Crime Commission:

> A drive against organized crime usually uncovers political corruption. . . . Politicians will not act unless the public so demands; but much of the urban public wants the services provided by organized crime . . . and much of the public does not see or understand the effects of organized crime in society.

JUST CALL "THE DOCTOR" FOR A LOAN [2]

They call him "the Doctor." You will meet him, if such is your misfortune, in the swankiest nightclubs, his curvaceous young bride dangling on his arm. "'Meet my friend, the Doctor," the maître d' will say, performing the introductions. "The Doctor" is always most charming. A man in his fifties, he dresses like the owner of a million-dollar wardrobe. It is hard to imagine that he is in reality a hybrid—a species of spider-vulture who spins a web in which to enmesh his victim so he can pick clean the bones.

Though names cannot be used in this portrait, the Doctor (a nickname of unknown derivation) is no figment of the imagination. He exists. He is, authorities say, one of the largest and most vicious loan sharks operating in New York, just a step down the ladder from Carlo Gambino, probably the most powerful of the reigning chieftains of the city's five

[2] From article by Fred J. Cook, free-lance writer. New York *Times Magazine.* p 34+. Ja. 28, '68. © 1968 by The New York Times Company. Reprinted by permission.

Mafia families. Detectives who get up with the Doctor in the morning and follow him through his daily routine until they put him to bed at night know the pattern of his days by heart —and are completely frustrated because he operates the safest and most remunerative racket in the underworld.

He has no visible means of support, but he has put up his new bride in an expensively furnished mansion in one of the finer residential sections of the city. He never "works," as other humans know the term, but when he has been stopped and questioned by police, he has never had less than $7,000 in sweet cash upon his person—and sometimes he has had as much as $15,000. "You can never charge him with vagrancy," one prosecutor says, with a sour smile. Unlike a master bookie, he has no fixed headquarters, no elaborate telephone setup, no army of runners. He simply circulates. And in the best and most expensive places. And among the "best" people.

The far reach of such an operator was brought home to New Yorkers recently when former Water Commissioner James L. Marcus was indicted [and later convicted—Ed.] on charges of participating in a $40,000 kickback scheme on a city contract. According to investigators, Marcus was in deep financial trouble on several fronts, not the least of which was a reported $50,000 loan-shark debt to Mafia mobster Antonio (Tony Ducks) Corallo. Corallo was arrested with Marcus as his alleged partner in the kickback scheme. Later, two men were charged with taking part in a plot to murder a Government witness in the Marcus case. The episode, as reported, is similar to innumerable less publicized events in at least two ways: (1) the shark's victim was an intelligent, experienced person—professional people and substantial businessmen are the loan shark's favorite targets; (2) the victim found that when he was over a barrel with a loan shark, he was over a barrel with the Mafia—and that is being over a nasty barrel indeed.

Big Change Only

The popular conception of the loan shark as a two-bit hoodlum lending $5 on Monday and collecting $6 the next—the typical "six for five" operative—is an anachronism bearing virtually no relation to current reality. As Sergeant Ralph Salerno, the now-retired racket expert of the city's Bureau of Criminal Investigation (BCI), told the New York State Commission of Investigation in its loan-shark probe three years ago: "No self-respecting loan shark . . . would ever want to admit, even to his best friend, that he has loaned less than $100."

At the same hearings, then Assistant District Attorney Frank Rogers, of New York County, testified: "A loan shark that we know lent a million dollars in the morning and a million dollars in the afternoon." Loan-sharking is so remunerative, he said, that one mob boss had pyramided $500,000 into $7.5 million in about five years—and there were, in New York County alone, "at least ten men who are comparable to him."

The conclusion of all the expert witnesses was that loan-sharking is, on a national scale, a multi-billion-dollar resource of the underworld and that, while its gross take is less than gambling, it is preferred to gambling because it is so safe it almost defies prosecution.

This safety factor (which breaks down only when the shark is caught using violence to enforce collection or committing some other overt crime, as is charged in the Marcus case) is probably the reason that top mob bosses have been more openly connected with loan-sharking than with more risky enterprises, such as gambling and narcotics. . . . There are, all investigators agree, four operating levels [in loan-sharking]. On the top level is the family boss. Just under him are his trusted principal lieutenants. The lieutenants have their own subordinates to whom they funnel money for investment, and these third-echelon underlings, besides lending out much of it themselves split up the rest of the money and pass it down to the fourth and lowest level, the working bookie and street-corner hoodlum. Sergeant Salerno gave a graphic description of the way it all works. He said:

> A big racket boss could have a Christmas party in his home, to which he invites ten trusted lieutenants. He doesn't have to write their names down. He knows their names. They are friends of his. . . . He can take one million dollars, which is not an inconceivable amount of cash, and distribute that, $100,000 per man to these ten men. All he has to tell them is, "I want 1 per cent a week. I don't care what *you* get for it. But *I* want 1 per cent a week."
>
> He does not have to record their names. He does not have to record the amount. They are easy enough to remember. And if you stop to think that, 365 days later, at the next year's Christmas party, the only problem this gang leader has is where he is going to find five more men to hand out half a million dollars that he earned in the last year on the same terms. . . .

This usurious interest (the gang chieftain's 1 per cent a week becomes 52 per cent a year) is known in the trade as "vigorish"—or "the vig." (There is a theory that the term derives from the word "vicarage" and refers to the contributions given the vicar by his parishioners.) Naturally, the rate goes up as the money is filtered through the various echelons, and each takes its cut. On the second level, where the principal lieutenants dwell, the vigorish may amount to 1.5 or 2 per cent a week, and on the lowest operating level, where most ordinary loans are made, it will be 5 per cent a week— 260 per cent a year. And the underworld, ruthless and insatiable, has a whole arsenal of neat devices by which even this horrendous figure can be hiked.

Big Money Mover

The Doctor is one of those top-level lieutenants who would be invited to the big chief's Christmas party. Only in his case, he would probably not be given a piddling $100,000 to put to work, but something more like a million. "He is a

big, big money mover," says one detective. "They trust him.
He has hundreds of thousands of dollars working at any one
time."

Rarely, if ever, does the Doctor participate in the direct
lending of his hoard of cash. He works through his sub-
alterns, parceling out his share of the underworld treasury
among as many as thirty underlings on the third echelon of
the pyramid; they make the actual loans and collections and,
in turn, put some of the money to work through street-corner
bookies and hoods. Under such circumstances, life for the
Doctor becomes one unvarying round of seemingly innocent
social contacts. . . .

Inevitably, with a business as intricate as the Doctor's it
becomes necessary, as it is not in a more streamlined operation, to keep some detailed records. It is fairly simple for the
family boss who has parceled out $1 million in chunks of
$100,000 to each of ten principal lieutenants to keep his
accounts in his head; but when you split up hundreds of
thousands of dollars into hundreds of chunks, the transactions become too complicated. Even an agile brain cannot
retain the details without the help of a written record. Authorities have been successful in obtaining one such account
sheet of the Doctor's. It contains a long column of figures
that look as if they were taken from a bank's daily ledger.
Scanning the column at random, one notices amounts ranging from $13,000 to $43,000, each representing a loan. Some
of the loans are identified only by nickname or initial; others
have names spelled out beside them—including names of
subsidiary Mafia figures to whom the Doctor apparently had
funneled some of his money.

"We're sure this sheet represents loan-sharking business,"
the prosecutor who has it says, "but when we questioned the
Doctor about it, his alibi was that this was just an ancient
record, representing transactions from years and years ago
when he was in the bookmaking business."

Even when authorities get an indubitably current record,
it is extremely difficult to make much sense, still less a legal

case, out of the mysterious chicken scratches. One investigative unit recently came into possession of a red-covered, loose-leaf pocket notebook containing the record of transactions of a bookie-shark on the lowest level of the Doctor's ring. The flyleaf carries an unexplained notation: $15,000.

"This apparently was the money entrusted to him to lend out," a detective says.

The $15,000 item is followed by these other unexplained entries: $7,300, $3,900, $700. Out at the side of the page, the last sum is broken down into three other amounts: $250, $350, $100—apparently representing three smaller loans that made up the $700.

Who got the money? There is no way of telling.

"The guy who had this book carried it in his head," the detective says. "He knows who got the $7,300, who got the $3,900; he doesn't have to put down names."

Some of the inside pages of the notebook do contain more information. In transactions involving week-by-week payments over periods of several months, the shark had to keep a careful record. But even here the entries tell little. There are designations like "Brother," "Billy," "Fred." Just who they are is anybody's guess. One of these accountings shows that $500 was lent to be paid back at a rate of $50 a week for twelve weeks—a mere $600 for $500. Regular payments were made, except for one week. However, the borrower paid $100 the next week, was never delinquent again and the account was marked closed at the end of the twelve weeks.

Not all borrowers were so lucky. One account in this book deals with a loan that started out at $11,600. The borrower—whose name appeared beside the figures—made regular payments at the start, but then the burden obviously became too heavy. His payments lapsed for weeks. Penalties were assessed. These and the accumulations of vigorish boosted the indebtedness, despite what had been paid, to $16,898. There the account ends—permanently. The man who borrowed but could not pay was found murdered in a city alleyway, and investigators trying to solve the case are operating on the theory that he paid with his life for having had the bad judgment to cost the syndicate money.

The Borrower Be Warned

Such gory episodes point up a fact of life: the borrower is always at the mercy of the shark, and the shark, backed by all the awesome, terroristic power of the Mafia, is utterly ruthless. Coupled with his ruthlessness is a devilish cunning that is always devising new ways of getting people in his power—and then driving them right through a wall. . . .

The trouble gets just as deep as the loan shark in his generosity chooses to make it, for the shark makes up the rules of the game as he goes along, and the other player, the borrower, hasn't a thing in the world to say about it. If a borrower defaults for a couple of weeks or a month, the shark can assess any penalty that comes into his usurious mind—and the borrower has to pay or flee the country or risk being dumped in some dank gutter.

Frank Rogers, in his testimony before the Commission of Investigation, cited a case that began with a $6,000 loan to a businessman. The borrower made three payments, then missed two. For this heinous offense, the loan shark decided that the $6,000 would now be converted into $12,000, with the accompanying double vigorish. When the hapless borrower could not begin to pay this suddenly doubled load, the shark upped the principal to $17,000, then $25,000. "Just by simple mandate from the loan shark," Rogers testified, "you are in an irreversible situation. He says, 'This is the loan,' and that is it."

Once a victim has been driven completely through the wall by such devices, the shark sometimes grins his suddenly friendly smile and says, "O. K., I'm now your partner. I own half your business."

This doesn't mean he's really forgiving anything; he's simply stopped piling it on. But he still expects his vigorish on the old loan—and half his new "partner's" profits besides. The situation then rapidly deteriorates to the point of utter hopelessness, which is what the shark wants. Then he may say magnanimously, "Look, we will swap even. We will forget the loan, you forget the business. It is now all mine." The entire process, Rogers said, sometimes takes less than six months.

Such takeovers, Rogers told the investigation commission, run the gamut "from nightclubs to optical stores to brick companies." And, as testimony before the commission showed, to Wall Street brokerage houses and banks.

The loan shark, then, is the indispensable "money-mover" of the underworld. He takes "black" money tainted by its derivation from the gambling or narcotics rackets and turns it "white" by funneling it into channels of legitimate trade. In so doing, he exacts usurious interest that doubles the black-white money in no time; and, by his special decrees, by his imposition of impossible penalties, he greases the way for the underworld takeover of entire businesses. . . .

Vulnerable Businessmen

Why do supposedly sensible men get themselves into such binds? . . . [One victim] who lost all gave the commission a succinct answer: "I needed the money."

It is a refrain that is heard again and again. Certain kinds of businesses are especially vulnerable. In the garment business, an uncertain and cyclical industry, the owner of a dress factory often finds himself caught in a sudden squeeze; either money is tight or he does not have the kind of credit he needs at a bank—so he goes to a loan shark. Many a tavern owner begins business after spending years as a cook or bartender. He does not have much capital. By the time he has rented and furnished his place, he is running short of funds with which to lay in the costly supply of varied liquors that he needs to woo a well-paying clientele—so he goes to the loan shark. In the construction industry, capital can be tied up in long-term projects; when the crush for cash for a new venture becomes acute, a sum like $1 million may be needed the day after tomorrow—and so the construction company executive, too, goes to the loan shark....

Such is the unsavory picture. What can be done about it?

There must certainly be increased public understanding of the problem. Prosecuting officials have shouted themselves hoarse in the past, but the public still seems to think of the loan shark as an accommodating fellow who is offering a valuable service. The Commission of Investigation was told of one contractor who borrowed $1 million from a second-echelon loan shark for a construction project. The contractor began to list for the loan shark all the collateral he could put up to guarantee the loan.

The shark wasn't interested. "Your body is your collateral," he told the contractor, and with these words, for the first time, the contractor understood the kind of a deal he was entering.

The public *must* be made to understand, officials say, that when a man borrows from a loan shark, his body is, indeed, his collateral. There is a lien on his life. "Anyone who borrows from a loan shark is leaving himself open to strongarm methods," one prosecutor said. "People should borrow only from legitimate sources; otherwise, they are borrowing, not just money, but a sackful of trouble."

THE MOB AND THE STOCK MARKET [3]

Maintenance of the highest standard of ethics and integrity in our capital markets is essential not only for the protection of the investor but for the entire American economy.

[3] From "Infiltration of the Securities Industry," by Louis J. Lefkowitz, Attorney General of New York State. *Annals of the American Academy of Political and Social Science.* 347:52-7. My. '63. Reprinted by permission.

The importance of preserving confidence in our security, real estate, and other capital markets cannot be stressed too strongly, for there are few Americans who are not affected by their rise and fall.

Millions of Americans who are investors and who hold life-insurance policies have a real interest in the great capital markets. Insurance companies and banking institutions, within the limitations of law, are substantial investors in the bonds and stocks of corporations. Beneficiaries of pension funds and holders of investment-company shares have a similar interest. And the families of millions of citizens who directly own shares of corporations are vitally concerned.

Because our capital wealth is so broadly held, the securities markets provide the mechanism by which business raises the capital required to serve the economic needs of our nation. They provide the means and the wherewithal by which industry may be broadly shared by the people.

But investors are willing to place their savings at the disposal of industry only if they have confidence in the integrity of these markets and the people who are instrumental in their operation. Doubt and suspicion retard the uninhibited public spending and investing which is the lifeblood of America's economy.

We have enacted laws aimed at eliminating the fraud and deception which not only harm the investor but also destroy public confidence in the honest dealer. But no matter how many laws are placed on the statute books, and no matter the care which is taken in their drafting, there are always to be found the few who search for the loophole which will permit them to prey upon the investor.

In the securities field, as in every line of human endeavor, we find the unscrupulous small segment which hides behind the cloak of respectability but operates in the shadowland of legality. Consideration of ethics and integrity is, to these commercial pirates, a hollow and meaningless concept.

The New York State Department of Law, which I head as the Attorney General of the state, is engaged continuously in a vigorous, unrelenting fight to ferret out the unprincipled operator and drive him out of business. At the same time, recognizing that the best protection against fraud and deception is an alert and wary investor, we are carrying on a broad educational program to enable the investor to recognize and avoid the schemes and devices used by the unscrupulous element.

But this fight to prevent victimizing of the investor and to preserve vital public confidence is the responsibility of the industry as well as governmental agencies. It is only by a coordinated effort between law-enforcement bodies and those who are faithful guardians of the investor's trust that we can cleanse the securities field of the small segment of shady operators who seek to bilk the investing public.

One important aspect of this problem is to curb infiltration of the securities business by criminals and criminal elements. . . .

Criminal Operations in Securities

There are various inroads of professional criminal operation which we have at one time or another witnessed in the securities business. The simplest to detect is the notorious ex-convict who attempts under his own or an assumed name to operate a brokerage house as principal.

Next, we have a situation where the criminal element will direct dummy figureheads with or without their own appearance at the business office of the securities firm. Various are the means for such operations. The principal may technically hire himself as "salesman," in order to be available for personal supervision. But, the more professional the criminal element, the more likely it is that a trusted lieutenant will supervise field operations—sometimes reporting only to another lieutenant to avoid identification of the principal. Such situations may result from initial cash investment by the underworld of moneys obtained from illegal activities.

An artful device for underworld infiltration of the securities industry involves direction of stock-price manipulation activities. In such cases, the underworld seeks control of a spurious company and several avenues for "unloading" its fraudulent securities. The principal earmarks of the success of such a venture are the establishment of fictional market prices and use of high-pressure literature or phone calls to "unload" the stock. After an initial small purchase, the investor is phoned by a professional "loader" and flagrant misrepresentations are made to induce heavy purchasing. Most importantly, professional criminal groups operate as a team effort to maximize every possible success in perpetration of the fraud.

An insidious method by which the underworld cancer has spread into some corners of Wall Street is loan-sharking. By carrying insolvent brokers, or "warehousing" their debt obligations, at enormous interest rates—sometimes as high as 60 per cent initially—the gangster has in the past become virtual ruler of several over-the-counter securities firms. As can be imagined, control of this type leads to additional gangsterism in business methods. Sometimes the debts are initiated by pressures caused by improvident gambling or excessive living expenses incurred by broker-dealers.

On occasion, the criminal take-over is a case of pure blackmail—based on an owner's indiscretion.

Several years ago, several gangsters just walked in and muscled their way into control of a brokerage firm under circumstances having all the elements of gangster extortion through fear of physical harm.

The problems posed to government would seem to be in two categories: (1) criminal elements openly operating and identifiable in the selling areas of the securities business; and (2) the criminal combine operating from outside the normal channels of the securities business. . . .

Attack on Infiltration

The first step in our attack on the danger of criminal infiltration was enactment by the New York State Legislature in 1958, on my recommendation, of an amendment to the Martin Act, to include the following new language:

Sec. 353 (2) Upon a showing by the attorney-general in an application for an injunction that any person engaged in the purchase, sale, offer to purchase or sell, issuance, exchange, promotion, negotiation, advertisement or distribution within this state of any security or securities, either as principal, partner, officer, agent, employee or otherwise, has ever been convicted by a court of competent jurisdiction in any state or county of any felony; or of any other criminal offense by any such court, whether or not constituting a felony, involving securities, the supreme court after a hearing may issue a permanent injunction awarding the relief applied for, or so much thereof as the court may deem proper, against such person shown to have been so convicted, in the form and manner provided for in subdivision one of this section in case of one who actually has or is engaged in any fraudulent practice.

Several dozen ex-convicts immediately exited Wall Street or were forced out by court injunctions obtained by the Securities Bureau of my office. So many left for New Jersey that the Jersey legislature a year later enacted its own stringent law, which even required fingerprinting of all applicants for a securities broker-dealer license.

Remaining as a major problem in New York, on which we then focused, were the hundreds of transient securities salesmen who flitted in and out of high-pressure over-the-counter firms. Many never used their own names, to avoid detection by routine government checks of their reputations or criminal records. With this in mind, New York State in 1959, on my recommendation, enacted the Salesman Registration Act, which for the first time in our state required securities salesmen to register. In addition, the new law made it unlawful for a broker to hire an unregistered salesman.

In my opinion, these two new statutes are responsible for reducing "boiler-rooming" to infrequent operations in place of regularly organized business in our state. And the gangster element which thrived on boiler-room activities found it more and more difficult to conduct business in New York. (The investing public is mulcted each year of millions of dollars by unscrupulous and criminal promoters operating out of "boiler rooms." The boiler room is a room lined with desks or cubicles, each with a salesman and telephone, where high-pressure peddling is done, over the telephone, of stocks of dubious value.)

But the underworld continues to pose a threat to the securities business.

Specialties and Scope

Once the organized underworld has moved into a securities operation it is able to buy or extort assistance in the securities field to help in the actual distribution of securities. We have found that their agents know the intricacies of securities manipulations, corporate finance, and public relations and are utilized effectively to initiate and supervise the nationwide or even worldwide distribution of securities in a fraudulent or illegal manner. There are specialists catering to the underworld who find "shell" corporations, mining corporations which can be given a romantic flavor, or a worthless electronic or missile corporation that can be promoted. There are specialists in cashing checks and in insuring payment, or forging or stealing necessary documents. There are specialists available to the underworld for writing and preparing attractive brochures and literature which have a sophisticated flavor. There are specialists who can contact traders in the over-the-counter securities houses who create, maintain, and manipulate a market. This is an organized effort which is so remakable in its efficiency that it requires expert skill to expose, eliminate, prevent, and prosecute.

The existence of a concerted drive by the organized underworld, when apparent, requires that all law-enforcement agencies exert the maximum of effort to prevent the spread and to eliminate this condition.

CRIME AND LABOR UNIONS [4]

Six years ago Senator John McClellan, the dour Arkansas Democrat, seemingly rang down the curtain on the labor union activities of two reputed Mafia stalwarts who allegedly had penetrated deeply into the Teamsters Union.

The pair, Antonio (Tony Ducks) Corallo and John (Johnny Dio) Dioguardi, had been described in Senate hearings in the late 1950's as veteran mobsters who invaded Teamsters locals in the New York City area and sought to capture control of Joint Council 16, central unit of the union around New York.

By the early 1960's they seemed to have been driven from power. In his 1962 book *Crime Without Punishment,* Senator McClellan said it was unlikely that "crooks and gangsters" such as Corallo and Dioguardi, "ousted from the ranks of labor leaders, will ever again be able to grab positions of power in organized labor."

There is bad news, Mr. McClellan. Corallo and Dioguardi are back.

Neither man is an officer or even a member of a Teamsters unit. But Federal investigators say that Tony Ducks and Johnny Dio now personally control at least seven of the fifty-six locals in Joint Council 16. The investigators are convinced that other gangsters, representing several Mafia "families," have a hold on nine other locals. Corallo and Dioguardi are "captains" in the Mafia family of the late Thomas (Three Finger Brown) Lucchese, according to Federal officials.

Disenchanted sources within the union corroborate that underworld influence on the Teamsters is extensive and growing, although one twenty-five-year veteran says the Federal estimate of its extent is "a little high." . . .

[4] From "Crime and Labor: Mobsters Grab Power in 16 Teamster Locals in the New York Area," by staff reporter Nicholas Gage. *Wall Street Journal.* p 1. Ja. 18, '68. Reprinted by permission.

The Payoff

For men like Corallo and Dioguardi, control of labor units means one thing—money. Over the years, underworld chieftains have developed a variety of methods for using union connections to enrich themselves. Loans from union funds are arranged for individuals willing to pay a "finder's fee" (10 per cent of the loan is an average figure). Pension and welfare funds or insurance programs go to brokers who are willing to share the commissions. An environment for profitable pilferage and theft from businesses is created.

Most lucrative is labor peace at a price. Companies plagued with work stoppages and inefficiency sometimes find that their problems vanish with a payment to the right man. (The deal isn't always for cash; one newspaper chain, not in New York, long has guaranteed that its delivery trucks run on time by declining to print unkind remarks about James R. Hoffa, the imprisoned general president of the Teamsters.)

One favorite instrument for profiting from involvement with labor is the "consulting firm" operated by gangsters. Companies with difficulties become clients, and their difficulties disappear. Dioguardi once had such a firm, Equitable Research Associates. A similar organization flourished for a time as S.G.S. Associates (the G in the name stood for Carlo Gambino, head of a New York Mafia family, while the two S's stood for two of his business associates).

New York State Investigation Commission hearings also showed how a union can achieve tremendous power over an industry. Alvin C. Schweizer, an official of Air Cargo Inc., testified that one man had the power to tie up the entire air freight industry in New York City.

The man? Harry Davidoff, Dioguardi's associate and the chief of Teamsters Local 295, whose members are air freight chauffeurs, handlers and warehousemen in the New York area.

A Tale of Intimidation

Davidoff took the Fifth Amendment at the SIC hearings. But various witnesses testified that he had used pressure and intimidation to force airlines to deal only with truckers who employ his men. One such story came from John Eschmann, part owner of Direct Airport Service Inc., Huntington, New York.

This company has a labor contract with a Teamster competitor, Amalgamated Union Local 355. Mr. Eschmann testified that Davidoff contacted National and Northwest airlines when they were considering business arrangements with Direct Airport last August. If the airlines signed with Mr. Eschmann's company, Davidoff allegedly threatened, they could expect endless labor troubles at Kennedy International Airport. The lines reportedly backed down. (Neither National nor Northwest will comment on the Eschmann testimony)....

Davidoff's Teamsters Local 295 pressures airlines to employ only truckers who are members of MITA [Metropolitan Import Truckmen's Association] investigators say. One independent trucker, Arthur J. Gibbard, told the SIC that an important client dropped his services after a telephone call from "a 295 delegate" threatened picketing against the shipper. Mr. Gibbard said that he previously had declined an invitation to join MITA from Philip Giocene, a felon friendly with Dioguardi....

The way things are now in New York, a trucker who wants any kind of air freight business has to sign a contract with Local 295 and belong to MITA [says Ralph F. Salerno, a former detective chief in the New York City Police Department, an acknowledged expert on organized crime and now a consultant to the National Council on Crime and Delinquency]. If you look hard enough at both organizations you'll see the shadow of Johnny Dio. This doesn't mean that Dio controls everything. I think it would be more accurate to say that there is an alliance of gangsters, the most conspicuous of whom is Dio.

Such an alliance injures the public at large as well as commercial interests. The State Investigation Commission was told that thefts . . . [in 1967] at Kennedy International Airport totaled $2.5 million, including large amounts of cash, diamonds and electronic equipment. Much pilferage probably isn't reported. "The situation at Kennedy is approaching conditions on the docks," says Paul Kelly, counsel to the commission. "Shippers close their eyes to it to avoid trouble with the union and simply pass on the cost to the consumer."

WHY ORGANIZED CRIME THRIVES [5]

"The extraordinary thing about organized crime is that America has tolerated it for so long." So concluded the National Crime Commission, and so do the facts reveal. An America that becomes outraged by symbolic gestures, such as flag-burnings or draft-card destruction on the part of a few, cannot seem to mount widespread oratory or action against systematic looting of society by corporations of criminality. One street rape can produce more sustained outcries than does the day-to-day illegal profiteering of organized crime.

This uncanny ability to neutralize potential opposition is a tribute to the skill, sophistication, and power of organized criminal groups. It has been seldom analyzed, seldom articulated, and too little understood in its full weight. The following offers some of the reasons why our society fails to act against organized crime.

Performance of Services

One way to get people on your side is to do something for them. Organized crime does this for all potential opposition. Much of the public wants to gamble in small, daily amounts, and organized crime complies. Customers for narcotics and quick, cash loans receive instant, curb-side service. The policeman seeking extra income can easily acquire a hand-

[5] From article by Henry S. Ruth, Jr., professor of law, University of Pennsylvania. *Annals of the American Academy of Political and Social Science*. 374: 113-22. N. '67. Reprinted by permission.

some weekly stipend for overlooking those criminal violations that the compliant "victims" do not want prosecuted
anyhow. The aspiring politician needs financing, and organized crime offers large amounts of cash requiring no public
accountability. These politicians become mayors, district
attorneys, judges, and legislators. Businessmen may need labor peace; they may need loans; they may need "successful
fires" from which insurance proceeds rescue a faltering enterprise; they may need a "fixer" who can smooth the path
through the possible governmental stumbling blocks of
zoning, licensing, and compliance with myriad regulations.
Organized crime provides all these services. Successful labor
organization requires discipline, unity, and a rapport with
business or, at least, the ability to frustrate that business
completely. Organized crime is available for these purposes
also. In cities, suburbs, and rural areas scattered throughout
almost all sectors of the nation, organized crime stands ready
to satisfy any reasonable desire, any reasonable ambition, of
anyone willing to cooperate with it. It will render less extensive, but yet very helpful, services to anyone already possessing social, economic, or political power. The price is
immunity from action against organized crime. Potential opposition is neutralized.

The National Crime Commission stated:

Consider the former way of life of Frank Costello, a man who
has repeatedly been called a leader of organized crime. He lived in
an expensive apartment on the corner of 72nd Street and Central
Park West in New York. He was often seen dining in well-known
restaurants in the company of judges, public officials, and prominent businessmen. Every morning he was shaved in the barbershop
of the Waldorf Astoria Hotel. On many weekends he played golf
at a country club on the fashionable North Shore of Long Island.
In short, though his reputation was common knowledge, he moved
around New York conspicuously and unashamedly, perhaps ostra-
cized by some people but more often accepted, greeted by journalists, recognized by children, accorded all the freedoms of a pros-
perous and successful man. On a society that treats such a man in
such a manner, organized crime has had an impact.

Fear

Fear has many forms and serves many purposes of organized crime. One can fear for one's own physical well-being or that of family and other loved ones. One can fear that the business to which a lifetime has been devoted will be destroyed. One can fear that a past moral dereliction may rise to the surface and destroy a promising political career or advanced employment status. Organized criminal groups utilize these and other forms of fear for continuing systems of extortion, usurious loans, maintenance of unity within the criminal organization, discouragement of informants and witnesses, and the securing of favorable action and inaction from public officials.

Selective fulfillment of threats gives the appearance of an ability to make any threat an actuality. Thus, only occasional violence is needed by organized crime to exploit in full the opportunities that the threat of violence affords. The economic and other rewards secured by threats are maximized without the public outrage and law-enforcement activity that would be engendered by continuous actual violence. As in any field of activity, the aura of overwhelming power has great residual benefit and induces respect and compliance beyond what actual power could or even would want to enforce. Fear is therefore useful to discourage opposition from any potential source, public or private. Individual fears also deter the initiation of collective opposition.

Fragmenting the Problem

Lack of knowledge about organized criminal groups has meant that the public, and even those directly concerned with combating organized crime, see only bits and pieces of what the groups are, what they do, and what effect they have upon society. One may see an article on gambling and organized crime or read about legislative hearings on narcotics and organized crime. A reporter may publish a story about organized crime's infiltration of legitimate business or a

Federal agency may spend years unraveling bankruptcy fraud schemes perpetrated by organized crime. With this fragmentation, very few persons are raising the question as to what social, political, economic, and criminal effects are produced by the fact that Cosa Nostra groups in practically all sectors of the nation are doing all these things all the time.

Fragmentation also builds up stereotypes in public conception of even organized crime's individual activities. For example, the idea that organized crime still controls and derives much income from prostitution has been perpetuated despite several years of indication to the contrary. Wholly irrelevant remedies, such as legalizing prostitution, are thus still being proposed as a partial counterthrust against organized crime.

Fragmentation of the problem also serves to hinder possible preventive efforts. Concentration upon gambling and loan-sharking alone deters analysis and planning based upon the broader and more correct conception that organized crime desires to, and does, participate in any criminal activity that offers high profit at low risk of detection.

Fragmentation also means that the public, being aware of only part of the problem, develops much less concern than if the total picture were available to them. Scholars, too, unable to perceive from existing public data that here, indeed, is a national problem deserving priority, have practically neglected organized crime as an area of study. . . .

Failures of Perspective

Popular representations of the scope of organized crime too often convey to the uninitiated the impression that these criminal groups operate in a separate world of crime that victimizes principally the greedy and the amoral, the seekers of a "fast buck," the persons who deserve what they get. Organized crime is therefore bracketed in a separate compartment as a phenomenon that certainly deserves attention sometime, but need not occupy a position of priority and significance, considering the wealth of other social and criminal problems. Indeed, the present Attorney General of the United States, Ramsey Clark, sees organized crime as a "tiny part" of the entire crime picture, though an important one. Improving life in the ghettos, saving youth from lives of crime, upgrading law enforcement and criminal justice—these are all seen as problems separate and apart from organized crime.

This narrow and shallow perspective does not survive an examination of the facts. From the standpoint of economic cost, the National Crime Commission stated that organized crime acquires about twice as much income from its illegal operations as criminals derive from all other kinds of criminal activity combined. And that is based upon conservative estimates of organized crime's net income from activities such as gambling, narcotics, and loan-sharking; it also excludes the millions of dollars that organized-crime groups acquire from infiltration of legitimate business.

There is a clear connection between so-called ordinary crimes and organized crime. Former Attorney General Katzenbach noted in 1965 that:

It is racketeers' involvement in narcotics which causes substantial theft and robbery, committed by addicts to support their hunger.

It is the racketeer's method of dealing with those who stand in his way which establishes examples of violence for others.

Organized crime is known as a sponsor of burglaries, hijacking, and bank robberies. The National Crime Commission pointed out that trucking, construction, and waterfront shipping companies, in return for assurance that business operations will not be interrupted by labor discord, countenance pilferage sponsored by organized crime on company property....

Little research and study has been attempted concerning organized crime's influence and effect upon life in the ghettos. Certainly, the police corruption that youths observe in the slums must affect their view of the power structure and of the appropriateness of respect for law and its enforcement officers. Said Mr. Katzenbach: "Young people in the slums cannot be expected to obey and respect laws if the guardians of the law are on the 'take.' " Certainly, organized crime feeds upon and seeks to perpetuate the depravity of the slums. Said an underworld figure: "You make more money out of a Harlem than a Scarsdale [the latter being a wealthy New York City suburb]." Certainly, the heroes of young persons in the deprived areas are those possessing all the indicia of power and influence, that is, the racketeers. Said an organized-crime participant: "Younger inmates [in two Massachusetts prisons] would do anything to get in with these people, figuring that they would become big men." The measure of respect for organized-crime figures among slum youth was recognized by the New York City Youth Board in calling upon three such leaders to help settle violence in the East New York section [of Brooklyn].

A group of youths in a large city, whose favorite pastime was disrupting a numbers operation by stealing and relocating numbers slips and records secreted by runners at various hiding places in the neighborhood, once told me that they saw life in their community as racket figures with public officials running the world. Even their school teacher, at the behest of a racket operator, had scolded the boys for hiding "the action." In their view, norms and standards had to be developed from within themselves. The adult world provided nothing worthy of emulation.

Concluded the National Crime Commission:

In many ways organized crime is the most sinister kind of crime in America. . . . [It] is not merely a few preying upon a few. In a very real sense it is dedicated to subverting not only American institutions, but the very decency and integrity that are the most cherished attributes of a free society. As the leaders of Cosa Nostra and their racketeering allies pursue their conspiracy unmolested, in open and continuous defiance of the law, they preach a sermon that all too many Americans heed: The government is for sale; lawlessness is the road to wealth; honesty is a pitfall and morality a trap for suckers.

Too many Americans heed the advice that organized crime is a "tiny part" of the crime problem. The limited perspective which most of the public and its governmental servants possess about organized crime is perhaps the severest detriment to the construction of a strong countereffort.

III. CRIME AND THE POLICE

EDITOR'S INTRODUCTION

Law enforcement in the United States reflects the country's hallowed traditions of local autonomy. Instead of one central police force (as in most other countries), the United States has about 40,000 separate law enforcement agencies—and they vary greatly in performance. Although many do their work in an efficient and compassionate manner, many others are inadequate. Especially in rural areas, local police forces are likely to be understaffed, undertrained, and inefficient.

Further burdening law enforcement work is the problem of conflicting jurisdictions. A police officer's power may stop at the county line, but organized crime, for example, never respects county boundaries.

The first article in this section, prepared by the editors of *Congressional Digest,* summarizes the basic steps in the law enforcement process. In the second selection, the novelist and playwright Bruce Jay Friedman gives a vivid description of the work of a pair of Chicago homicide detectives on the beat. This is followed by an interview with O. W. Wilson, then superintendent of the Chicago police department, whose work has drawn widespread praise for reducing crime and improving community relations. The next article, by a lawyer, Richard H. Kuh, describes the controversy surrounding the police practice of "stopping and frisking" persons considered suspicious, without necessarily making an arrest. The fifth article, taken from *Senior Scholastic,* examines the issue of wiretapping and "bugging" and the problems of balancing the individual's right to privacy against society's need to protect itself. The next selection, by *National Observer* staff reporter Robert Ostermann, discusses New York State's computerized information system. The last article in the section, by attorney and law professor Morris Ploscowe, calls for fundamental changes in law investigation and police organization in order to eliminate the threat of organized crime to our society.

BASIC STEPS OF THE ENFORCEMENT PROCESS [1]

Justice in most criminal cases is administered in the United States through one of two separate but generally parallel systems of courts—a Federal system which includes both trial and appellate courts, in which are tried violations of Federal law; and a state system consisting of several levels of trial courts and one or more appellate court levels. The state courts and their procedures are established by state constitutions or laws, and are charged with enforcing the laws of the state and its component political subdivisions. Most offenses against person or property represent violations of state rather than Federal law and are, accordingly, tried in the state court systems.

At the apex of both systems is the United States Supreme Court, which under the Constitution has original jurisdiction in specified categories of cases, and appellate jurisdiction in many other areas.

The Process of State Law Enforcement

The initial step in criminal law enforcement is normally taken by an officer of one of the several levels of police authority—state, county, or municipal—existing within the state. Following investigation of an offense, police follow arrest procedures which are generally similar for all levels of police within the state. Except in cases where an offense occurs in the presence of the arresting authority, an arrest warrant must first be obtained. This may be issued by a justice of the

[1] Article in *Congressional Digest*. 46:194. Ag-S. '67. Reprinted by permission.

peace or other designated authority on the complaint of an aggrieved citizen, by request of the police, or as the result of an indictment by a grand jury.

Following arrest, the suspect is in the custody of police and is normally "booked"—the particulars of the offense, his identity, and related information made an official record at the police station in whose jurisdiction the offense occurred. The suspect is also photographed and fingerprinted in most instances.

After booking, which concludes the formalities of arrest, an individual must generally be brought before a justice of the peace or other magistrate whose responsibility is to make a preliminary assessement of the apparent facts in the case and to take those steps necessary to guarantee the availability of the suspect for further judicial process—either by ordering his temporary incarceration or by setting the amount of his bail bond. At this time a date is generally fixed when the accused must appear before a court of limited jurisdiction, either for trial in the case of a lesser offense, or for preliminary hearing of the charges in the case of a major offense.

At the preliminary hearing, conducted before a court of limited jurisdiction, the police charge is read to the suspect, and the court makes a finding of whether there was probable cause for the arrest. In some instances, charges may be dismissed by such courts if found insubstantial; where charges are found to have reasonable substance, the court customarily remands the case to a grand jury for further procedure. The level of bail bond set for the accused is also subject to review at most preliminary hearings.

The prosecution of offenders is normally the responsibility of the state's attorney (or district attorney) for the jurisdiction in which the offense occurred. His office prepares the case against the accused, conducts any necessary additional investigation, and presents the state's case to the grand jury, where applicable, and in the trial court. In most jurisdictions the state's attorney is an elective officer, responsible to the electorate; he normally serves as an adviser to the police in the enforcement of law.

Stated most simply, the police may be said to investigate and arrest, the state's attorney to investigate and prosecute, and the courts to adjudicate the guilt or innocence of the accused.

If the grand jury—which in most states is regarded as an adjunct to the investigative and prosecutive role served by the state's attorney—finds probable cause, it indicts the suspect. Normally, an accused person does not appear before a grand jury, since its role is investigative rather than judicial.

Upon indictment, the suspect is arraigned before a judicial officer of the trial court, the charges are read to him, his plea of guilt or innocence is noted, the identity of his counsel—if he has one—is ascertained, or provision is made for securing counsel, and a tentative date for his trial may be set.

At trial, the accused is defended by his own or, in cases of indigence, court-appointed counsel; is prosecuted by the state's attorney or one of his assistants; and the case is tried by a justice of the court before a jury, unless the accused has waived his right to a jury trial, in which case the presiding justice makes the determination of guilt or innocence on the basis of the testimony and evidence presented.

CHARGE: MURDER [2]

I spent part of last January with the detective division in Chicago, and it took me a week to realize the things I saw weren't being taped as a dark-horse entry in NBC's new fall lineup....

Notified of a homicide, a relative falls back in the great tradition of television shock. "My God! Who in the world

[2] From article "Arrested by Detectives Valesares and Sullivan—Charge: Murder," by the novelist and playwright Bruce Jay Friedman. *Saturday Evening Post.* 240:38-47. Ap. 22, '67. Reprinted by permission of Russell & Volkening, Inc., as agents for the author. Copyright © 1967 by Curtis Publishing Company, Inc.

would've wanted to hurt that nice man?" . . . "Me kill him?" says a Rod Serling-wise suspect in another case, "why, that man was like a daddy to me." . . . "I don't talk to coppers," snarls a young South Side punk and obvious late-movie addict. . . . "Go ahead and frame us," barks his friend, an Edward G. Robinson buff. . . . "All right," the detective teases back, handing them a subtle concoction of Coburn-Marvin-Duff and middle-period Dane Clark, "I'll slap a frame on you so good you'll hang on the wall for forty years."

Yet finally, there are some big differences. There is no way to wrap up a real murder and make it go away in thirty minutes with three short breaks for a word from our sponsor. Crime and real violence have a smell to them that simply doesn't come through on prime time. There is no way to pan in on the hate-stitched mouth of a woman whose father has just been stabbed to death. No flick has ever picked up the smell of dead blood, the things people use to mop it up, the volcanic calm that comes over frightened people involved in a homicide. . . .

Real violence doesn't require effects, montages, camera angles, establishing shots. Mostly it is the particular smell of violence that does not survive the trip from life to actors to camera across TV tubes and into the living room—the smell of rooms in which terrible things have happened, the smell of guilty sweat, the smell of serious gunpowder. . . .

Captain Otto Kreuzer is the chief of Chicago's 1,200 detectives, and it was his idea that before zeroing in on one or two of his men for this story, I ought to see a comfortable sampling of them—detectives who specialize in armed robbery, homicide, auto theft, sex and aggravated assault.

In my talk with him, Kreuzer put a lot of emphasis on the social underpinnings of crime; he used the word "compassion" quite often, saying it each time with enormous ceremony and conviction. I did not think that unusual until I had spent some time working in the detective division. There is much talk—all of it somehow expected—about police-shackling, about the limiting powers of the Supreme

Court's Miranda and Escobedo decisions. "The Fifth Amendment says a man doesn't have to convict himself," a detective sergeant said to me, "but it sure as hell used to help." [*Miranda v. Arizona* and *Escobedo v. Illinois* were two recent U.S. Supreme Court decisions dealing with procedures to be followed by law enforcement officers following the arrest of a person accused of a crime. In *Escobedo v. Illinois* (1964) the Court ruled out a confession as usable evidence in court if the police questioned a suspect without permitting him to confer with a lawyer or without advising the suspect of his right to remain silent. In *Miranda v. Arizona* (1966), the Court expanded on its earlier Escobedo ruling by spelling out the right of a suspect to avoid self-incrimination during police interrogation.—Ed.]

If the detectives are not exactly cheerful about the new rulings, they struck me as being more or less resigned to them and determined to go about their business in the face of them. One does not have to be a bleeding heart to see quickly that they retain awesome power. They have the guns, the intelligence, the techniques, and there is that manner they have of "dropping in" on people. I honestly don't think they realize the kind of havoc one of those little unexpected visits can produce. The hoods, of course, are used to seeing them— but anyone concerned about so-called police-shackling needs only to observe the terrifying "calm" that comes over a banker or an internist when two representatives of the law decide to drop by on some little matter that happened four months ago.

While my detectives were being rounded up, I took a tour of Chicago's dazzling police headquarters and communications center. It is the envy of the world, and police officials all the way from Hamburg come over to look at it. Its best feature is that Chicago police can answer a call for help faster than any police in history. Crime is now "data-systemed," "despatched," "regulated," "administered." You feel that a criminal might feel terribly elevated by it all, might enjoy a sense of status, as though he, too, in his own small way, were doing his bit for the IBM team. In the detective division there are scaled maps of the city in which different types of crimes are charted with multicolored pins. Voyeurs get one color pin on the sex-crime chart, indecent-exposure people another—so that detectives can tell at a glance whether a small wave is building up in a particular neighborhood. I noticed one clump of similarly colored pins that seemed to be piling up on the armed-robbery chart. The armed brigand in this case turned out to be a man who had been calling restaurants, asking that pizza be sent to a certain address, then lying in wait for the delivery man, hitting him over the head and stealing his money (also, presumably, the pizza). He had pulled half a dozen jobs, but now he was being "data-systemed" and "processed," and before long would be snatched from the ranks of underworld specialists. . . .

After detectives' roll call at their headquarters . . . [Detectives Pete Valesares and John L. Sullivan] picked me up at my hotel one morning at 0900 (military time is used in the Chicago Police Department). A newsstand clerk had advised me to remain in the hotel for my entire stay, that I was crazy to go out into the Chicago streets. "Big as you are, they'll leap on your back, snatch your glasses and grab your wallet. They work in teams."

While waiting in the lobby, I stood with my newspaper up over my face, Alfred Hitchcock-movie style, just to get into the swing of things. Their car, or "squad," on this day was a Plymouth '66, equipped with radio gear but not particularly souped up. Neither felt any particular craving for a James Bond tire-slasher of a vehicle. I sat in the back next to John's attaché case which is marked "John L. Sullivan— Crime Detection." He calls it his "Clue Box." At the roll call both men had checked to see whether any new homicides or "fresh ones" had come in the night before and, having found the well dry, were now going out to work on their unsolved murders of the near past. John's favorite was a four-month-old gang shooting of a youth whom the killers had mistaken for someone else. A new lead had tumbled in from a "friend," as a spin-off from another case, and we were off to track it down. "You hate to forget a juvenile murder," said John, "since there are at least two hundred kids out on the street who know your man." Sooner or later, someone would start to brag about it, to say "Guess who I shot?" at some pool hall —since that was really the only reason to do it in the first place.

I had always felt the sets for Harold Pinter plays were the ultimate in grayness until I saw the South Side of Chicago in January. It is a grim, thickly populated area, made up of working-class Negroes, Italians, Lithuanians, Poles, who live in beat-up single-family homes and three-story apartment houses. Pete and John took me on a cruise of their district, and our excursion had much the same flavor as a Marine reconnaissance mission into Cong country. The area is gang-inhabited, each of the warring factions staking out its boundaries on the sides of stores and buildings with giant scrawls that said, "Blackstone Rangers," "Devil's Disciples," "Apache Rangers." Pete said it was virtually impossible to survive in this part of Chicago if you did not belong to one of the gangs, but that gang activity slowed down in cold weather. . . .

We ran through the area—Emma's Eat Shop, Bob's Recreation, Upper Room Healing Center, First Pentecostal Church of Christ Inc., Bush's Soul Bar-B-Que, Al's Action Lounge—until Pete suggested a coffee break, and John reluctantly said all right. He had figured you wasted three hundred hours a year on those "breaks" and imagine how much digging you could do in that time. We took seats in the rear of a restaurant, John drinking ice-cold Diet Pepsi, which he orders regularly through the day, often along with banana-cream pie. Pete said that detectives would generally sit in the rear of public places or at least with their backs to the wall. He felt that he could generally spot a detective by the way he walked into a room, looked around, took his time being seated, by the way he carried himself. He felt that a detective was somewhat more poised than the average man.

We left the restaurant and drove over to see the young man who might have some new information on the four-month-old gang slaying. . . . We met our man at a place on South Vernon: a low-echelon gambler and ladies' man in his early twenties with a kind of boneless, easy-going calypso style. He wore a bandanna and did not take his eyes off the television set once during the interrogation. We sat there easily, comfortably, four fellows having a little midday chat, Pete tossing in an occasional jive expression ("So you got anything cool for us, babe?"), but for the most part allowing John to work out of his strength with juveniles. ("I spend two hours with a kid and wind up invoking the Blessed Virgin Mary," Pete had said. "Then John does his older-brother routine and cracks the case in five minutes.") This one seemed a fruitless interview, but Pete and John had put in a good word for the fellow after a recent street rumble and had a feeling there might be a little return dividend rolling in.

As we prepared to leave, our man, eyes still fixed on daytime TV, mentioned a certain "mean, ugly dude who was shooting his mouth off down at the pool hall, about a month back." John didn't respond particularly, but in the car he said he felt a four-month-old slaying was about to be solved. "He knows who did it," John said, "but he has to figure out a way of telling us roundabout." The man would feed them a few pieces at a time, and when he had given them everything but the name, John and Pete would "guess" the man's identity. That way, no one would ever be able to say the informant was a stool pigeon.

Pete was pessimistic, however, and like the Hollywood writer who doesn't believe he has been paid until he has not only cashed the check but spent the money, he felt that no case was anywhere until the report said, "Arrested by Detectives Valesares and Sullivan. Charge: Murder." That, of course, is what it was all about, and when you had brought a case like that home you saw how trivial it was to make a burglary arrest—or any other arrest, for that matter.

A POLICEMAN LOOKS AT CRIME [3]

Q. Superintendent Wilson, is crime getting out of control?

A. Yes, it appears to me that it is. Crime has been increasing about five times more rapidly than our population, and this can't go on forever. Simple arithmetic will indicate that we will be in very serious trouble if this continues another decade or two.

Q. You recently said the time may come when law-abiding citizens will have to live in walled communities—

A. When I was attending the Governors' conference in Los Angeles this summer, I took a ride around the area and came across a real estate development for retired people which was just exactly as I described it—a community with a high masonry wall surrounding it, and armed guards at the gates.

In other words, it was sort of a penitentiary in reverse—the good people inside and the bad people outside.

I think this condition is being reproduced in many cities in our country where the residents, through a sense of fear, do not undertake to enjoy the sidewalks and parks of the community after dark, but withdraw into their homes behind barred doors.

It seems to me we are in a serious situation when our society reaches the point where it is necessary for the good people to bar themselves behind locked doors to protect themselves against the marauders.

Q. What do you think can be done about rising crime?

A. In all honesty, we must recognize that some of it grows out of the burgeoning youth population. Crime, after all, is a function of youth—a lack of maturity—and many criminals outgrow their criminal behavior.

[3] Interview with O. W. Wilson, superintendent of the Chicago police department (1960-1967), former dean of the School of Criminology, University of California (1950-1960). Reprinted from *U.S. News & World Report*. 61:51-2. Ag. 1, '66.

Another important factor is the disadvantaged people who seek to gain the satisfaction of their needs, or fancied needs, through criminal activity. The reasons go back to the educational differential, the cultural lack, the economic problems, the lack of employability and job opportunity. But these are problems for society as a whole, not just the police.

Q. Are these new problems?

A. Yes, in the sense that they have increased in recent years.

Q. Do you find a growing contempt for the law itself?

A. This is a factor, too. It is found, not among the law-abiding, but in the attitude of those engaged in criminal actions.

Possibly some of this is due to the great attention being given now to civil rights. We tend to think of this in terms of the rights of minority groups, but I think the effect of the agitation goes far beyond that, to the point where concern about individual rights gives the criminal an edge, an advantage he has not had in the past.

For example, our officers are often confronted by juveniles who will shake their fingers in the face of the police officer and will say, "You can't touch me—I'm a juvenile." With older offenders, a somewhat similar situation develops, where one will say, "This is an invasion of my privacy. This is an invasion of my rights as a citizen."

All of this tends to destroy the deterrent power of authority. The juveniles and adult offenders I described are, in effect, shaking their fists at all authority.

Q. Is this part of a breakdown in American morals?

A. Yes, I think so. There is not only lack of respect for police authority, but for all our institutions—our courts, the church, parents, the home. In every situation where there is an authority figure, some people are rebelling against that figure. People today simply seem insistent on being above authority.

Q. Is this attitude confined to certain groups?

A. It's mostly confined to the lawless, the disadvantaged, the child from a broken home. I don't think this attitude is representative of our law-abiding citizens, including those from minority groups and the great majority of juveniles who are today just as responsible as they ever have been in the history of our country. The trouble comes from people who have a sense of frustration, of not having all the things they think they should have, along with a feeling they have the right to these things now.

For example, you could not say to any man, "You have no right to own a Cadillac automobile." As an individual, I don't plan ever to exercise this right, because I'll never be able to afford it. But there are people who feel it is not only their right to have a Cadillac, but that they have the right to have it now, without regard to how they get it. They fail to see the need for accomplishments, for earning and winning rewards.

Q. Do they get this idea from speeches by public officials sometimes? What is encouraging the growth of this idea?

A. I don't know, beyond the fact that some civil-rights leaders do give the concept to disadvantaged people that they have the right to have things. And, as a matter of fact, in some situations they do use the word "now."

Q. Do you expect more riots around the country?

A. I wouldn't be surprised.

Q. Are these riots becoming too big a problem for police?

A. Yes. In Chicago, on two occasions, we've been forced to call out the National Guard. Whether there will be a resurgence of vandalism and window-smashing and looting and arson after the Guardsmen leave remains to be seen.

Q. Do you see any answer to the riots?

A. I think there is a long-range answer—the correction of the inequities we're all aware of: higher educational standards, improved economic opportunities, a catching up on the cultural lag, a strengthening of spiritual values. All of these things in the long run must be brought to bear on the problem if it is to be solved permanently, and obviously it must be solved. It will be solved, but not overnight.

Q. In the meantime, what does the country face?

A. We're faced with the prospect of having to curb lawlessness. And this we intend to do.

Q. How can that be done?

A. By effective police patrols. And if the situation gets beyond the capacity of the police patrols of the community then they have no alternative but to call for the National Guard.

Q. Is crime growing in the suburbs, too?

A. Yes, it is.

Q. How do you explain that?

A. I suppose there is a development in suburban communities of the same kind of problems we have in a large city.

Q. Are parents partly to blame?

A. Yes. There is a breakdown in family control. We have an undisciplined society, and it's undisciplined because people seem more concerned with discovering some excuse for the behavior of an individual than anything else. Having discovered there is an explanation for his behavior, they use that as an excuse for the misbehavior.

I don't think our forebears were ever concerned about why a person misbehaves. If he misbehaved, this called for a remedial action. We are straying away from the principle of holding the individual responsible for his conduct, and are excusing his conduct in all too many cases—some very serious cases.

Q. Are courts too lenient in handling criminals?

A. I wouldn't want to criticize the courts. It's the system for the administration of criminal justice that is faltering. I'm not being critical of individual judges, or judges as a class, but rather of the whole system of criminal law and its procedure.

Q. Are court rulings handicapping police seriously in enforcing the law?

A. In my judgment, yes.

Q. Do criminals have less reason to fear punishment now than they did twenty or thirty years ago?

A. Yes, I think this is true.

Q. Is that a factor in the crime wave?

A. Yes.

Q. Have you seen any signs that police are developing a "what's the use" attitude in the face of their problems?

A. This is a danger. I don't think it exists so far as Chicago police officers are concerned. They are a well-disciplined body of men, and I don't believe they have a feeling of frustration.

Q. How would you describe the state of police morale?

A. In Chicago, morale is high. I'm not able to speak on the question outside of this city.

Q. Is it growing harder to recruit policemen?

A. Yes, recruiting is a problem. Our current success in this area is the result of our having lowered the age requirement to twenty years from twenty-one, and the minimum-height requirement from 5 feet 8 inches to 5 feet 7 inches. But we are losing more and more men to better-paying jobs.

Q. Are cries of police brutality making police work more difficult?

A. Yes, indeed. It creates a situation where police officers are reluctant to be aggressive, lest they be accused of being brutal. We don't condone brutality, but we do expect our officers to overcome force that is used in resisting arrest. But, in the face of the continual accusations of police brutality, I'm confident there are some who say, "It isn't worth the gamble," and would rather let an individual go than use force necessary to overcome resistance.

Q. Is there any truth to charges of police brutality?

A. Oh, I suppose in individual instances it's conceivable there may be. We make a very intensive investigation of every such allegation in Chicago. We have a squad of sergeants who are dedicated to this work, and they have come up with a few cases where brutality charges were sustained. In these cases, disciplinary action has been taken against the men. Percentage-wise this is very small, compared with the number of allegations filed.

Q. Do you think larger police forces can curb crime?

A. Yes, we must have more police. We're going to have to spend more money on crime control. This is inevitable. People aren't going to be eager to have this done, but I think they will be driven to it.

Q. Do you think a civilian board to review police action in cases where brutality is charged would help the situation?

A. I think it would destroy discipline in the Chicago police department if we had one.

Discipline is a function of command. This is my responsibility. I recognize a tendency of police officers to close in around an officer who is charged with some irregularity. I have the machinery and determination to penetrate this "blue curtain," as some people call it, and take suitable action where we find an officer has been remiss.

If we have a civilian-review board, that board then creates a situation where I, as the head of the police department, am confronted by an adversary group which the entire department will tend to unite against.

Therefore, if we had a civilian-review board, my discipline would be less effective than it is today.

THE PROS AND CONS OF STOP AND FRISK [4]

Samuel Lasky, an off-duty New York City patrolman, was showering in his sixth-floor Mount Vernon apartment one afternoon in the summer of 1964 when he heard a noise at his front door. He went to the peephole and saw two men

[4] From article by Richard H. Kuh, a New York attorney. *Reporter.* 38:30-1. F. 8, '68. Copyright © 1968 by The Reporter Magazine Company. Reprinted by permission of Paul R. Reynolds Inc., 599 Fifth Avenue, New York, N.Y. 10017.

tiptoeing in the hall. He immediately phoned the local police, threw on some clothes, and returned to his door. The two men were heading quietly toward the stairs. With his service revolver in hand. Lasky ran into the hall. The tiptoers ran, too, but Lasky succeeded in apprehending one of them, John Francis Peters, who claimed that he had been looking for a girl friend, a married woman, in the building. Chivalrously, he refused to divulge her name. Lasky frisked Peters—that is, he patted Peters's clothing to see if he was carrying a weapon. He felt a hard object, which on inspection turned out to be a plastic case containing picks, wrenches, and a tension bar.

Peters was charged with possession of burglars' tools. His attorney sought to have the charge dismissed on the ground that Peters's detention and frisking were in violation of his constitutional rights against unlawful search and seizure. When this argument proved unsuccessful, Peters pleaded guilty, reserving his rights, under New York State procedure, to appeal. And appeal he did. Ultimately, after taking the case through the state's appellate courts without success, Peters pressed his claim in the United States Supreme Court.

Is Suspicion Enough?

Last December 11 and 12 [1967], Peters's case was argued before the Justices in Washington, along with two other cases involving "stop and frisk," one from New York and one from Ohio. At this writing, the three cases are *sub judice*—fully argued but as yet undecided.

"Stop and frisk" is the police power to stop someone—forcibly, if resisted—without formally placing him under arrest, when his actions, although not obviously criminal, arouse strong suspicion. For instance, a patrolman on his beat hears a woman scream inside an apartment building and moments later sees a man leaving the building. The policeman knows of no crime; but shouldn't he stop the man and ask a few pertinent questions, or perhaps detain him while the source of the scream is being checked? Without the stop-and-frisk power, he could not intervene.

In this and hundreds of similar situations, the police clearly have no power to arrest the suspect. They can make an arrest only when they believe their prisoner has committed or is committing a specific known crime, and when they are ready to charge him with it, book him at a local station house, and bring him to the criminal courts to answer the charge. Short of that, they rely on the stop-and-frisk power, which involves far less of an intrusion or deprivation of freedom. They need only have a reasonable suspicion of criminal conduct, not a reasonable cause to believe a specific crime has been committed. After a field investigation, including possibly a quick search, the suspect must be turned loose or, if further information has been turned up, he must be formally charged with a crime and arrested. . . .

The President's Commission on Law Enforcement and the Administration of Justice, although favoring the right of police to stop suspects whether or not they cooperate voluntarily, noted in its 1967 Task Force Report on the Police:

> Misuse of field interrogation . . . is causing serious friction with minority groups in many localities. This is becoming particularly true as more police departments adopt "aggressive patrol" in which officers are encouraged routinely to stop and question persons on the street who are unknown to them, who are suspicious, or whose purpose for being abroad is not readily evident. . . . Both minority group leaders and persons sympathetic to minority groups throughout the country were almost unanimous in labeling field interrogation as a principal problem in police-community relations.

This alarm was more pointedly noted in a legal brief submitted to the Supreme Court by the NAACP Legal Defense and Educational Fund: "The evidence is weighty and uncontradicted that stop-and-frisk power is employed by the police most frequently against the inhabitants of our inner cities, racial minorities and the underprivileged."

One of our ablest judges, Charles D. Breitel of New York, in urging the American Law Institute—a congress of leading lawyers, judges, and law professors—to approve the power of stopping on suspicion, stated that the most likely victims of street crimes are the poor and members of minority groups; these are the persons most in need of the protections that stop and frisk affords. But the corollary of extensive stopping on suspicion in slum areas is that law-abiding residents of such areas will be stopped far more often than will law-abiding persons in other areas. The occasional inconvenience of stop and frisk to the majority may be so frequent as to suggest willful harassment to the minority.

The claims of harassment are understandable, but they may be overstressed. In New York State, stop and frisk has had statutory ratification since July 1, 1964. When the statute was passed, an Emergency Committee for Public Safety pledged to "proceed to establishing and providing free legal dissent for any persons oppressed under the new laws." Although this and other pressure groups have tried unsuccessfully to repeal the state law, their inability to find any cases that dramatize the evils they foresaw strongly suggests that the law's abuses have not been significant. None of the cases now before the Supreme Court appear to involve slapdash, arrogant police action against members of minority groups, and no particular case has arisen—as opposed to broad condemnatory generalities—in which it has even been alleged that the stop-and-frisk power has been misused discriminatorily.

Practical Guidance

What is needed, rather than a blanket ratification or a blanket condemnation by the Supreme Court of stopping on suspicion, is a rapprochement that will preserve the stopping power while refraining from such abuses of it as may further strain racial relations. This will require legislation that carefully defines and limits the stopping power, and judicial action that ratifies stopping on suspicion but only under circumstances that make that stopping reasonable.

In addition, this rapprochement can be furthered through enforced police regulations that inform patrolmen in the field just what they are supposed to do and not to do. After New York State's stop-and-frisk law was passed, the Combined Council of Law Enforcement Officials (consisting of representatives of all the state's enforcement agencies: police, sheriffs, prosecutors, and others) took steps to inform the more than fifty thousand police in the state, in considerable detail, just what was expected of them under the law. The 1967 Report of the President's Commission on Law Enforcement noted that the Council's bulletin "affords the patrolman practical guidance for his actions, including examples, factual variables, and guiding principles. In effect, this carries a New York stop-and-frisk statutory provision into the street situations in which it is administered."

In formulating its guidelines, which incorporated the limitations of the state law, the Council sought to map dispassionately what it thought most persons would agree was reasonable police authority and what were reasonable limitations upon that authority. The guidelines said that an officer was not to stop anyone unless he was prepared to explain his specific reason for doing so. He could not use a firearm or nightstick. Persons were to be stopped only when felonies and certain major misdemeanors were suspected. The extent of the search that might accompany any stopping was limited: it was not to be a pretext for obtaining evidence but solely for the officer's protection against hidden weapons. The suspect's detention was to be brief, just long enough to ask a few questions designed to allay or confirm the officer's suspicions, and questioning had to proceed where the stopping took place—on the street, in a nearby hallway, or in the police car.

Through this kind of self-regulation, backed by legislatively or judicially imposed restraints, police can weed out those ills—abuses toward minority groups and high-handed treatment of suspects—that stop-and-frisk opponents understandably fear. In this way, the improved ability of the police to protect all of us through preventive measures can be preserved.

[On June 10, 1968, the Supreme Court upheld New York State's stop-and-frisk law. The Court upheld the right of police to search suspects when, in the words of Chief Justice Earl Warren, "a reasonably prudent man in the circumstances would be warranted in the belief that his safety or that of others was in danger."—Ed.]

ELECTRONIC EAVESDROPPING [5]

For rare moments of enforced separation, those Caped Crusaders of Gotham City, Batman and Robin, have their "Super Bat Television Transmitter" to keep in touch. "Channel D" keeps Mr. Waverly informed of the latest exploits of UNCLE's Napoleon and Ilya. (Those THRUSH men always seem to forget to check Ilya's tie clasp or the hollowed-out heel of Napeoleon's shoe.) But Ben Jamil's "007 Spy Transmitter" makes Batman and UNCLE's creations seem as old-hat as smoke signals.

Ben Jamil? What TV channel is he on? you ask.

None. Ben Jamil is a real-life person, whose real-life electronic creations would make any TV scriptwriter turn green with envy. He is one of a growing breed of experts whose specialty is the "bug"—not the crawling type but the electronic variety. These experts are specialists in electronic eavesdropping.

The "007 Spy Transmitter" is a handy little eavesdropping device. It is smaller than a postage stamp and can thus be easily hidden in a pocket or a pack of cigarettes. It can pick up a whispered conversation in one room and broadcast it to a larger radio receiver located in an adjoining room.

[5] From "Electronic Eavesdropping: Is Ours a Bugged Society?" *Senior Scholastic.* 90:10-13. Ap. 14, '67. Reprinted by permission from *Senior Scholastic,* © 1967 by Scholastic Magazines, Inc.

"Bugs" such as this are much more than harmless little gadgets. They are, among other things, a multimillion-dollar business. Apparently a lot of people are interested in hearing what other people are saying.

But many people are gravely worried that we are fast on the road to becoming a "bugged" society: a society where very few people can be absolutely certain that their private comments are not being overheard. In short, many commentators believe this electronic wizardry is rapidly putting our right to privacy in serious danger.

Electronic snooping devices are now so easy to acquire and so effective that practically anyone with an itch to eavesdrop—and with the money to back up that itch—can do it. . . .

[In 1966] a United States Senate subcommittee chaired by Senator Edward Long (Democrat, Missouri) took a long hard look at electronic snooping in the United States. Witnesses before the subcommittee gave a chilling picture of how widespread snooping has become.

Who does this snooping? At the top of the list, according to the Senate subcommittee, is the government—Federal, state, and local. Government law enforcement officers have been using wiretaps and "bugs" for years. The subcommittee reported that Federal Government agencies such as the Internal Revenue Service, the Federal Bureau of Investigation (FBI), the Central Intelligence Agency (CIA), and even the Food and Drug Administration commonly used electronic snooping to gain information during investigations. Not far behind, according to the subcommittee, are state and local law enforcement officers. . . .

How to safeguard "the little man from the big ear," as [former] Federal Communications Commission Chairman E. William Henry has put it, is a particularly knotty problem. It involves the right of each person to his privacy. "The right to be alone," said the late Supreme Court Justice Louis Brandeis forty years ago, "is the most comprehensive of rights and the most valued by civilized man."

But in the world of postage-stamp-thin transmitters, the right to be alone is also one of the most difficult rights to protect. Technology has so completely outpaced the law that individual citizens today have little legal protection against electronic snooping. The technology of snooping may be space age, but our eavesdropping laws are, in the opinion of the critics, "horse and buggy" relics.

First of all, the right of privacy, itself, is not spelled out in the Constitution. The Fourth Amendment guards citizens against "unreasonable search and seizure." The framers of the Constitution were concerned with police breaking into private homes, but these framers knew nothing of telephones and tape recorders—to say nothing of printed circuits, transistors, or "bugged" martinis.

Our laws today reflect this. Thus it is illegal for the police to break into a home and search it without a court-issued search warrant. At the same time, most states have no legal restrictions against anyone planting a "bug" in that same house which will pick up every sound made within.

The laws covering electronic snooping are a hodgepodge of conflicting, confusing, and generally disobeyed statutes. The law recognizes two categories of electronic snooping. The first is wiretapping: splicing into a telephone line to pick up a phone conversation. The other is bugging—eavesdropping by using a hidden microphone.

Wiretapping

The only Federal law on the books dealing with wiretapping makes it a crime to tap a phone *and* (the *and* is important) divulge any information gained from the tap. The United States Justice Department has interpreted this wording to mean that Government agents *can* wiretap but that none of the information gained can be disclosed to the courts or to others outside the Government agency doing the wiretapping. In a number of cases involving wiretapping that have come before the courts in recent years, the courts seem to have accepted this interpretation.

State laws on wiretapping are a tangle of confusion. Eight states (California, Florida, Illinois, Kentucky, Michigan, New Jersey, Pennsylvania, and Wisconsin) ban all wiretapping. Five states (Maryland, Massachusetts, Nevada, New York, and Oregon) allow police wiretapping, but only with court permission. One state (Louisiana) allows only the police to tap without a court warrant. In the other thirty-six states, there are no laws directly aimed at controlling wiretapping.

Bugging

There is no Federal law covering electronic "bugging." Several states specifically outlaw it, but only one (Maryland) bans the manufacture and sale of "bugs."

There is one significant limitation on "bugging," but it is valid only in Federal courts. These courts have ruled that evidence gathered through "bugging" is admissible only if it was not the result of trespassing on the subject's property. Since it is difficult to plant a "bug" without trespassing, this has cut down on the use of evidence secured by "bugging" in Federal cases. (In 1963 the United States Supreme Court ruled that evidence gathered by a tape recorder hidden on an agent's body was not a trespass.)

But as the technology of "bugging" becomes more sophisticated, this ruling is likely to fade in importance. For example, under development is a device which will bounce radar beams off a windowpane. The windowpane vibrates as people inside talk. The radar beam will pick up these vibrations and send them back to a monitoring device which will reproduce the conversation going on inside.

If nothing else, the development of ultrasophisticated "bugs" has forced many people on all levels of government to consider the broad implications of the electronics revolution on our society. The question many officials are puzzling over is this: Wiretapping and "bugging" are valuable weapons in the fight against crime. But is their value worth the chipping away of our privacy?

"Ban-the-bug" adherents say No, it certainly is *not* worth the price. Writes United States Supreme Court Justice William O. Douglas:

The dangers posed by wiretapping and electronic surveillance strike at the very heart of the democratic philosophy. The citizen is completely unaware of the invasion of his privacy. The invasion of privacy is not limited to him, but extends to his friends and acquaintances—to anyone who happens to talk on the telephone with the suspect or who happens to come within the range of the electronic device.

Says Senator Long:

Unfortunately, electronic gadgetry has "grabbed" the law enforcement community and given it what has been described as the "Dick Tracy syndrome." Wiretapping and eavesdropping have often replaced solid investigative work.

The real problem [Long continues] is one of chipping away. Our right to privacy (which admittedly is hard to define) is being rapidly chipped away. If something is not done to reverse the process, soon it will be gone.

Many believe, however, that a limited amount of court-authorized eavesdropping by police is absolutely necessary to fight crime. Organized crime, they argue, has its own code of conduct which provides harsh penalties, often death, to those who inform. Law enforcement agencies have thus had little success in recruiting paid informers within the syndicates. A selective law which would allow law enforcement agencies to get a warrant to eavesdrop would be a valuable tool in crime fighting, they argue.

Says O. W. Wilson, [former] superintendent of police in Chicago:

Law enforcement is asking only for authority to tap the telephones of a relatively few selected targets—the telephones used by organized gangsters . . . and only then when sufficient evidence of crime can be introduced to satisfy a court that probable cause exists for the use of a tap on that particular telephone.

Wiretapping is not unconstitutional; but even if it were, the Constitution does not make any of our rights absolute. Our homes are our castles, but they are not immune against search and seizure —only against *unreasonable* search and seizure. And so it should be with our telephone communications.

For the time being, at least, Federal Government eavesdropping has been severely curtailed. President Johnson has ordered a halt to all Federal bugging and wiretapping with one exception: eavesdropping by the Government in national security cases. In his message to Congress on crime . . . [early in 1967], the President called for a law banning all eavesdropping, public or Government, except in national security cases. (LBJ's advisers were split on this question. About half of his crime commission reportedly backed legalized Government eavesdropping in criminal cases.) Indications are that this proposal will face stiff opposition from congressmen who want to legalize Government eavesdropping in crime investigations. . . .

Less than twenty years ago, British writer George Orwell published his now-famous book *1984*, in which he described life on earth in that year. Orwell imagined a totalitarian government that used electronic spying and psychological brainwashing to maintain itself in power. By means of closed circuit television, Big Brother and his henchmen knew almost everything that every citizen said or did—twenty-four hours a day, seven days a week.

Wrote Orwell:

The telescreen received and transmitted simultaneously. Any sound that Winston [a main character] made, above the level of a very low whisper, would be picked up by it; moreover, so long as he remained within the field of vision, . . . he could be seen as well as heard. There was, of course, no way of knowing whether you were being watched at any given moment. . . . You had to live—did live, from habit that became instinct—in the assumption that every sound you made was overheard, and, except in darkness, every movement scrutinized.

Orwell's nightmare world of thought control and constant snooping seemed farfetched to many in 1949, when the book was published. In those days, closed circuit television, such as Big Brother's system, was considered way-out.

But even Orwell, with his vivid imagination, didn't foresee the fantastic advances in electronic snooping that have been made in less than two decades. Closed circuit television is definitely not way-out today. Will postage-stamp-sized bugs and other electronic snooping gadgets that seem so farfetched today be commonplace in a few years? And will unscrupulous men attempt to exploit these gadgets for evil purposes?

These are the perplexing problems lawmakers and concerned citizens must face as society grapples to strike a balance between its right to fight crime and the right of individuals to be protected against the all-seeing eye of Big Brother.

THE COMPUTER AND CRIME [6]

[In 1967] one of the most remarkable institutions in contemporary law enforcement completes the final phase of its preparations and becomes operational. Then it will be possible in a matter of minutes for information to be sifted, analyzed, assembled into significant patterns, and made available to the policemen confronting crime in the front lines.

The institution is the New York State Identification and Intelligence System, already dubbed NYSIIS by everyone connected with it, in whose complex of computers will be stored every possible scrap of information relating to the administration of criminal justice in the State of New York. . . .

"The trouble in the past," says NYSIIS director Robert R. J. Gallati, a former New York City police official and holder of four law degrees, "is that crime data has been scattered all over the state in thousands of different offices. No

[6] From "The Computer vs. Crime," a chapter in *Crime in America,* by Robert Ostermann, staff reporter, *National Observer.* (Newsbook) National Observer. Silver Spring, Md. '66. p 62-75. Reprinted by permission.

one really knew what anyone else had in his files. The same stuff got passed around. You didn't know where to look for what you needed or how to go about getting the information at the moment you needed it most."

What kind of information is Dr. Gallati talking about? Accurate personal appearance data; arrests records; personal and family histories; aliases and disguises used; probation, prison, and parole experience; photographs and fingerprints; patterns of criminal performance; handwriting samples; travels; friends and enemies. In short, anything that can be used to specify an individual, to identify and distinguish him from other persons like him. . . .

The NYSIIS thesis states that the key to successful law enforcement is information and the adequate sharing of information by all criminal justice agencies possessing it. One indisputable fact supports the thesis: Most crimes are committed by people who have already committed previous crimes. Therefore ready access to comprehensive information is one of the best ways to speed identification of the guilty and to spare the innocent.

No one pretends that "ready access to comprehensive information" is the rule—anywhere. And certainly not in New York State, where in 1958 an abortive investigation dramatized beyond dispute the gravity of what has come to be known in law enforcement circles as the "information crisis."

The preceding year, 1957, a small peaceful town situated southwest of Binghamton, New York, and only a couple of miles from the New York-Pennsylvania border had leaped into the nation's headlines. Overnight Apalachin, New York, became notorious as a kind of super crime capital of the United States.

The label and reputation were acquired unintentionally by this harmless community of some nine hundred persons. It happened because the Barbara estate is in Apalachin. And it was on the Barbara estate that one hundred or more of the master figures in American organized crime decided to convene. Tipped off to the meeting, the New York State Police descended on the convention of crime lords, held many of them for questioning, and the ancient thesis of a national criminal empire and criminal hierarchy had new life pumped into it.

Authorities then proceeded to track down the answers to two main questions about the Apalachin meeting: Why had it been called? Who were the conferees? It was believed that knowledge about the second would lead to answering the first.

Eliot H. Lumbard, a New York City lawyer with a deep commitment to the improvement of criminal justice in all its branches, was chief counsel to the state commission established in 1958 to conduct the investigation. A prodigious amount of work lay ahead of him and the commission before they would learn how inconclusive and sterile their inquiries had been.

The commission walked into a bureaucratic morass. Somewhere "out there" to be searched through were the activity files of more than 3,600 state and local agencies concerned with the administration of criminal justice. Files containing an estimated 60 million forms.

A single example of what the commission found: Just one of the major criminals at the Apalachin meeting was the subject of two hundred separate, official police files in an area covering many hundreds of miles. And there were dozens like him.

The commission plowed slowly through mountains of paper. Two years and thousands of man-hours later, according to Mr. Lumbard, all of the state's files on the Apalachin congress members still hadn't been accumulated or studied. The files that had been searched often yielded disappointing results. Their contents were unoriginal and repetitive, of little use for the purposes of prosecution. . . .

Mr. Lumbard retained a stinging memory of his frustrations during those two years. In 1961 he was appointed to Governor Nelson Rockefeller's staff as special assistant counsel for law enforcement. High on his list of priorities was the assignment to find answers to the problems encountered in the Apalachin investigation, as well as to discover a way to master the continuing flood of files and paper that day after day poured into criminal justice agencies in the state. . . .

"In essence," says Dr. Gallati, "what was needed was a way to squeeze geography. All that information had to be gotten into one place. It had to be quickly available. And it had to be kept up to date."

The answer—electronic data processing—was simplicity itself. Simplicity, that is, if you consider "simple" the kind of device that can record and store a library full of information on a few reels of plastic tape or on disks a couple of feet in diameter. . . .

NYSIIS is not a police force. Dr. Gallati makes this fact emphatically clear. It does no investigating or arresting and has no authority for these functions. No other agency charged with administering some phase of criminal justice need fear its autonomy and responsibilities are in jeopardy. . . .

To one who has seen the monotonous rows of ceiling-high file cabinets containing the state's criminal records, the coming economy in space seems miraculous. The actual information contained in those 479,000 file folders will end up on some 20 to 25 reels of magnetic tape about one foot across. In a matter of minutes (estimated maximum, two hours) the data on these tapes can be searched and the appropriate information extracted. . . .

Dr. Gallati is firmly optimistic about NYSIIS' potential as a crime deterrent. One area of particular concern to him is auto theft, which in many cases is the first expedition into crime taken by the juvenile offender. He believes that discouraging a youth from "borrowing" (he deliberately chooses the term) a car may turn him aside from the future steps into crime that seem inevitably to follow auto theft.

"If they are aware the odds are against their getting away with it, it should help to curb juvenile delinquency," Dr. Gallati asserts.

The odds definitely are going to be against them when the Gallati method of apprehending auto thieves goes into operation. In essence, it involves linking a closed-circuit network of all-seeing television cameras, perhaps as many as four hundred, to the NYSIIS computer system.

The idea has its origins in an experimental demonstration conducted at the New York World's Fair several years ago. Strategically located police officers would call in license numbers from moving cars to a computer on the Fair grounds. These numbers were checked by the computer against wanted numbers. When the numbers matched, the computer would dispatch the officers to investigate.

The experiment turned out a surprising success. Of New York City cars screened 1 in every 67 was wanted for some reason; throughout the rest of the state the ratio was 1 to 300 cars. Authorities felt the program had proved itself as a means to control automobile thefts, which rose to more than 40,000 in the state in 1964. But the cost in manpower was prohibitive.

Enter the computer. Along with other crime data like fraudulent checks, laundry marks, stock and auto registration forgeries, and descriptions of stolen property NYSIIS computers will maintain an up-to-date record of license plates from vehicles stolen or otherwise wanted by the police.

Television cameras are to be installed at highway- and bridge-toll booths, stop signs, and traffic lights to scan the passing plates. It takes 25/1000 of a second to "read" these numbers into the computer. In the time it takes a driver to get into high gear the word could be back to police to stop the car. The computer, Dr. Gallati explains, can respond almost instantaneously to hundreds of simultaneous inquiries. . . .

Can computers be used to predict crime? The answer you give to that question depends on what you understand by the word "predict."

Understood literally, in the sense of fixing a time, place, date, and person of a future criminal act, a computer isn't likely to predict. But the word has alternative meanings. It's a common enough experience for officers investigating a crime to discern definite signposts to the crime in data available before the fact. Unfortunately no one then was in a position to see their bearing on the future.

But suppose this bearing could be discovered; it's just here that the computer plays an invaluable part. Because of the speed with which it can sift vast accumulations of facts and detect relationships between them it can discover the "signposts" in time for effective preventive action to be taken.

Richard Johnson, who has extensive computer experience in industry, cites the case of the bad check passer, the "paper hanger" in criminal jargon. All the details known of his previous working methods *(modus operandi)* can be fed into the computer to establish definite patterns of behavior. Perhaps it turns out that he always works his game in suburban shopping centers with an A&P supermarket, always passes the check in late afternoon, and (for a reason no one knows) always wears a certain color jacket.

"It wouldn't be impossible to narrow down the selection of possible targets to a number that could be placed under surveillance," Mr. Johnson suggests.

This kind of predicting is one of the answers Mr. Johnson proposes when he asks the rhetorical question of what you do with a system like NYSIIS after it's established and is functioning as an information-sharing agency. "It can do so much more," he says. "And if you don't make it work for you, you're wasting it."

He forecasts NYSIIS' greatest value will be discovered to lie in its capabilities to perform research that would be impossible to develop through conventional manual techniques. Much of this research would undoubtedly be in the related areas of the administration of criminal justice: in probation and parole work; in upgrading the quality of sentencing offenders; in applying the best rehabilitative resources to convicted offenders in prisons and other correctional institutions.

NEW APPROACHES TO THE CONTROL OF ORGANIZED CRIME [7]

Organized crime has deep roots in our economy and in our culture. It has evolved from the relatively simple, brawling, larcenous, predatory stick-up gangs of the nineteenth century to more complex forms of nationwide crime syndicates involved in gambling, prostitution, and industrial, commercial, and labor racketeering. Whether the form is simple or complex, the object has always been the same—the pursuit of the quick and easy buck. Prohibition provided an enormous impetus to the development of organized crime. Gambling and prostitution had already become relatively well organized prior to Prohibition. Prohibition, however, broadened the scope of organized criminal gangs and provided golden opportunities for them. There was fierce competition for the gold in the liquor traffic. This led to innumerable gang killings and gang wars. Eventually, however, criminal gangs learned that it was more advantageous to divide territories and profits than to kill each other. Gang leaders discovered that they lived longer and made more money if they cooperated rather than fought. Gang leaders also discovered that, in the distribution of illicit liquor, as in the supply of other illicit commodities, protection from law enforcement was vital to success. But, once protection was bought for liquor, it could also be purchased for other criminal rackets. Protection from law enforcement has always been one of the pillars of organized crime.

Emergence of Organized Crime

Organized crime emerged from the repeal of Prohibition, the Depression, and World War II as a continuing menace to our social, political, and economic institutions. It continued

[7] From article by Morris Ploscowe, lawyer, New York University law professor, and author of *Organized Crime and Law Enforcement. Annals of the American Academy of Political and Social Science.* 347:74-81. My '63. Reprinted by permission.

many of the same activities which it had controlled for generations and expanded others. Gambling in all of its variegated forms—bookmaking, policy, lotteries, slot machines, punch boards, bingo, gambling casinos, and so forth—continued to be one of the most lucrative sources of revenue for organized crime. Prostitution is of lesser importance today because of the changing sexual morality and the increasing amateur competition. The distribution of narcotic drugs, however, has brought rich rewards to those gang bosses willing to undertake the substantial risks of this traffic. But, along with the supply of frankly illegal commodities, organized crime has penetrated more and more areas of legitimate business and legitimate areas of our economy. The supply of liquor is today a legitimate, licensed business, yet it is an open question as to how many distilleries, wholesale liquor companies, retail liquor stores, taverns, and night clubs are controlled by the mobsters, either directly or through respectable fronts. Similar questions may be asked with respect to such things as the operation of trotting and horse-racing tracks, sporting enterprises, garbage-disposal companies, distribution of juke boxes, and other coin-vending machines, garment-manufacturing concerns, laundry and linen supply houses, loan companies, trucking companies, and the like. The McClellan Committee [the Subcommittee on Criminal Laws and Procedures of the Senate Committee on the Judiciary, chaired by Senator John McClellan of Arkansas] uncovered shocking evidence of the penetration of organized criminal elements into labor unions. The loot from this area is substantial as union treasuries and union welfare funds increase in size. In addition, control of labor unions makes possible kickbacks from employers for favorable union contracts, extortion through strike threats, and related practices.

Muscle and murder continue to be the ultimate weapons on which organized crime rests. They are used to finish off competitors, to silence informers, to eliminate recalcitrant or double-crossing members of a gang, to intimidate businessmen and to impose the will of the top gang bosses. Gang leaders have learned the value of using specialized, outside killers who murder on contract—the Murder Incorporated gang of Brooklyn was one such gang. They have also learned the value of keeping the use of muscle and murder to a minimum through adjustment and compromise of gang differences.

Criminal gangs and criminal syndicates continue to cooperate with each other. This does not mean that there is a national crime syndicate controlling all organized crime throughout the country. It is the writer's belief that, although there are large criminal syndicates which operate in many cities throughout the country, a good deal of organized crime is the work of local gangs which have pursued their activities for years in defiance of local law enforcement. However, such local gangs may have loose relationships with broader criminal syndicates.

Political protection from law enforcement and governmental noninterference with gang activities are still fundamental to the operation of organized criminal gangs. The record in this area is a sorry one. Innumerable police officers throughout the country have taken mob money so that gambling and prostitution operations will not be interfered with. On occasion, even the dirty money of the narcotics mob has found its way into police pockets. Wherever there is a so-called "open city" where gamblers and prostitutes operate openly, a substantial part of the police department is cooperating with criminal gangs. Mob money is used not only for direct payments to police and law-enforcement officials, it is also used to insure the election of key officials who will be sympathetic to its aims. Frank Costello's power in New York City politics during the 1940's is typical of what may be found in other large cities. The usual labels of Republican and Democratic have little meaning to organized-crime chieftains. What they are interested in are officials who will do the mob's bidding when the chips are down, and protection from interference is needed.

Needed Fundamental Improvements

It is obvious from even this sketchy description that there can be no simple panaceas and easy solutions to the problems of organized crime. If this cancerous threat to our economic and social system is to be eliminated, we must come to grips with fundamentals which involve such things as changes and improvements in substantive criminal laws, readjustment of Federal-state relations, elimination of bureaucratic and departmental isolation in dealing with organized crime, strengthening criminal procedures, improving the quality of local law enforcement, and eliminating the "fix," without which organized crime could not flourish. Some proposals will be considered in the following pages. They are designed basically to decrease the revenues available to organized crime and to strengthen immensely the law-enforcement effort to deal with organized crime.

Legalization of Drug Distribution

Legalization of the distribution of narcotic drugs to chronic addicts under strict medical and clinical controls would be one means of cutting down revenue to organized crime.

There are many thousands of narcotic addicts whose sole supply of opiate drugs comes from organized crime. The revenues from this illicit traffic are enormous. So long as an addict cannot get his drug legally, he will continue to patronize the minions of organized crime. The narcotic addict is, in the writer's opinion, a sick individual, with a physiological need for opiate drugs, for whom no known cure against a relapse has ever been discovered. If he could be handled on a medical basis with his major need for the drug supplied through legitimate medical and clinical channels, a good part of the illicit market for opiate drugs could be eliminated. The flow of gold from the drug traffic into the pockets of organized crime would be curtailed.

Stiffened Gambling Enforcement

The same approach of legalization cannot be used toward gambling, which provides huge sums to organized crime. Nevada is a showcase example of the social, cultural, and economic cost of legalized gambling, as well as a demonstration that legalization does not drive criminal mobs out of the gambling business.

The strengthening of the enforcement of gambling laws involves a far-flung effort on the Federal, state, and local levels. On the Federal level, considerable progress has been made in dealing with big-time gambling. A Federal statute has finally been passed, after many years of effort, prohibiting the transmission of gambling information and bets and wagers across state lines through the use of wire communication facilities. Wire services controlled by mobsters, transmitting rapid information about horse races and other sports events, had been the heart of organized crime's control of gambling for over half a century. In addition to the aforementioned statute, eliminating wire services to gamblers, Attorney General Kennedy . . . also secured the passage of bills prohibiting the transportation in interstate commerce of records of bets and wagers or policy numbers. Of vital importance in the Federal control of gambling activities is also the new statute prohibiting interstate travel in furtherance of illicit enterprises, such as illicit gambling activity.

These statutes and others, such as the requirement that gamblers pay wagering taxes [since declared unconstitutional by the United States Supreme Court—Ed.], now make it possible for Federal law-enforcement authorities to cope with the interstate aspects of gambling activity. It is to be hoped that an all-out effort will be made in this area by the Federal Government.

Gambling, however, remains essentially an activity which violates state and local laws. A primary requirement for stiffer law enforcement in connection with gambling is adequate state antigambling laws. . . .

The control of gambling on the state and local levels should not be hampered by inadequate, poorly drafted, old-fashioned laws which have not kept pace with modern methods of gambling.

Much more important than the substantive laws relating to gambling are the procedures used to detect and prosecute gambling violations and to enforce gambling laws. Law-enforcement agencies paralyzed by the "fix" will not enforce even the best of gambling laws. Light fines meted out to minor figures in the gambling rackets simply perpetuate gambling activities and give the public the illusion of enforcement. How to improve the enforcement of gambling laws at the state and local levels presents vital problems of eliminating police inefficiency and corruption, strengthening and making our criminal procedures more realistic, dropping the hypertechnical rules on search and seizure and illegally obtained evidence, authorizing the use of such means as wiretapping in the enforcement of gambling laws, making possible the cooperation of law-enforcement agencies in different areas of a state, improving the relationships between the police and prosecuting attorneys, and the introduction of more realistic sentencing practices in gambling cases. Any one of these problems can be the subject of a separate essay in this volume.

Investigative Coordination

Information about organized crime and the professional criminals who dominate it is absolutely vital to any program for dealing effectively with organized crime. Such information is not easy to come by. It is obtainable only through careful, involved, and difficult investigations. Many such investigations have already been made by Federal and state law-enforcement agencies, and considerable material about organized crime and criminals exists in their files. A fundamental problem in dealing with organized crime has been how to pool such information so that effective attacks can be made upon specific mobsters or specific organized criminal activities. Usually each agency, state or Federal, jealously guards the information that it has acquired and resents the necessity of passing this information to an outside agency. The present Organized Crime Unit in the Federal Department of Justice has helped to break down this isolation of law-enforcement agencies in the Federal Government. It is obvious that this Organized Crime Unit of the Department of Justice can serve to coordinate the efforts of all Federal law-enforcement agencies and spearhead the Federal Government's attack on organized crime. The Unit should be strengthened in terms of manpower, money, and investigative and prosecuting procedures, so that effective work can be done. One of the great advantages of the Unit is that it can use all existing Federal statutes in the drive on organized crime. It is not limited to the enforcement of a single law, as are many Federal agencies.

Enhanced State Activity

Antiracketeering units similar to the Federal one should be organized in the states, and there should be greater state supervision of local law enforcement.

If it is desirable to break down the isolation of Federal law-enforcement agencies, it is likewise desirable to eliminate the isolation and inertia of local law-enforcement agencies when they are confronted with organized criminal activities. It is also desirable to gather in one place information which local law-enforcement agencies may have available concerning local mobs and the activities of local professional criminals. This necessarily requires the expansion of state activity in connection with local law enforcement. Some years ago, the American Bar Association Commission on Organized Crime formulated a Model State Department of Justice Act. The major purpose of this model act was to provide for greater state supervision, through the attorney general's office of the state, of local prosecuting and law-enforcement agencies. This model act made possible the kind of direction, pooling of information, and cooperative effort of law-enforcement agencies which is vital if organized crime is to be dealt with adequately at the state and local level.

Some states have recognized the need for greater state effort in dealing with organized crime and the local corruption which it breeds. In New York, for example, there have been a number of successful investigations and prosecutions of organized criminal activities by the State Department of Investigation. Such activities have been virtually unmolested for years by local enforcement agencies. The work of such agencies as the New York State Department of Investigation makes it clear that local autonomy in law enforcement and local control of police and prosecuting agencies must be modified if strong barriers are to be erected against organized crime.

Improved Policing

Steps should be taken to improve police efficiency and to eliminate police corruption in dealing with gambling and organized crime.

Shortly after the Kefauver investigations [Senator Estes Kefauver (Democrat, Tennessee), Chairman of the Senate Crime Investigating Committee, held a series of televised hearings on the influence of national crime syndicates in 1950-1951.—Ed.], the writer and Professor Don L. Kooken of the University of Indiana summarized the police problem as follows:

To a considerable degree, law enforcement has broken down at all levels, national, state and local. Police officials entrusted with the security of the public have betrayed their trust. They have permitted the growth of organized crime to go unchallenged, until government itself is threatened.

The breakdown in police service, however, goes far beyond the lack of integrity or corruption of specific officials. Scores of police studies and surveys made throughout the country in the past few years have demonstrated that the inefficiency of police departments in dealing with crime is due to such factors as inadequate administrative organization, the brevity of tenure of police department heads, the poor selection of police personnel with respect to physical, mental and moral standards, the deficiency or the complete lack of police training standards, the defective personnel methods used by police departments, especially the methods of discipline, the inadequate techniques of criminal investigation and detection that are employed, the inadequate use of scientific aids in police operations and in the investigation of crime and apprehension of offenders, the lack of coordination and cooperation between police departments, etc.

We suggested that state-wide effort was necessary to eliminate police inefficiency and improve police methods of dealing with organized crime. We proposed a Model Police Council Act for the American Bar Association Commission on Organized Crime. We still believe that this act can be a useful tool in the development of better methods of policing and in the elimination of evils which investigations reveal. The proposed act makes possible uniform methods of recruiting and training police officers throughout the state as well as the maintenance of decent standards of policing through inspections of police departments and otherwise.

Some such radical approach to local police departments as that provided for in the Model Police Council Act is necessary if local police departments are to meet the massive threat of organized crime in their communities.

Law-Enforcement Procedures

Available procedures against criminals should be strengthened so that law-enforcement agencies will not be hampered in the enforcement of laws relating to organized crime.

If sumptuary laws, such as the prohibitions against gambling, are to be enforced effectively, we may have to sacrifice some of the protections which we throw around individual liberties. Wiretapping, for example, may be called "dirty business," yet any law-enforcement agency is hampered in dealing wth organized crime unless it can tap telephone wires legally. Similarly, when the Supreme Court of the United States declares invalid traditional state rules concerning the use of illegally obtained evidence, it is to be expected that professional criminal activities will be widely benefited. When outstanding arrests are negated by a hypertechnical application of the rules relating to search and seizure, then law enforcement is further discouraged in attempting to deal with organized crime. It has become popular to take the Fifth Amendment when questioned by authorities concerning criminal activities. Unless a state has a realistic law making it possible to compel testimony of underlings through a grant of immunity, the wall of silence around organized crime cannot be pierced. The provision of many state laws that even misdemeanors occuring in connection with organized criminal activities may be tried by juries hampers still further the development of any realistic program of dealing with organized crime.

It is obvious that some hard thinking and realistic examination must be made of our present rules of criminal procedure and evidence before progress can be made in the repression of organized crime.

We have mentioned some of the new approaches to the control of organized crime. Adequately implemented, they can go far toward curtailing the massive threat of organized crime to our social and economic system.

IV. CRIME AND THE COURTS

EDITOR'S INTRODUCTION

The court system, the President's Crime Commission has noted, is "the central crucial institution in the criminal justice system. . . . It is the institution around which the rest of the system is in large measure responsible." It is probably because of this crucial role that the courts today—and particularly the United States Supreme Court—are so often subjected to bitter criticism. The courts are persistently accused of contributing to, and by some of even creating, the "crime crisis." Much of this criticism stems from Supreme Court rulings setting out procedures to be followed by police during the questioning of suspects—rules which the critics say "handcuff" the police.

But the courts perform a wide array of functions in addition to the controversial appellate functions of the Supreme Court. These functions and the structure of the U.S. court system are outlined in the first selection in this section, excerpted from *Senior Scholastic*. The next selection is an excerpt from the Supreme Court's 1966 ruling in *Miranda vs. Arizona*—a landmark case in the treatment of suspects by police. This is followed by two articles taking issue in various degrees with the Court's rulings. The first, by Eugene H. Methvin, takes the Court to task for being too lenient with criminals. The second, by Jon O. Newman, United States attorney for the District of Connecticut, attempts to chart a middle course between the Court and its sharper critics by suggesting that judges be given more flexibility in admitting evidence into trials.

The final selection, by Robert Cipes, a lawyer and writer, discusses the American Bar Association's Reardon report and the fuel it has added to the ancient controversy between the press and lawyers on how much publicity should be allowed in court cases.

THE COURTS: THE PYRAMID OF U.S. JUSTICE [1]

Time-honored ceremony attends the opening of a session of the United States Supreme Court. Spectators stand, voices hush, a gavel raps, and nine black-robed judges file into the stately courtroom from behind a red velvet curtain. "Oyez, oyez, oyez," intones the Marshal of the Court, chanting an old Anglo-Norman word for "hear ye." Then, with solemnity, the nine eminent, black-robed Justices begin another working day.

This is the court that many people think of when they think of "the courts." It is the court whose decisions are subjected to close study in law schools and judicial chambers around the country. It is the court whose decisions often stir lively controversy from the halls of Congress to small-town barber shops. It is *the* Court—with a capital "C."

Yet the Supreme Court of the United States handles only a tiny handful of the tens of thousands of cases considered each year in the nation's courts. The individual who becomes involved in a court case is far more likely to find himself dealing with a lower state or Federal court. And the opinions which that individual has of the U.S. system of court justice are likely to be heavily influenced by what he sees in these lower courts.

Many of these lower courts would impress almost any observer as models of even-handed justice and dignity. Judges and attorneys may devote long hours to a thorough inquiry into all sides of a case, even those cases that many people might consider "unimportant."

However, in some lower courts throughout the country, dignity can be lacking and serious inquiry stifled. Howard

[1] From article in *Senior Scholastic.* 92:18-20. N. 30, '67. Reprinted by permission from *Senior Scholastic,* © 1967 by Scholastic Magazines, Inc.

James, a reporter for *The Christian Science Monitor,* tells of instances during a nationwide tour of state courts this year [1967], when he saw judges reading newspapers or talking on the telephone while witnesses testified—even in cases where there was no jury and the judge was entirely responsible for the verdict. President Johnson's Commission on Law Enforcement and Administration of Justice asserts that many lower courts dispense "assembly-line justice" under shocking conditions.

One reason, says the President's commission, is that the lower courts are simply overloaded. Each year the backlog of cases gets bigger. In some parts of the country, delays of up to five or six years in settling a case (from original filing to final verdict) are not uncommon.

This backlog affects all levels of the U.S. court system—the Federal system as well as the fifty separate state court systems. Many factors help cause this backlog. Among them are:

The Automobile. About 10 million auto accidents occur each year. In civil courts, damage suits growing out of auto collisions account for 50 to 90 per cent of all cases. Of the 102 million drivers in the United States, 30 million are expected to be charged with some traffic offense in the course of the current year.

Rising Population and Crime. The population of the United States grows by some 2.25 million each year, and more people mean more problems involving lawsuits. Moreover, the crime rate is rising even faster than the population—placing an ever heavier burden on the courts.

"The Law Explosion." Each year Congress passes hundreds of bills that set up new laws or new administrative procedures that have the effect of laws. State legislatures and city councils pass still more laws. As these laws are applied, the courts must act as umpires when disputes arise.

Numerous plans have been proposed—some of which have already been adopted—to modernize the nation's various court systems to better handle the rising number of cases. Just one example: New York City's criminal courts plan to make permanent a round-the-clock operation that was tried on an experimental basis earlier this year. By keeping the courts open all night, New York hopes to spare many defendants from having to spend a night in jail awaiting arraignment.

It is important to remember that there are fifty-one *different* and *separate* court systems in the United States. Only at the top—the United States Supreme Court—are the fifty-one systems joined. It is important, too, to recall that each of the fifty states makes laws. That means that each of the state courts is enforcing slightly different laws, based on the fifty different state constitutions.

Each of the separate systems is in the form of a pyramid, with large numbers of "inferior" or "trial" courts at the bottom and a handful of courts above to handle appeals (these are called appellate courts). At the top of each system is one court, which in most states is called a supreme court. Here, then, are the court systems in brief:

State and Local Courts

No single outline can adequately summarize all of the fifty state systems. Each state is free to devise its own judicial structure and to use its own labeling. New York State, for example, calls some lower courts "Supreme Courts," while terming its highest court the Court of Appeals. Other states have other peculiarities in naming their courts.

State courts have been called "the backbone of the United States judicial system." As against some 400 judges in all Federal courts there are roughly 8,000 state court justices, including justices of the peace. Here is a very general outline of state court systems, starting at the lowest level:

Inferior Trial Courts. At the very bottom of the judicial structure are courts for minor offenses, usually misdemeanors (as opposed to felonies). In many states these are not formal courts staffed by judges. Instead they are run by justices of the peace, who need not necessarily be lawyers. (Many states are eliminating justices of the peace and replacing them with regular judges.) In most cities, courts at this level would be called Magistrates Court, Police Court, or Municipal Court. They would handle such offenses as traffic violations, petty theft, and public drunkenness.

Trial Courts. These are courts of general jurisdiction with authority to try all types of cases under both civil and criminal law. Their names vary widely from state to state: Court of Common Pleas, District Court, Superior Court, Circuit Court, and even Supreme Court. Here is where the vast number of important cases in the state judicial system begins. Such courts may have one judge or several (the Superior Court in Los Angeles has 120). In many major cities such courts are divided so that individual judges handle only specific types of cases. One judge would handle only juvenile offenders, another criminal trials, another divorce proceedings, and so on.

Specialized Trial Courts. In some states, instead of splitting up the general trial courts, separate courts have been created to deal with specialized problems. . . . Such courts would include Probate or Surrogate Court (which handles deceased persons' wills and estates), Divorce Court, Family Court, and Juvenile Court.

Intermediate Appellate Courts. Less populated states generally do not have courts at this level, but at least fifteen states with larger populations have created appeals courts to reduce the workload of the state's highest court. . . .

Final Appellate Court. Usually called the Supreme Court, this court functions within the state system much as the United States Supreme Court does in the Federal system. It is the final judge on matters relating to the state's constitution. It can reverse any decision of lower courts within the state system, and the court's ruling is binding on all state courts. Unless the case involves "a substantial Federal question," the matter stops there and cannot be appealed to the United States Supreme Court.

Federal Courts

United States courts handle a more narrow range of cases than do state courts. They may decide only those types of cases for which the United States Constitution gives specific authority. Section 2 of Article III of the Constitution spells these out. The principal ones are:

(1) "Controversies to which the United States shall be a party" (that is, when the Federal Government is suing or being sued).

(2) "Cases involving controversies between two or more states, or between a state and citizens of another state, or between citizens of different states."

(3) "All cases in law and equity arising under this Constitution, the laws of the United States, and treaties made, or which shall be made, under their authority.". . .

District Courts. These are the lowest Federal courts. They have original jurisdiction only, and do not review cases from other courts. . . .

In general, Federal district courts are limited to three types of cases: prosecutions for Federal crimes (such as kidnaping, transporting stolen goods across a state line, counterfeiting money, or narcotics violations), civil claims based on Federal law, and civil claims between residents of two or more states. The United States Government or one of its agencies is a party to a large share of District Court cases.

Courts of Appeals. Originally called Circuit Courts, these are intermediate appellate courts that were created to ease the work of the United States Supreme Court. There are eleven Courts of Appeals, each with from three to nine judges. Ten circuits include three or more states each; the eleventh deals only with the District of Columbia.

Courts of Appeals do just what their name implies—consider appeals from the District Courts, and from administrative agencies (such as the Internal Revenue Service or Interstate Commerce Commission). . . .

United States Supreme Court. This is the only court created by the United States Constitution, and thus the only Federal court that Congress could not abolish tomorrow if it wished. The Court receives about 3,000 cases a year, but gives full-scale consideration to only some 250 of these. With responsibility under the Constitution equal to that of the President and Congress, the Supreme Court has the power to overrule Federal legislation that it considers to be in contradiction to the Constitution. It thus considers cases involving some of the most significant legal issues of the day.

MIRANDA V. ARIZONA [2]

[Ernesto Miranda, a twenty-five-year-old mentally retarded Arizona man, was arrested in 1962 and charged with kidnap and rape. After he was identified in a police lineup, Miranda freely confessed the crime. He was convicted the next year and sentenced to twenty-thirty years in prison. In appealing the conviction, Miranda's court-appointed lawyer agreed that no physical or psychological pressure had been applied during the police interrogation of the suspect. However, the lawyer pointed out that Miranda had not been warned that his statements could be used against him and that Miranda should have been provided with legal counsel at the time of interrogation, even though he did not know enough to request it. By a 5 to 4 vote, the Supreme Court overturned Miranda's conviction. Here are excerpts from the Court ruling.—Ed.]

The cases before us raise questions which go to the roots of our concepts of American criminal jurisprudence: the restraints society must observe consistent with the Federal Constitution in prosecuting individuals for crime. More specifically, we deal with the admissibility of statements obtained from an individual who is subjected to custodial

[2] From the Supreme Court opinion, by Chief Justice Earl Warren, in *Miranda v. Arizona,* a case involving the Fifth Amendment protections against self-incrimination. *United States Reports.* 384 U.S. 436 (1966). Supt. of Docs. Washington, D.C. 20402. '67.

police interrogation and the necessity for procedures which assure that the individual is accorded his privilege under the Fifth Amendment to the Constitution not to be compelled to incriminate himself.

We dealt with certain phases of this problem recently in *Escobedo v. Illinois* [378 U.S. 478 (1964)]. There, . . . law enforcement officials took the defendant into custody and interrogated him in a police station for the purpose of obtaining a confession. The police did not effectively advise him of his right to remain silent or of his right to consult with his attorney. Rather, they confronted him with an alleged accomplice who accused him of having perpetrated a murder.

When the defendant denied the accusation and said "I didn't shoot Manuel, you did it," they handcuffed him and took him to an interrogation room. There, while handcuffed and standing, he was questioned for four hours until he confessed.

During this interrogation, the police denied his request to speak to his attorney, and they prevented his retained attorney, who had come to the police station, from consulting with him. At his trial, the state, over his objection, introduced the confession against him. We held that the statements thus made were constitutionally inadmissible. . . .

[*Escobedo*] was but an explication of basic rights that are enshrined in our Constitution—that "no person . . . shall be compelled in any criminal case to be a witness against himself," and that "the accused shall . . . have the assistance of counsel"—rights which were put in jeopardy in that case through official overbearing.

These precious rights were fixed in our Constitution only after centuries of persecution and struggle. And in the words of Chief Justice [John] Marshall, they were secured "for ages to come and . . . designed to approach immortality as nearly as human institutions can approach it." . . .

Our decision [in *Miranda v. Arizona*] in no way creates a constitutional straitjacket which will handicap sound efforts at reform, nor is it intended to have this effect. We encourage Congress and the states to continue their laudable search for increasingly effective ways of protecting the rights of the individual while promoting efficient enforcement of our criminal laws. However, unless we are shown other procedures which are at least as effective in apprising accused persons of their right of silence and in assuring a continuous opportunity to exercise it, the following safeguards must be observed:

At the outset, if a person in custody is to be subjected to interrogation, he must first be informed in clear and unequivocal terms that he has the right to remain silent. For those unaware of the privilege, the warning is needed simply to make them aware of it—the threshold requirement for an intelligent decision as to its exercise.

More important, such a warning is an absolute prerequisite in overcoming the inherent pressures of the interrogation atmosphere. It is not just the subnormal or woefully ignorant who succumb to an interrogator's imprecations, whether implied or expressly stated, that the interrogation will continue until a confession is obtained or that silence in the face of accusation is itself damning and will bode ill when presented to a jury. Further, the warning will show the individual that his interrogators are prepared to recognize his privilege should he choose to exercise it.

The Fifth Amendment privilege is so fundamental to our system of constitutional rule, and the expedient of giving an adequate warning as to the availability of the privilege so simple, we will not pause to inquire in individual cases whether the defendant was aware of his rights without a warning being given. Assessments of the knowledge the defendant possessed, based on information as to his age, education, intelligence, or prior contact with authorities, can never be more than speculation; a warning is a clearcut fact. More important, whatever the background of the person interrogated, a warning at the time of the interrogation is indispensable to overcome its pressures and to insure that the individual knows he is free to exercise the privilege at that point in time.

This warning is needed in order to make him aware, not only of the privilege, but also of the consequences of forgoing it. It is only through an awareness of these consequences that there can be any assurance of real understanding and intelligent exercise of the privilege. Moreover, this warning may serve to make the individual more acutely aware that he is faced with a phase of the adversary system— that he is not in the presence of persons acting solely in his interest.

The circumstances surrounding in-custody interrogation can operate very quickly to overbear the will of one merely made aware of his privilege by his interrogators. Therefore, the right to have counsel present at the interrogation is indispensable to the protection of the Fifth Amendment privilege under the system we delineate today. Our aim is to assure that the individual's right to choose between silence and speech remains unfettered throughout the interrogation process. A once-stated warning, delivered by those who will conduct the interrogation, cannot itself suffice to that end among those who must require knowledge of their rights.

A mere warning given by the interrogators is not alone sufficient to accomplish that end. Prosecutors themselves claim that the admonishment of the right to remain silent without more "will benefit only the recidivist and the professional." Even preliminary advice given to the accused by his own attorney can be swiftly overcome by the secret interrogation process. Thus, the need for counsel to protect the Fifth Amendment privilege comprehends not merely a right to consult with counsel prior to questioning, but also to have counsel present during any questioning if the defendant so desires.

An individual need not make a preinterrogation request for a lawyer. While such request affirmatively secures his right to have one, his failure to ask for a lawyer does not constitute a waiver. No effective waiver of the right to counsel during interrogation can be recognized unless specifically made after the warnings we here delineate have been given. The accused who does not know his rights and therefore does not make a request may be the person who most needs counsel. . . .

Accordingly we hold that an individual held for interrogation must be clearly informed that he has the right to consult with a lawyer and to have the lawyer with him during interrogation during the system for protecting the privilege we delineate today. As with the warnings of the right to remain silent and that anything stated can be used in evidence against him, this warning is an absolute prerequisite to interrogation. No amount of circumstantial evidence that the person may have been aware of this right will suffice to stand in its stead. Only through such a warning is there ascertainable assurance that the accused was aware of this right.

If an individual indicates that he wishes the assistance of counsel before any interrogation occurs, the authorities cannot rationally ignore or deny his request on the basis that the individual does not have or cannot afford a retained attorney. The financial ability of the individual has no relationship to the scope of the rights involved here.

In fact, were we to limit these constitutional rights to those who can retain an attorney, our decisions today would be of little significance. The cases before us as well as the vast majority of confession cases with which we have dealt in the past involve those unable to retain counsel. While authorities are not required to relieve the accused of his poverty, they have the obligation not to take advantage of indigence in the administration of justice. . . .

In order fully to apprise a person interrogated of the extent of his rights under this system then, it is necessary to warn him not only that he has the right to consult with an attorney, but also that if he is indigent a lawyer will be appointed to represent him. Without this additional warning, the admonition of the right to consult with counsel would often be understood as meaning only that he can consult with a lawyer if he has one or has the funds to obtain one.

Once warnings have been given, the subsequent procedure is clear. If the individual indicates in any manner, at any time prior to or during questioning, that he wishes to remain silent, the interrogation must cease. At this point he has shown that he intends to exercise his Fifth Amendment privilege; any statement taken after the person invokes his privilege cannot be other than the product of compulsion, subtle or otherwise. Without the right to cut off questioning, the setting of in-custody interrogation operates on the individual to overcome free choice in producing a statement after the privilege has been once invoked.

If the individual states that he wants an attorney, the interrogation must cease until an attorney is present. At that time, the individual must have an opportunity to confer with the attorney and to have him present during any subsequent questioning. If the individual cannot obtain an attorney and he indicates that he wants one before speaking to police, they must respect his decision to remain silent.

This does not mean, as some have suggested, that each police station must have a "station house lawyer" present at all times to advise prisoners. It does mean, however, that if police propose to interrogate a person they must make known to him that he is entitled to a lawyer and that, if he cannot afford one, a lawyer will be provided for him prior to any interrogation. If authorities conclude that they will not provide counsel during a reasonable period of time in which investigation in the field is carried out, they may do so without violating the person's Fifth Amendment privilege so long as they do not question him during that time. . . .

Our decision is not intended to hamper the traditional function of police officers in investigating crime. When an individual is in custody on probable cause, the police may, of course, seek out evidence in the field to be used at trial against him. Such investigation may include inquiry of persons not under restraint.

General on-the-scene questioning as to facts surrounding a crime or other general questioning of citizens in the fact-finding process is not affected by our holding. It is an act of responsible citizenship for individuals to give whatever information they may have to aid in law enforcement. In such situations the compelling atmosphere inherent in the process of in-custody interrogation is not necessarily present.

In dealing with statements obtained through interrogation, we do not purport to find all confessions inadmissible. Confessions remain a proper element in law enforcement. Any statement given freely and voluntarily without any compelling influences is, of course, admissible in evidence.

There is no requirement that police stop a person who enters a police station and states that he wishes to confess to a crime, or a person who calls the police to offer a confession or any other statement he desires to make. Volunteered statements of any kind are not barred by the Fifth Amendment and their admissibility is not affected by our holding today.

To summarize, we hold that when an individual is taken into custody or otherwise deprived of his freedom by the authorities and is subjected to questioning, the privilege against self-incrimination is jeopardized. Procedural safeguards must be employed to protect the privilege, and unless other fully effective means are adopted to notify the person of his right of silence and to assure that the exercise of the right will be scrupulously honored, the following measures are required:

He must be warned prior to any questioning that he has the right to remain silent, that anything he says can be used against him in a court of law, that he has the right to the presence of an attorney, and that if he cannot afford an attorney one will be appointed for him prior to any questioning if he so desires.

LET'S HAVE JUSTICE FOR NON-CRIMINALS TOO! [3]

In a Washington, D.C., courtroom, Federal Judge George L. Hart faced the jury and shook his finger angrily at forty-one-year-old James W. Killough, on trial before him for murder.

On three separate occasions this man voluntarily confessed foully killing his wife and throwing her body on a dump like a piece of garbage. He led police there. Yet the United States Court of Appeals has seen fit to throw the confessions out. Though it makes me almost physically ill, I must direct a verdict of acquittal. I feel I'm presiding not over a search for truth but over an impossible farce. We know the man is guilty, but we sit here blind, deaf and dumb, and we can't admit what we know. Tonight felons can sleep better.

Thus, in a spectacle now being repeated across the nation, after confessing a murder the confessor walked free, a scoffing example of the "impossible farce" the Supreme Court has made of American justice. For, in a series of rulings over the past nine years, the Court has progressively handcuffed the police, turned trial judges into automatons, and blindfolded juries, all to the immense benefit of criminals.

Last June 13 [1966] the Court went further than ever before in a decision the New York *Times* called "an overhasty trespass into the legislative area, . . . lacking either constitutional warrant or constructive effect." Chief Justice Earl Warren, in a razor-thin five-four decision [*Miranda v. Arizona*], announced a new interpretation of the 175-year-old Fifth Amendment: now it requires that police, in questioning suspects, not only first warn them of their right to silence, but even furnish a lawyer and allow him to sit in on the interrogation if the suspect wishes. Moreover, if the suspect "indicates in any manner" that he does not want to answer questions, the police must stop.

[3] From article by Eugene H. Methvin. *Reader's Digest*. 89:53-60. D. '66. Reprinted with permission from the December 1966 *Reader's Digest*. Copyright 1966 by The Reader's Digest Assn., Inc.

Dissenting thunderously, Justice Byron R. White said the Court's ruling "has no significant support in the history or language of the Fifth Amendment" and "in some cases will return a killer, a rapist or other criminal to the streets to repeat his crime whenever it pleases him. As a consequence, there will not be a gain but a loss in human dignity."

"I Did It!"

Justice White's prediction was speedily verified. Consider these two cases.

1. After a $10,000 fire almost killed a sleeping housewife and her three children, a Washington policeman answered a radio call. Two men walked up to him. "This is the guy who set the fire," said one. The policeman blinked, looked at the other and asked, "What have you got to say?" "I did it!" the man blurted. A painter who showed up for work drunk and was ordered off the job, he had returned at night to explode a Molotov-cocktail firebomb in the home.

At the arson trial, his lawyer argued that the mere presence of the uniformed policeman psychologically coerced him, thereby violating his Fifth Amendment privilege against self-incrimination. Incredibly, the judge excluded the confession from the jury. (However, in this case a conviction was obtained on other evidence.)

2. A young probationer in Cleveland admitted killing another youth. But because police neglected to warn him of his rights, Judge Angelo J. Gagliardo had to let him go.

There is no question in my mind that this is anything but a willful, deliberate act of murder without any justification [Judge Gagliardo fumed]. Some day members of the Supreme Court will engage themselves in the practical problems of life in a modern urban society, and deal with realities rather than theories that place individual rights far above the community.

Since Chief Justice Warren announced the new rules, Philadelphia police are finding that 56 per cent of the suspects they arrest refuse to answer police questions. In Brooklyn, police find four times as many suspects as before—96 out of 239—arrested in homicide, robbery, felonious assault and rape cases are refusing to make statements. "Most of these men will walk the streets as free men," warns District Attorney Aaron E. Koota. "These vicious crimes may never be solved." Police in Boston, Washington, Cleveland, Los Angeles, San Francisco and Memphis report similar results, and the percentages can be expected to increase in every U.S. city.

The Supreme Court's foray into legislating rules for police conduct springs from one of the oldest riddles of American criminal justice: How can we ensure that police obey the rules protecting individual liberties, yet have enough freedom themselves to protect society against criminals? . . .

Hair-Split Decisions

In undertaking to police the police, basically a legislative and executive function, the Supreme Court until recently operated under Justice Cardozo's wise injunction: "Justice, though due to the accused, is due to the accuser also. The concept of fairness must not be strained till it is narrowed to a filament. We are to keep the balance true."

Now, as Dean Erwin Griswold of the Harvard Law School points out, the Court has become "absolutist." It is pursuing defensible doctrines beyond the realm of rationality and common sense. Such extremism has spread like moral rot throughout Federal and state appellate courts until, as the then Attorney General Nicholas Katzenbach last year [1965] protested: "The judges have left the public behind, and even among judges the margins of consensus have been passed."

Take, for example, the crucial problem of search and seizure. "It must be remembered that what the Constitution forbids is not all searches and seizures, but unreasonable searches and seizures," says [Supreme Court] Justice Potter Stewart. But judges are handing down increasingly unreasonable decrees on what constitutes reasonable police conduct. Consider:

In Tucson a policeman followed a suspected stolen car. The driver parked and went into a college fraternity house. The officer crawled under the car, looked at the transmission serial number and, sure enough, it matched one on the list of stolen property.

In Washington, police had a tip that a known prostitute had illegal dope. They went to her rooming house, knocked on the door, then started inside to find her room. At that moment she dashed past them and dropped a small package into a garbage can under the front porch. The officers looked in the garbage can and found a package of narcotics.

In each of these cases, hair-splitting judges ruled the searches "unreasonable," dismissed the evidence and turned the defendants loose upon the community, as a "lesson" to police.

Yet the reasonable citizen is likely to agree with Federal Judge Warren Burger's acid dissent in the garbage-can case: The police would have been derelict in their duty if they had *not* done precisely what they did. Judge Burger declared, "I cannot find a constitutional right to privacy in the garbage pail of a rooming house." He denounced the "unfortunate trend of judicial decisions which stretch and strain to give the guilty not the same but vastly more protection than the law-abiding citizen."

The Meaning of Mallory

Until 1957, noncoercive police interrogations were taken for granted. Then came the Mallory case. After police questioning and a lie-detector test, Andrew Mallory, a Washington, D.C., handyman, confessed to raping a woman in the apartment house where he lived. But the Supreme Court freed Mallory by—in effect—writing a new rule for Federal law-enforcement officers. The Court said taking Mallory to the police station for questioning represented an "unnecessary delay" in presenting him before an arraigning magistrate, and his confession therefore could not be used in evidence.

The net results? Thirty-three months after Mallory's release he attacked another woman in a Philadelphia apartment. This time he got a ten-to-twenty-year sentence. His Philadelphia victim was, as one Justice Department lawyer told me sardonically, "deprived of her constitutional right to equal protection of the laws by the Supreme Court, without due process of law."

Unnecessary delay in Mallory's case meant seven and a half hours. In 1962 the courts said "three hours" was unreasonable; in 1964, thirty minutes; in 1965, *five* minutes.

Since the *Mallory* decision applied only to Federal officers, federally ruled Washington, D.C., was the only city affected. But there the impact was devastating. In the five years before *Mallory,* with crime rising nationally, Washington's police had reduced serious crimes 37 per cent. But thereafter the rate began to climb sharply, and in nine years it has gone up 124 per cent. Holdups, purse-snatchings and muggings, down a third before *Mallory,* skyrocketed 305 per cent—five times the national increase. Worse, the rate of police success in solving crimes has been cut in half, to an all-time low. . . .

Congress has the clear duty and power to curb the Supreme Court's extremism; Article III of the Constitution lays on the legislators the responsibility to make "exceptions and regulations" for the Court's appellate jurisdiction. Thus, declare the classic essays in *The Federalist,* Congress "would certainly have full power to provide that in appeals to the Supreme Court there should be no reexamination of facts where they had been tried by juries." Or it clearly could permit the jury to decide finally whether a confession is voluntary within the Fifth Amendment's terms. What could be a more democratic way of enforcing standards upon police and safeguarding individual rights?

Moreover, state legislatures have a heavy duty to provide safeguards against "squeal room" secrecy and the occasional instances of police abuse. "It's time the American people tell policemen how they want the law enforced, and back them to the hilt in doing it," says former New York City Police Commissioner Michael J. Murphy. "We want and need legislative guidelines. Virtually every policeman in America wants to obey the Constitution—if somebody will only tell him what it says."

One fact is clear: Police must be allowed a fair opportunity to do their job. To police its 200 million people the United States has 397,000 state and local law-enforcement officers. Only 70,000 are on duty on any 4 P.M.-to-midnight shift. With 7600 serious crimes reported every day (on the average), and untold thousands more unreported, police already have to pick and choose which they will investigate. Says Quinn Tamm, executive director of the International Association of Chiefs of Police, "It would be grand if the officer could play Sherlock Holmes and contemplate all aspects of a case for hours on end. But he has fifteen cases, and, in the real world, many of them simply cannot be solved without questioning." Even vast increases in police manpower and scientific techniques will not prevent a substantial loss in law-enforcement effectiveness. Some form of interrogation is necessary.

The American Law Institute, representing 1800 law professors, judges, prosecuting and defense attorneys, is working on a Model Code that provides police authority to "stop and frisk" citizens on the streets in suspicious circumstances, question them for twenty minutes without formal arrest, and question them at the police station up to four hours. They must warn the subject of his rights, and tape-record the station-house sessions so judges and jurors can be sure what goes on. On their own, New Orleans police have even installed a television-tape device so they can later show courts the whole interrogation process.

Find Out the Truth

The Supreme Court today is rewriting the Bill of Rights. Dominating this process are five Justices who apparently prefer turning patently guilty criminals loose if the slightest flyspeck can be found on police conduct. But, as Brooklyn's erudite prosecutor William I. Siegel reminded them last spring, "No human institution is perfect, and we cannot require from a prosecutorial apparatus a level of perfection not found anywhere else in human affairs. 'Ideal' is by definition unobtainable. The true function of a court is to find out where the truth lies." Even Chief Justice Warren has recognized that the Court is ill-fitted to "police the police" on a case-by-case basis, and has urged legislative action.

A wholesale revision of state and Federal laws is urgent. . . . If nothing is done, we will live under a system prescribed not by elected representatives but by a committee of five lawyers sitting in a faraway marble palace and unaccountable to anyone at the ballot box for the results of their legislating.

So extreme have the present Court rulings become that Federal Appeals Judge Wilbur K. Miller spoke for millions when he protested in Washington's Killough murder, "Nice people have some rights, too!"

COPS, COURTS, AND CONGRESS [4]

Supreme Court decisions in the field of law enforcement have spurred a bitter national debate. Some police officials believe they have been "handcuffed." A few even claim the new restrictions on police searches and questioning of suspects have "caused" the current increase in crime.

On the other hand, many attorneys and legal scholars insist the Court has done no more than provide needed protections for constitutional rights that would otherwise be violated. And they argue that these protections are needed to keep to a minimum the risk of convicting innocent people.

The controversy now involves the highest echelons of the national Government. Congressional hearings have been held on proposed laws and constitutional amendments to over-

[4] From article by Jon O. Newman, United States Attorney, District of Connecticut. *New Republic.* 156:16-20. Mr. 18, '67. Reprinted by permission of *The New Republic*, © 1967, Harrison-Blaine of New Jersey, Inc.

come the effects of Supreme Court decisions, and more hearings are planned. Recently seven members of the President's Commission on Law Enforcement and Administration of Justice urged serious consideration of far-reaching changes in the Fifth Amendment.

Of the many recent Supreme Court decisions on criminal law, there are two at the center of the controversy—*Mapp v. Ohio* in 1961 and *Miranda v. Arizona* in 1966. In both, a defendant was convicted for violating the laws of a state. The Supreme Court reversed both convictions and, in doing so, announced new rules to be followed by police and courts in all the states in all criminal cases.

To date the major battle has raged over whether the new rules governing the police are necessary to protect the rights of individual citizens or too restrictive to permit the police to protect the safety of all citizens. This dispute has obscured a second, very practical problem: even if the police rules are accepted, what should happen to the defendant when a policeman fails to observe the new rules? Should the policeman's error *always* benefit the accused? Is it always necessary, as Cardozo put it, that "the criminal is to go free because the constable has blundered"?

In *Mapp* the Supreme Court dealt with police searches and seizures. The Constitution's Fourth Amendment prohibits "unreasonable" searches, a somewhat vague standard which the Court has been defining over the years. In general, a search is "reasonable" if it occurs during a lawful arrest, or if a search warrant has been issued based on some solid evidence. The Ohio police officers in the *Mapp* case had committed an unreasonable search. No member of the Supreme Court doubted this, and even the lawyers for Ohio did not seriously dispute the point. But the issue was: Could the evidence unlawfully seized—dirty pictures—be used at trial as part of the case against Miss Mapp? On this question, a five-man majority of the Court said No and reversed the conviction for possession of pornography.

The Supreme Court announced a new rule that whenever police obtain evidence by an unlawful search, the evidence cannot be used at trial. Previously, the Court had allowed each state to decide for itself whether evidence illegally obtained would be admissible in its courts. Nearly half the states had kept the historic common law rule that evidence, if reliable, is admissible no matter how it came into the hands of the police. A gun that fired fatal bullets and that bore the defendant's fingerprints could be considered by a jury even though the police lacked a search warrant when they found the gun in the defendant's home. Under the new rule, the jury would never know about the gun and the defendant might well go free.

In *Miranda* the Court faced the difficult problem of police questioning of arrested suspects. The constitutional rule in this area, the Fifth Amendment, says no person shall be "compelled" to be a witness against himself. Again, the constitutional standard is not too clear, and Court decisions have filled out the meaning. A defendant cannot be required to testify at his trial and a suspect, being questioned before trial, cannot be subjected to any physical or psychological form of compulsion to extract a confession.

The Arizona police officers in the *Miranda* case obtained a confession of kidnaping and rape from the defendant. The questioning took two hours, there was no claim of physical abuse and the claim of psychological pressure was not convincing. In short, it could not fairly be said that the confession had been "compelled," and no member of the Court said otherwise.

Nevertheless, the Court went on to consider two other questions: Should there be a new rule to govern police when they question suspects, and can a confession obtained in violation of the new rule be used at trial to obtain a conviction? A five-man majority of the Court said Yes to the first question and No to the second.

The new rule announced in *Miranda* requires that all questioning of arrested suspects must be preceded by a clear warning to the suspect that he can remain silent, that what he says can be used against him, and that before answering he can consult with a lawyer, whether or not he is able to afford one. If a suspect freely agrees to be questioned after hearing these rights, then his confession passes muster under the Fifth Amendment. The Court said the new rule was necessary to guard against the possibility of a compelled confession.

Echoing *Mapp,* the Court also ruled that whenever the police fail to give the required warning, any statement made by the accused cannot be used against him at trial. Previously, the Court had tested the confession of a suspect solely by the standard of voluntariness. If the statement was voluntarily made, it could be used; otherwise it could not. And whether the suspect had been warned of his rights used to be only one of the many factors the Court would consider in deciding whether a statement was voluntary. Thus, if a suspect was adult, reasonably intelligent, and familiar with criminal proceedings, a confession made after only twenty minutes of questioning would have been admissible at his trial despite the absence of a warning as to his rights. But a statement obtained only after prolonged questioning of a youth of low intelligence might well be considered involuntary and therefore kept out at the trial. Of course, under the test of voluntariness, any evidence of physical coercion automatically vetoed use of a confession.

The critics of the *Mapp* and *Miranda* rules surely go too far when they claim that these new restrictions are somehow "causing" an increase in crime. People commit crimes for many reasons, but it is absurd to contend that a teen-ager deciding whether to steal a car goes ahead because he knows that if he is caught, the police will have to warn him before they can question him.

The more temperate critics do have a point when they observe that these restrictions will make the apprehension and prosecution of criminals less likely in *some* instances. However, there is scarcely any valid data to show that rates of detection or conviction are significantly lowered by observance of the new rules, though some decreases have been reported. But there is no dispute that as a result of the new rules, some convicted felons are set free, and charges against some dangerous criminals are dropped because a successful prosecution is impossible. A man who confessed to the brutal murder of his wife and children recently walked out of a New York City courtroom because of *Miranda* rule violations. The new rules have also freed hundreds of others whose guilt was absolutely clear.

Those who support the new rules often overstate their case in claiming that they are necessary to avoid convicting the innocent. Certainly the *Mapp* rule against using illegally obtained evidence cannot possibly add to the protection of an innocent person. If he is innocent, the most illegal search in the world will not produce evidence to convict him.

The *Miranda* rule comes closer to affecting the risk of convicting the innocent, but the relationship is more theoretical than real. Obviously, if a person is compelled to confess to a crime he did not commit and thereby convicted, the grossest miscarriage of justice occurs. The celebrated *Whitmore* case reminds us that this can happen. Yet what effect do the *Miranda* rules have? Any police officers corruptly bent on coercing an innocent man to confess will not be deterred one whit. They will falsely testify that they gave the required warnings and the suspect freely confessed.

When the Police Overstep the Rules

Nevertheless, there is a strong case for the basic protections involved in both *Mapp* and *Miranda*. *Mapp* seeks to protect the right of privacy—the hallmark of a free and civilized society. Few would seriously argue that police officers should be allowed to make unreasonable searches of homes and offices, even if the Constitution did not prohibit such tactics. And the best rationale for *Miranda* is simply elemental fairness. If a person does have the right not to answer police questions (which all concede), does it not make sense to tell him about that right and let him decide if he wants to exercise it? What good is a right if it remains unknown?

Let's agree that police officers should not make unreasonable searches and should not question suspects without advising them of their rights. The second problem remains: what happens when the rules are not observed? Does it necessarily follow that any time police overstep these rules, the evidence obtained cannot be used with the result that the defendant very likely goes free?

In *Mapp* the Supreme Court said that evidence unlawfully obtained must be excluded from a criminal trial because there was no other effective way to make sure that police observed the rule against unreasonable searches. Indeed, the other possible restraints upon the police had not over the years proved effective. In many states a police officer who searches unlawfully can be sued for money damages or prosecuted criminally, but successful suits against policemen are rare, and convictions almost nonexistent. Internal discipline by police departments has been used sporadically.

Thus the Supreme Court felt it faced the choice of either relying on these ineffective sanctions and always allowing the use of illegally seized evidence, or using the more reliable weapon of always excluding unlawful evidence. It chose the latter, believing that a police officer will not search unlawfully if he knows that whatever he would obtain could not be used to convict anyone.

The Sensible Middle Ground

There is, however, another choice: a flexible rule that excludes illegally seized evidence in most cases. Such a rule would very likely be just as much a restraint on improper police conduct as the *Mapp* rule of automatic exclusion. Most police officers conscientiously try to follow the rules laid down by the Constitution and the courts. For most of them, the likelihood that evidence obtained unlawfully will not be used at trial is sufficient to deter them from making illegal searches. They want to see criminals prosecuted successfully, and they will not deliberately break the rules, especially as long as there is a serious risk that their misconduct will free the accused. But these policemen are not further restrained by a rule of automatic exclusion. The threat of probable exclusion suffices.

As for the handful of unscrupulous policemen, the absolute rule of exclusion does not deter them at all. They take the attitude that their job is to catch the guilty man, whether by fair means or foul. If he is later freed by the courts because of police misconduct, they simply criticize the courts and go right on ignoring the rules.

If a flexible rule would not lessen the restraints on the police, would it have any benefits? Simply this: in appropriate cases a menace to society would be put in jail instead of being freed to rob, rape or murder. If society can gain that advantage without encouraging police misconduct, it is worth a try.

How would a flexible rule work? The decision to admit or exclude unlawfully obtained evidence would be left to the discretion of the trial judge, to be exercised with regard to certain specific criteria. Among these would be the kind of illegality, the good faith of the police, the seriousness of the crime, and the prosecution's need for the evidence.

A search may be unlawful because the police officer's warrant had some technical defect. That might be overlooked, but not an illegality due to the officer's careless failure to bother to get a warrant at all. Similarly, evidence might be allowed if obtained by an officer who had to make an on-the-spot decision whether to stop and get a warrant or search without one when he feared evidence would be removed and destroyed. But evidence would be kept out where the police officer not only overstepped the rules, but had no plausible excuse for doing so. These decisions might go in favor of admissibility where the crime is murder, and against admissibility in prosecutions for breach of the peace. The evidence would almost always be kept out if the prosecution had other evidence to make a case. But if, without the unlawfully seized evidence the prosecution has no case at all, the trial judge might decide to let the jury see it. No one factor would control. The trial judge would exercise his discretion after weighing all the relevant criteria. . . .

A similar approach should be used to deal with interrogation of suspects. The rules announced in *Miranda* requiring advice as to rights should be followed. But not every statement obtained in violation of these rules need be excluded. Here again, just the threat of probable exclusion will insure that most police officers will give the necessary warnings. And the few who flout the rules are not deterred by automatic exclusion. They either take credit for "breaking" the case and ignore the lack of successful prosecution or they falsely testify that the *Miranda* rules were complied with.

The trial judge should have discretion to admit or reject confessions even though the *Miranda* rules are not strictly followed. Of course, if the evidence shows that the confession is not voluntary, it would automatically be excluded. The risk of unreliability is too high to be tolerated, and any form of coercion is too hostile to our concepts of fairness. But if the officer gave substantially the *Miranda* warning, or if he forgot to give any warning under the pressure of a midnight street arrest of an armed hoodlum, or if the crime is serious, or the prosecution must fail without the confession, a trial judge should be permitted to weigh all these factors and then decide whether to admit or exclude the confession.

CONTROLLING CRIME NEWS [5]

Four days after the assassination of President Kennedy, the New York *Times* published a letter from its own managing editor, Turner Catledge. Catledge wrote that a *Times*

[5] From article by Robert M. Cipes, lawyer and writer. *Atlantic.* 220:47-53. Ag. '67. Copyright © 1967 by Robert M. Cipes. All rights reserved. Reprinted by permission. (This material appears in Chapter 5 of the author's book *The Crime War.* New American Library. New York. '68.)

news report had erred when it referred to Lee Harvey Oswald as "President Kennedy's assassin." Said Catledge: "Although Oswald was accused of the assassination and the Dallas police thought they had an airtight case against him, he was never tried and convicted. Under the American system of justice, he is innocent until proved guilty. Future articles and headlines will reflect that fact."

While such posthumous regard for Oswald's rights is overdone, it reflects growing concern with standards of crime reporting. There are surely more significant issues of public affairs, yet because the prerogatives of the press are involved, there are few which have generated so much newspaper space and such heated debate. In response to the Warren Commission Report, and with tensions heightened by a recent spate of sensational trials, the legal and journalistic professions are groping for standards which will bridge the uneasy gap between the constitutional rights of the press and those of the accused. An American Bar Association committee has drafted a tentative code to regulate crime publicity, which has met with almost uniform condemnation by newspaper publishers and editors. . . .

The publicizing of sensational crime is as old as crime itself. In America, with its dual institutions of trial by jury and assertive journalism, the key issue is the influence of publicity on the minds of jurors. One critic posed it this way: "In the case of a particularly audacious crime that has been widely discussed, it is utterly impossible that any man of common intelligence, and not wholly secluded from society, should be found who had not formed an opinion." This was in 1846. During the newspaper circulation wars at the turn of the century, Arthur Train called yellow journalism the "most vicious factor in the administration of criminal justice." Train damned the newspapers for creating false sympathy for defendants, rather than bias against them. This does not change the issue, of course; it simply illustrates a difference in environment.

Each decade has had its *causes célèbres,* and each *cause célèbre* has produced a wave of revulsion and talk of curbing excessive publicity. But it has remained just that—talk—with no tangible reforms. This time *may* be different. One result of the Warren Report was the appointment of the ABA [American Bar Association] committee to study publicity. It is known as the Reardon Committee, after its chairman, Justice Paul Reardon of the Massachusetts Supreme Court. Last October [1966], after two years of work, the committee released its recommendations. It found that most prejudicial material is not the result of independent news reporting but originates with law enforcement officers and lawyers (both prosecution and defense). Hence the committee recommends strong controls over all participants in a criminal case. Its theory is that by drying up the source, most offensive material will not find its way into the newspapers. The committee would not entirely immunize the press. It could be punished for contempt of court but only for flagrant abuses which affect the jury's verdict. . . .

Consistent with a resolve to clean its own house, the ABA committee begins by proposing a change in the canons of legal ethics. This would prevent lawyers from releasing any information or opinion about a criminal case with which they are associated "if there is a reasonable likelihood that such dissemination will interfere with a fair trial or otherwise prejudice the due administration of justice." The committee feels that the existing canon on publicity (adopted sixty years ago) is too general, and it has rarely been enforced. The new canon would bar lawyers' statements about the following: a defendant's prior criminal record or information as to his character or reputation; the existence or contents of any confession; the performance of any examination or tests or the defendant's refusal to submit to such an examination; the testimony of prospective witnesses; the possibility that the defendant will plead guilty; and any opinion as to the defendant's guilt or innocence, although a defense attorney may state that his client denies the charges.

During the trial itself, no lawyer can release or authorize any statement relating to the case, except that he may quote from or refer without comment to public records in the case. Lawyers who violated the canon would be subject to disciplinary action, which could mean suspension or disbarment. The restrictions are similar to those laid down by the Justice Department two years ago for Federal prosecutions. It is in state courts, however, that most crimes of violence are tried and that the worst publicity abuses occur. . . .

The Reardon Committee assumes that since most offensive publicity comes from the mouths of the trial participants, controlling them will indirectly cure abuses by the press. But what happens when the press acts on its own, when an editor personally initiates a prosecution? This was pretty much the situation in the Sheppard case. [Dr. Samuel Sheppard of Cleveland, Ohio, was arrested in 1954 and charged with killing his wife. He was found guilty and sentenced to life imprisonment.—Ed.] Federal District Judge Weinman, in reversing Dr. Sheppard's conviction in 1964, sized it up accurately in these words:

> If ever there was a trial by newspaper, this is a perfect example. And the most insidious violator was the Cleveland *Press*. For some reason that paper took upon itself the role of accuser, judge, and jury. The journalistic value of its front page editorials, the screaming, slanted headlines and the nonobjective reporting was nil, but they were calculated to inflame and prejudice the public. Such a complete disregard for propriety results in a grave injustice not only to the individual involved but to the community in general. . . . If ever a newspaper did a disservice to its profession; if ever the cause of freedom of the press was set back, this was it.

Only a month after the Sheppard case was decided by the Supreme Court, an event occurred which was to throw an already fuzzy subject into a state of confusion. On July 14, 1966, eight Chicago student nurses were slain in their dormitory. Effective police investigation quickly produced a suspect, Richard F. Speck, whose fingerprints were found in the dormitory and who was identified from a photograph by the lone survivor. Speck's photo was plastered on every front

page as a massive manhunt began. As a result of this publicity he was soon recognized by a physician treating him
after a suicide attempt.

In April, Speck was convicted of the eight murders and
sentenced to death. Since prejudicial publicity is bound to
be an argument on appeal, it is worth examining what that
publicity was. The first question is the propriety of news
disclosures before Speck's arrest. Taking the Reardon Report as a guideline, it specifically permits the police to release any information necessary to aid in the defendant's
apprehension or to warn the public of any dangers he may
present. Clearly there is a public interest in stopping a dangerous criminal before he commits further violence. Thus
the Chicago police acted properly in publishing Speck's picture and conducting the manhunt. It was not necessary, however, to announce positively and repeatedly that Speck was
"the killer," nor to disclose all the damaging evidence against
him, especially the fingerprint evidence (the accuracy of
which became a key issue at the trial). Even if disclosures
were necessary to aid in Speck's apprehension, public interest
in the disclosures ends when the suspect is arrested. Here,
however, the police superintendent compounded earlier in-
jury by adding even stronger public assurances of Speck's
guilt.

As the trial date approached, the judge granted a change
of venue from Chicago to Peoria. Though any difference in
the degree of news coverage was doubtful, the prosecuting
attorney did not oppose the motion. Like the judge, he would
do everything possible to preserve the conviction that would
almost certainly be obtained.

Shortly before trial, the judge issued a fourteen-point order regulating reporters. It covered everything from sketch-
ing in the courtroom (prohibited) to the consequence of
visiting the men's room during trial (loss of one's place).
More seriously, reporters were allowed to print only what
occurred in open court (a ban going far beyond anything
recommended by the Reardon Report). To make this worse,

they were forbidden to purchase transcripts—a strange way to ensure the accuracy of their reports.

The formal purpose of the trial judge was of course to protect the rights of defendant Speck. The actual purpose was to protect the state's conviction against reversal, and his own judicial rectitude. Without clear guidelines, the tendency of any trial judge, particularly in this era of close appellate oversight, is to err on the side of caution. Had the Reardon proposals been in effect in the Illinois courts during the Speck trial, the fourteen-point fiasco would never have occurred. All of which suggests that uniform standards in the end may be the press's best protection against arbitrary censorship.

It took six weeks to pick a jury in the Speck case, longer than it took to try the case. Partly this was because of the enormity of the crime; one murder gives each side 20 peremptory challenges, eight murders required 160. A "peremptory" challenge is exercised without stating any reason. It differs from a challenge "for cause" which the court exercises; there were also many of these in the Speck case, on grounds of opposition to capital punishment or an acknowledged belief in Speck's guilt.

For a crime like the Chicago massacre this six-week ritual is perhaps inevitable; the Reardon proposals would not avoid it. Indeed, by setting higher standards for jury selection they might actually aggravate the *voir dire* process. [*Voir dire* refers to a prospective juror's oath binding him to answer truthfully on his qualifications to serve.—Ed.] A juror who has formed an opinion about the defendant's guilt will be challenged for cause "unless the examination shows unequivocally that he can be impartial." And any juror who remembers any significant prejudicial information will be challenged "without regard to his testimony as to his state of mind."

The committee's conclusions about juror prejudice jibe with the results of a University of Chicago study. It found that pretrial examination is "grossly ineffective" to screen out bias; jurors often lie in a desire to be chosen, feeling that rejection reflects on their good faith. But existing rules, while irrational in assuming that court instructions can cure bias, at least have the pragmatic virtue of getting a jury selected. The *voir dire* examination in the Speck case might still be going on were the Reardon proposals in effect. Perhaps this only emphasizes the need to concentrate on the early stages of a case, before publicity has done its damage. Yet even here it would be visionary to expect perfect control. "There are some crimes so terrible," as the late Mark DeWolfe Howe said of the Speck case, "that you can't expect either the police or the press to observe the normal rules."

I have described the committee's indirect controls over publicity. How about controls placed directly on the press? Can a court legally hold a newspaper editor or publisher in contempt, as is commonly done under English rules? The Reardon Committee is convinced that the contempt power may be used, providing that it is limited to narrow and clearly defined situations. The committee attributes infrequent use of the power not so much to lack of authority as to the fact that courts have placed so few restraints on the press in the first place; in other words, there has been no occasion for enforcement. The Supreme Court has never passed upon use of the contempt power in a criminal *jury* trial, though it has reversed contempt convictions in several nonjury cases.

Under the committee's code there are two types of cases in which contempt may be appropriate. One is where a person, going beyond public records, makes a statement willfully designed to affect the outcome of a trial and which seriously threatens to have that effect. This applies, however, only when a jury trial is in progress, and thus may be criticized as too narrow. The type of pretrial poisoning which took place in the Sheppard case, for example, would not even be punishable under this clause. The committee has taken pains to come within the "clear and present danger" test which the Supreme Court created for First Amendment restrictions. No new legislation would be necessary to authorize this use of contempt, says the committee, except in a few states and in the Federal courts.

The second type of case permits contempt action against anyone (including a reporter) who violates a judge's order not to release information produced in a hearing closed to the public. This means that a judge cannot control disclosures (for example, of an inadmissible confession) unless he engages in the rather drastic procedure of closing his courtroom. If he follows the common practice of holding a hearing outside the jury's presence, he cannot prevent a reporter from disclosing what went on in the hearing. He can only request the reporter's cooperation. This is the present practice, and the Reardon Committee would not change it.

Last February [1967], another in the series of press-bar reports came out. This one was by a committee of the Bar Association of the City of New York, chaired by seventy-eight-year-old Judge Harold R. Medina of the Federal court of appeals. The Medina Report differs from the Reardon Report in denying power to hold news media in contempt and power to impose judicial controls on police. It is stronger than Reardon, however, in the restrictions it would place on lawyers, such as the duty to pressure clients and witnesses not to make out-of-court statements.

Judge Medina concluded his report "with a feeling of optimism," but unfortunately it proved to be misplaced. The judge was sure that the reluctance shown by news media was due to a threat to their independence and their constitutional rights. "Once it becomes firmly established that these fundamental rights are not in jeopardy and that their contribution to the purification of the judicial process is a voluntary one . . . their cooperation will be more generously forthcoming." Judge Medina, like Justice Tom Clark before him, was unprepared for the press's ungenerous treatment. "A code of silence," a "policy of secrecy in law enforcement," said the American Society of Newspaper Editors. "Frankly, I think those people don't realize who their friends are," Medina lamented.

The Editors' group believes that "putting prior restraint on news sources is equivalent to putting prior restraint on the press." What the drying up of "live" sources really means, however, is that the laborious task of digging out the facts must be done independently. Independent reporting of crime news is now largely a myth, according to a leading trial lawyer, Milton R. Wessel. He writes, "A large number of criminal indictments themselves would go completely unnoticed if not highlighted by a tip from the police or the district attorney, and sometimes by the defense counsel." Getting crime news without assistance between indictment and trial is even more difficult. "Absent an official tip of some kind, the reporter has no way of knowing what applications or motions will be heard." And covering the trial, says Wessel, is the most difficult, time-consuming job of all. "The press can't afford to assign full-time reporters . . . to any but the most exceptional cases. Stenographic transcripts are much too expensive, usually not available in time, frequently incomprehensible without exhibits and long study."

Recognizing that without help publicity will be limited, participants in a trial often point out to the press significant matters in the record, advise them when an "interesting" witness will testify. These officials, says Wessel, adopt "the fiction that they are merely reciting what is public, ignoring that it is not otherwise available and in any event they are editorializing by selecting episodes that they consider favorable. These comments . . . actually serve to create partisan news and prejudicial comment, which for practical reasons would never otherwise exist."

This is not mere theory. Wessel's point was proven in a long criminal trial in which both he and this author participated. At Wessel's request, the trial judge directed all participants to withhold any comment concerning the case until its conclusion. No restriction was placed upon the press itself, but it was arranged that "off the record" tips, summaries, and digests would not be given to reporters, nor would anyone furnish free copies of transcripts to them. Despite the obvious public interest in the case, writes Wessel, and trial disclosures of relatively sensational matter, "the amazing result was that there was absolutely no public comment anywhere about it for over a month following the beginning of trial." When one reporter finally did come upon the case, it was so difficult for him to follow that he ended up writing his articles on the theme "No Publicity in Fraud Trial." Wessel does not suggest that drying up present sources will foreclose press coverage; he believes that it will encourage the press to select and concentrate on those cases which are truly newsworthy. . . .

To understand the malaise of the American press I think we must look beyond the courtroom and the police station. The press was given its privileged status in order to question and, if necessary, counteract the exercise of government power. In that function it is defaulting. Writing in the *New York Review of Books,* Andrew Kopkind has described the real sources of news suppression: "In ways which journalists themselves perceive only dimly or not at all, they are bought, or compromised, or manipulated into confirming the official lies: not the little ones, which they delight in exposing, but the big ones, which they do not normally think of as lies at all, and which they cannot distinguish from the truth."

The press has been tilting at windmills in this noisy debate about crime news, dissipating energies which might be better spent in a larger struggle, already deferred too long. The press is off fighting brushfires while its own house is burning down.

V. CRIME, PUNISHMENT, AND PREVENTION

EDITOR'S INTRODUCTION

The articles in this section treat two separate aspects of crime prevention: the treatment of offenders to keep them from slipping back into a pattern of criminal behavior and action on the community level to prevent crime.

If there is any one indication of just how thoroughly the United States has failed to cope with crime, it is in the rate of recidivism—a technical term applied to the criminal who is a "repeater" and shuttles in and out of prisons. According to the President's Crime Commission "these repeated offenders constitute the hard core of the crime problem." One study quoted by the Commission indicates that about half of the parolees released in a three-year period in California were back in prison within another three years. One basic reason may be that the United States has never formulated a coherent philosophy of how offenders should be treated. Our theories of correction seem to alternate among the desires for revenge, deterrence, and rehabilitation.

The first article in this section, by Senator Edward M. Kennedy, gives a general overview of the U.S. crime problem with an array of suggestions covering law enforcement, sentencing, and parole policy and a concerted attack on hard-core poverty. In the second article, free-lance writer Samuel Grafton examines the role of punishment, parole, and probation and suggests that punishment should fit not only the crime but the criminal. The next selection contains excerpts from a speech by United States District Court Judge Warren E. Burger, who argues that the complex U.S. criminal justice system with its checks and reviews may be contributing to crime by building up prisoner hostility. This is followed by an article by University of Illinois sociology Professor Daniel Glaser describing society's objectives in imprisoning criminals.

Switching to society's role in preventing crime, the next two selections examine the question of gun control. The first selection is excerpted from testimony favoring gun control legislation given by Nicholas deB. Katzenbach (then Attorney General, now Under Secretary of State) before a subcommittee of the Senate Judiciary Committee; the second is an excerpt from testimony by Michigan Democratic Representative John D. Dingell opposing the legislation, given before the same committee. The next article, by William Bowen, an editor of *Fortune* magazine, argues that crime in the cities is "an unnecessary crisis." Bowen cites the examples of Atlanta and Chicago to prove his contention that aggressive and enlightened law enforcement combined with community cooperation can put a real dent in the crime rate. In the last selection, the President's Crime Commission makes a number of suggestions for a coordinated attack on crime in America.

A PLAN OF ACTION [1]

Day after day, newspaper headlines attest to the bitter truth of what every American knows: that crime in this country is increasing. Despite our wealth, our technological advances, our enlightened social legislation, we are failing to meet the first responsibility of government—the maintenance of law and order and of personal security. Today fear is a part of the daily lives of many Americans—whether they are walking alone on a dark street, or working in a shop, or driving a cab, or even sitting in their own homes. . . .

Each of these examples represents a different type of social problem. If we are to deal effectively with crime, there-

[1] From article by Senator Edward Kennedy, Democratic Senator from Massachusetts. *Saturday Evening Post*. 240:28-9. F. 11, '67. Reprinted by permission.

fore, we must reject pat answers and instead seek a program of crime control—a blueprint for action—that gives special attention to each different problem.

Consider, for example, the very special problem of drug addiction. For far too long we have treated addicts as if they were ordinary criminals, rather than victims of a serious disease. Because of our ignorance and indifference, we have failed both ourselves and the addicts, while their numbers have multiplied until there are today an estimated 100,000 addicts in the United States.

A new approach to this growing malignancy has long been required. Following California's pioneer program initiated in 1961, Congress passed legislation last session which would permit addicts in Federal cases to be placed under medical treatment rather than sent to prison. Because about half of those committed under the California program have subsequently returned to their communities and have not gone back to narcotics, there is good reason to believe that this Federal program will return many addicts to a normal life. If other states will follow this lead, medical treatment for addicts could make a significant contribution to our national fight against crime.

An equally significant part of any anticrime program, I feel, must be legislation to control the sale of firearms. Our Senate Juvenile Delinquency Subcommittee heard testimony indicating overwhelmingly that the present mail-order business in guns makes it ridiculously easy for juveniles, criminals, even lunatics to obtain firearms for less than the price of a pair of shoes. I know of no other country where it is as easy for dangerous and misguided members of society to obtain firearms as it is in the United States. Each year about a million weapons are sold by mail order, thousands to persons with criminal records. J. Edgar Hoover has stated that the "easy accessibility of firearms is a significant factor in the murders committed in the United States today." Nothing could testify more vividly to the truth of this warning than the example of Charles Joseph Whitman, who stood on top of the Texas University tower one horrible day last summer and shot fifteen people to death, wounding thirty-one others.

In the aftermath of that terrible tragedy some voices were heard calling for an end to easy accessibility of guns. But the outcry was short-lived, and without strong public support the proposed Federal legislation did not pass. Those of us in the Congress who are concerned about the need for effective gun controls require the active support of the American people, if we are ever to realize this goal, and I urge all Americans to demand effective new laws. [See "Why We Need a Gun Control Law" and "Guns Don't Cause Crime—People Do," below.—Ed.]

Our failure to fight crime successfully can be attributed only in part to such factors as the absence of gun controls and the lack of effective treatment programs for drug addiction. There is a much larger failure: Despite the dedicated efforts of many thousands of individuals, the traditional processes of our criminal justice system—the police, the courts, the correctional agencies, the probation and parole services— simply are not performing adequately.

Almost everyone will agree that the job of the policeman is more difficult today than it has been at any other time in our history. Even as the crime rate continues to grow, our concern for the protection of individual rights increasingly restrains the policeman's freedom of action. Unfair charges of police brutality are often made, and in many communities the policeman is treated abusively and contemptuously. In addition he is now often called upon not merely for police duties but also for the dangerous and strenuous job of riot control. Yet the sad fact is that police departments almost everywhere are understaffed and ill-equipped, and the low pay levels fail to attract enough of the high-quality personnel we need.

If this diagnosis is correct, then the prescription seems obvious: Devote the resources and attention necessary to hire more policemen, attract highly qualified men to police work, develop new techniques of police administration, apply the advances of modern science and technology to crime prevention and crime detection, and improve public understanding and support of our law-enforcement agencies.

There is every indication that, if we follow this prescription, we can make significant progress in combating crime. Take, for example, the experience of Chicago over the last six years under the outstanding leadership of Police Chief O. W. Wilson. Chief Wilson is a perfect example of the kind of man we must attract to police work in greater numbers. A former dean of the school of criminology at Berkeley, he is the author of *Police Administration,* the classic work in the field. When Mayor Daley brought Chief Wilson to Chicago in 1960, criminal activity was rising sharply in Chicago as it was in most large American cities. But whereas the trend has continued upward elsewhere, it has been on the downgrade in Chicago since Wilson took over. [O. W. Wilson retired as Chicago superintendent of police in August 1967.— Ed.]

How did he do it? To begin with, he had the unqualified support of the mayor and the city. With this kind of backing, both financial and political, Wilson introduced business-administration techniques and modern computer technology to police work. The computer system gives Chicago police almost instantaneous access to a vast range of important information on wanted persons and stolen property, and also keeps track of the kind and amount of crime going on in various parts of the city so that more policemen can be allocated to the areas most in need of protection.

This kind of information system made it possible for Wilson to implement his theory of aggressive preventive patrol, which actually minimizes the opportunity for crime by making police patrols as frequent and as conspicuous as possible, particularly in the areas of highest criminal activity.

In addition Wilson raised pay scales and substituted civilians in a host of office jobs, thus releasing over a thousand policemen for patrol work. He also encouraged Negro recruitment, stressed community-relations training, and impressed upon Chicagoans the fact that, if the police are to be successful in combating crime, they need the aid of the average citizen.

On April 13, 1964, he launched "Operation Crime Stop." The program is keyed to a card which reminds the holder that the police need the eyes and the ears of private citizens, provides a central number to call if a suspicious person or incident is seen, and indicates the information the police will need to respond effectively. The program has been remarkably successful. Some 7,600 offenders have been arrested by the Chicago police as a result of Crime Stop calls.

I believe this kind of program should be adopted in cities throughout the country; it would remind Americans that crime prevention is not solely the responsibility of the police, and it would serve to refute the notion, which I dispute, that Americans are not willing to involve themselves in the safety of others. Programs like Operation Crime Stop demonstrate that, though the problems of crime are massive and complex, citizens and communities can play an effective part in solving them. . . .

Chief Wilson's success in Chicago proves that good men and good ideas can greatly improve the quality of law enforcement. Wilson's kind of operation is expensive (Chicago's police budget has gone up almost 45 per cent in the last six years), but considering that crime costs run into billions of dollars annually—more than we are spending on Vietnam—money spent on effective crime prevention is definitely money well spent.

The same sort of diagnosis and the same sort of prescription can be made for our state prison systems. These systems have been too long ignored and denied the resources they need to modernize and to attract high quality personnel. A correctional system cannot live up to its name unless it can rehabilitate as well as confine. Criminal correction should be viewed as a process, beginning as soon as the lawbreaker is apprehended, which treats a criminal as an individual, teaches him the skills of a trade and the duties of citizenship and assists him materially in finding a job and returning to his community. To do this effectively requires large numbers of skilled personnel working in the field of correctional rehabilitation. It also requires construction of new kinds of facilities and emphasis on programs which seek rehabilitation through skill-training and participation in community life.

For the most part our present correctional systems are ill-equipped to accomplish these tasks. A national survey recently completed by the President's Crime Commission indicates how badly the existing jails and prisons fall down on their job of rehabilitation. It shows there is an appalling shortage of skilled personnel in this field. Of the 20,000 employees in local correction institutions, only about 5 per cent are involved in training and treatment—the vast majority of personnel are capable of performing only custodial functions. Thirty per cent of the state-operated adult institutions provide no vocational training. . . .

As in the area of law enforcement, however, there are some places where progress is being made. Available evidence indicates that the longer you keep a man in prison, the more likely he is to revert to crime when he is released. So several states and communities are experimenting with ways to return the individual to community life earlier. In New England, both Vermont and the Federal prison at Danbury, Connecticut, have instituted successful programs which release prisoners into the community for work, under careful supervision; Wisconsin, North Carolina and California have pioneered similar techniques.

And in California, Richard McGee, who heads the state's Youth and Adult Correction Agency, has demonstrated that imaginative thinking, coupled with additional resources and personnel, can help enormously in our war against crime. When McGee came to California in 1944, the state's prison system comprised little more than several maximum-security prisons, such as San Quentin and Folsom, run by their wardens as independent empires. The emphasis was on custody, not on treatment. McGee has changed things dramatically. Now there is a whole range of facilities, from maximum-security prisons to open institutions like the California Institution for Men at Chino, where inmates live on an honor system without the constraints of prison walls.

Recognizing the importance of building bridges between inmates and community, McGee also set up trade-advisory councils, whose members are representatives of business and labor in those occupations for which inmates are being trained. These representatives visit correctional institutions, advise on the type of equipment, training facilities and programs needed, and assist the inmates in getting jobs after they are released.

Another California experiment involved paroling youthful offenders immediately upon conviction under careful community supervision. In an effort to test the project's effectiveness, a control group of delinquents similar to those returned to the community was sent through the conventional process. The behavior of each group following discharge was watched closely. The amazing finding: The boys treated in the experimental project have returned to criminal activity at a rate almost 50 per cent lower than that of the boys treated by the more conventional methods. I think, however, that the real significance of this project is California's determination to actually test these new methods—to find out what works and what does not work. This kind of willingness to search for new and better techniques and to test their effectiveness has not been the hallmark of our criminal justice system. . . .

I recommend that we establish grant programs in selected universities around the country to foster training and research—criminal justice academies, I call them in the legislation I have introduced. This idea is the brainchild of Sheldon Glueck, the eminent Harvard criminologist, and in my judgment it makes good sense. The establishment of such regional centers would help show the nation the importance we place on work in this field; it would raise the status of our nation's effort to combat crime; and it would attract more able people to careers in criminal justice.

OF CRIME AND PUNISHMENT [2]

Not far back, as history goes, there was no doubt about what to do with a convicted criminal. He was punished: hanged, jailed, or transported overseas. The guilty man "paid his debt to society," and that was that. In our century, punishment fell into disrepute. Its usefulness, to the criminal and to society, was sharply questioned. It was pointed out that centuries of hangings and floggings and jailings had failed to eliminate or even decrease crime. Clearly, another approach was called for, and the new professionals—the psychologists, the social workers, the penologists—supplied that new approach. Punishment went out of style, and in its place came a host of modern concepts: rehabilitation, psychiatric help, counseling, retraining.

Today, there is some suspicion that the Age of Enlightenment has been no more successful than the Dark Ages in preventing crime and reforming criminals. A heated debate rages between those who would revive the old concept of punishment and those who call for even greater "understanding" of the criminal. And, as is often the case during such debates among experts, a confused and bewildered public finds it almost impossible to evaluate the conflicting philosophies. When a stern judge hands down a clearly punitive maximum sentence on a youthful first offender, we are shocked and outraged. When a paroled criminal who has been given a clean psychiatric bill of health murders an aged storekeeper, we are aghast.

What are the merits of the case? Are we too hard on criminals or too soft on them? *McCall's* researchers talked to social workers and penologists, to law-enforcement officers and

[2] From article by Samuel Grafton, free-lance writer. *McCall's*. 92:73+. Je. '65. Reprinted by permission.

judges, to probation officers and youth workers throughout the country, in an effort to sift out the essentials of the debate.

"Stiffer and stiffer punishments never helped anybody," says Professor Howard F. Gill, expert on penal administration at American University in Washington, D.C. In Florida, J. Hopps Barker, Miami-area supervisor for the State Probation and Parole Commission, echoes the thoughts of hundreds of probation workers as he says: "When you punish someone, you build up resentment and hate. You pay for it later. All sorts of punishments have been tried. There was a time when pickpockets were publicly hanged, but other pickpockets took advantage of the large crowds attracted to the executions to ply their trade." ...

"Punishment is a deterrent," says Seymour Gelber, assistant state attorney in Dade County (Miami), Florida. "Look at the burglars who purposely go unarmed because they know they'll get lighter sentences if caught. You'd be amazed at the number of robberies that did not result in killings because of it. If a judge gives a stiff sentence, the news gets around. A judge in Key West got that reputation—five years for robbery, not six months or a year—and criminals stayed away. There's all this talk about going to the roots of the problem, better housing, better education. How's that going to stop some guy from mugging you when you're out in the street tonight? Severe penalties are the stopgap until we get the Great Society." Gelber's superior, State Attorney Richard E. Gerstein, urges county judges to hand down a ten-year sentence for every armed robbery. He thinks it is time for "responsible leadership in this country to stand up against lawlessness."

There is no one who doesn't want to stand up against lawlessness. The question is how to do it. When children and young people are involved, the controversy is particularly bitter. Thus, in Los Angeles (one of six major areas covered by *McCall's* researchers in this survey of crime and punishment), workers in the sheriff's office cite mournfully the case of two brothers—David, eleven, and Sam, thirteen. In a three-month period last year, David was arrested for burglary on five occasions—and promptly released to his parents each time, pending final determination, by probation officers. His brother, Sam, during an eight-month period, was arrested and similarly released five times for burglary, illegal entry, and petty theft. Los Angeles probation officers have the power to release juveniles on their own authority pending hearing, and they use it in about 40 per cent of the almost 25,000 annual juvenile arrests. As a result, there is frequently strain between arresting officers and probation workers:

> The juvenile takes his offense too lightly, and he and his friends are encouraged to break the law, because they know nothing will happen [complains one Los Angeles juvenile officer]. People think detention is harmful. . . . It may be unpleasant. It's not harmful. It often has a strong rehabilitative effect. . . .

The most massive effort along these lines has been mounted by Judge Lester H. Loble, in Helena, Montana, who has stunned the juvenile-court world by obtaining a law from the Montana legislature allowing full publicity for court proceedings involving juveniles charged with felonies. In most jurisdictions, such cases are heard in private, so as not to stigmatize the youthful offender for life. (In California, typically, these cases are considered "hearings," not trials, and no accusation of crime is laid against the youngster.) But in Judge Loble's court, any spectator may come and go, and the local newspaper gives full coverage, doing so even in one case in which the defendant was age thirteen. Judge Loble has sentenced a sixteen-year-old to five years in the state reformatory, for aggravated assault, and a seventeen-year-old, who pleaded guilty to slugging a gas-station attendant during an armed robbery, to ten years in state prison. Members of the "tough" party, all over the country, have been delighted by Judge Loble's work and have hailed it as a solution to the vast problem of youthful crime. It has been claimed that felonies in Helena have dropped 49 per cent, and several states are considering adopting "Loble Laws" of their own.

The social-service world has, of course, viewed these developments with horror. Professional workers with juveniles feel that everything they have tried to accomplish in sixty or seventy years is challenged. Eighteen other Montana judges with jurisdiction over juveniles have not chosen to go along with Judge Loble. The National Council on Crime and Delinquency, a voluntary citizens' group which, among other activities, works to upgrade local probation services, has attacked the claim that felonies have dropped in Helena and has declared: "Such figures as we have been able to obtain indicate that juvenile offenses have substantially increased not only in Helena but throughout the state of Montana since the passage of the 'Loble Law.' " Three other states—Arizona, Florida, and Georgia—which adopted laws allowing the publicizing of names of juvenile defendants even before Montana did, all show large increases in crimes typically committed by juveniles.

Debate over the point is sharp and bitter. "There is no question in my mind that in serious crimes the name should be used," says Milwaukee County Judge Christ T. Seraphim. "I don't buy the idea that if you give the young hoodlum love and understanding, he will stay out of trouble." But Juvenile Court Judge John J. Connelly, in Boston, declares that the whole point of juvenile court is that "children are immature and prone to make mistakes . . . their chances in later life should be protected."

The vehemence of the debate suggests that we may be in for another one of those swings of the pendulum that so often afflict our society. For hundreds of years, we punished criminals brutally, executing even children for minor thefts. For a generation, the softer, social-work approach has been in the ascendance, perhaps moving too far in the direction of believing that any criminal can be redeemed. Now the "get tough" movement is gaining force again. Surely, there must be methods that fall between the extremes of brutality and starry-eyed idealism.

One person who has managed to avoid the pitfalls of extremism and, over more than a quarter of a century, has worked toward a lucid, realistic, and compassionate view of crime and punishment is James V. Bennett, the now retired director of the Federal Bureau of Prisons.

Writing "Of Prisons and Justice," Mr. Bennett has summed up the four different threads that go into judicial thinking at the moment of sentencing:

Although many of us have abandoned the idea that the purpose of a sentence is to inflict pain and suffering on the miscreant, there are still some courts who remain emotionally convinced that the prime function of the sentence is to punish the criminal. With more validity, other judges hold that the sentence should be severe enough to deter others from committing similar crimes. Some courts, like so many police administrators, declare that criminals should be committed permanently, in order to incapacitate them from further crimes. And other courts, remembering that most offenders in actual fact do come out of prison someday, say that the sentence should be so formulated as to promote the rehabilitation of the individual prisoner.

Mr. Bennett holds that these factors—punishment, deterrence, incapacitation, rehabilitation—all play a part in the determination of a sentence. The problem with which responsible jurists, penologists, police administrators, and social workers alike must struggle is the relative weight to be given to each of the considerations.

Mr. Bennett believes that the key to the solution of this problem lies in "balancing the requirement of the law with the characteristics of the individual offender." "The current trend in the United States," he says, "is unmistakably in the direction of an individualized penal treatment, administered within the framework of a flexible criminal code."

Many questions need to be asked, many fine distinctions made, Mr. Bennett believes, in arriving at a sentence that will best serve society, in both the short run and the longer run when a culprit returns to freedom.

How old is the defendant, how set in a pattern of crime? Has he been driven to his crime under the spur of economic necessity, or has it stemmed from calculated greed and a desire for gain at whatever cost to others? Has the crime been motivated in part by a mental or physical defect that has handicapped him in his efforts to get a job or even obtain the acceptance of society? Is he an alcoholic, more in need of treatment than of imprisonment? Or is he a sociopath whose "tendencies and crimes now virtually dictate, in the absence of any dependable knowledge concerning the cause of his blindly impulsive conduct or how to treat it, that he be kept almost indefinitely in confinement"?

The process of making the punishment fit not only the crime but also the criminal depends on a large measure of judicial flexibility within the law, and this flexibility is provided by the growing use of probation, parole, and indeterminate sentences, which give prison officials a good deal of leeway in determining when it is safe to release a prisoner. . . .

There can be no doubt that expert probation work, conducted by trained men, carrying reasonably small case loads, can do an enormous amount of good. In a famous three-year Michigan experiment, the "Saginaw Project," the Michigan Crime and Delinquency Council (an affiliate of the National Council on Crime and Delinquency) helped the city of Saginaw set up an almost ideal probation procedure. Probation officers' case loads were cut virtually in half, to fewer than fifty; all public officials cooperated. The results were startling: The courts ended up by sending only 19 per cent of felony convicts to prison, instead of 36 per cent, relying on probation to handle many of these men. Only 17 per cent of probation cases ended in failure, as compared with 32 per cent before the experiment.

Parole, like probation, is another instrument by which a sentence can be tailored to the individual, and its success also depends on the amount of supervision and attention the parolee gets. In 1964, Robert F. Kennedy, then the Attorney General, reported that the violation rate among juveniles and youths paroled from Federal institutions had been running around 50 per cent—a dismaying figure.

After releasing the prisoner at the end of his term, society has a choice between dropping him back into ordinary life, forgetting about his welfare (or the harm he may still do to others), and keeping him in view until a reasonable future seems likely.

"Halfway houses" are perhaps the most promising innovation in dealing with the transition from prison to freedom. These are residences in which ex-prisoners can live for a time after release, while becoming adjusted to being on their own. Typical are Chicago's Saint Leonard's House, run by an Episcopal priest, and Saint Anthony's Inn, run by Catholics.

Unless an ex-prisoner is fortunate enough to get this kind of help, his situation on release is often quite tragic, and the results may be dangerous. He usually receives (besides the ill-fitting suit) from ten to twenty-five dollars. His not unnatural impulse is to eat a steak dinner and sleep between clean sheets at a decent hotel on his first night out. By morning, his money is spent, and often he has no recourse but to look up some ex-convict he knows and plan another crime.

For the average citizen, the idea of being cast adrift, without money or connections, in a perhaps unfamiliar city would seem a nightmare; it is our regular procedure with many ex-prisoners. Fortunately, we are becoming somewhat more sophisticated about the problem: The United States Bureau of Prisons now operates four guidance centers, recently started in New York, Chicago, Los Angeles, and Detroit. Using living quarters near downtown areas, the centers provide places in which ex-prisoners can live while becoming adjusted. Employment counselors and caseworkers offer assistance, and an official is on duty twenty-four hours a day, to give advice and help and to smooth emergencies.

About three hundred young men have passed through the Chicago center in four years; its officials feel it has been successful. Instead of half of these youthful ex-prisoners going back to crime, less than 30 per cent do—which is, in this troubled social area, a distinct success. . . .

In addition to rehabilitation of those who can be helped, the citizen is entitled to permanent protection against those who cannot be reformed.

We have to accept the reality that a large number of people cannot adapt to society and never will and must be kept off the streets [says Tim Murphy, assistant United States attorney in the Court of General Sessions, in Washington]. One reason men on probation don't get the attention they need is that too much time is wasted on hopeless cases. After a certain amount of bad conduct, you should forfeit the right to go free.

Estimates of the number of "unreachables" among prisoners vary from a figure of 10 per cent, offered by a Florida judge, to an estimate of 35 per cent, by Warden Jack Johnson of Cook County (Chicago) Jail. Johnson, a liberal on penal questions, feels that reform efforts have to be concentrated on the remaining 65 per cent.

Slowly the idea of preventive detention is gaining ground —the thought that we don't really have to wait to act until a confirmed criminal beats or stabs a citizen, but can stop him before he does so, on the basis of his previous bad record and the most responsible professional prediction of his future. England has a preventive-detention law, under which incorrigibles are sent to a Channel island, where they can live under fewer restrictions than in prison, but without unlimited opportunity to hurt others.

Perhaps the biggest contribution the ordinary citizen can make in this field, where even the professionals are struggling for valid answers, is to refuse to fall in with the swings of the pendulum. It is easy enough to join the hue and cry for a crackdown on crime, and visionary enough to believe that every criminal can be reformed. Responsible public opinion, aware of the complexities of the problem, can support those programs and those public officials that promise not miracles but a balanced view of an admittedly difficult problem. It can demand protection, mindful of the fact that protection is a matter not only of clapping people into jail but also of preparing for their release. It can insist on better police work and better correctional work—and on the appropriation of funds that will make this possible.

Moreover, it can recognize that the prevention of crime and the treatment of criminals are inextricably tied up with every aspect of our society—the slums and the schools, the police and the courts, our mental-health programs and our correctional institutions, the firearms laws and the narcotics laws, the level of unemployment, and the moral framework in which young people are reared.

THE VIEW OF A FEDERAL JUDGE [3]

We often hear the claim that the breakdown of law and order is due to this decision or that decision of some court—most often of the Supreme Court.

It would be good if things were that simple, for, if the overruling of one or two opinions would solve the problems of crime, I suspect the Supreme Court would be willing to reconsider.

It is no aid to sensible public discourse to attribute the crime problem to any one decision or any one court.

Unfortunately, the problems and their solutions are far too complex to be resolved so easily. Let's probe into it.

Our whole history as a nation reflects a fear of the power of government and a great concern for individual liberty, and these feelings led us to place many protections around persons accused of crime. This has resulted in the development of a system of criminal justice in which it is often very difficult to convict even those who are plainly guilty. You know that this was a response to the abuses which people had suffered from the absolutist attitudes of rulers in Europe and in England in the sixteenth and seventeenth centuries.

[3] Excerpts from "Justice and the Search for Order," a speech by Judge Warren E. Burger of the United States Court of Appeals, Washington, D.C., delivered at Ripon College, Ripon, Wisconsin, March 25, 1967. Text from *U.S. News & World Report.* 63:70-3. Ag. 7, '67.

During the middle of this century—that is, from about 1933 to 1966—we have witnessed more profound changes in the law of criminal justice than at any other period in our history.

In addition to court decisions, there have been many legislative enactments in both Congress and state legislatures which have enlarged the protections of a person who is accused of crime.

No nation on earth goes to such lengths or takes such pains to provide safeguards as we do, once an accused person is called before the bar of justice and until his case is completed.

But governments exist chiefly to foster the rights and interests of its citizens—to protect their homes and property, their persons and their lives. If a government fails in this basic duty, it is not redeemed by providing even the most perfect system for the protection of the rights of defendants in the criminal courts.

It is a truism of political philosophy rooted in history that nations and societies often perish from an excess of their own basic principle. In the vernacular of ordinary people, we have expressed this by saying, "Too much of a good thing is not good." . . .

Our system of criminal justice, like our entire political structure, was based on the idea of striking a fair balance between the needs of society and the rights of the individual.

In short, we tried to establish order while protecting liberty. It is from this we derive the description of the American system as one of ordered liberty. To maintain this ordered liberty we must maintain a reasonable balance between the collective need and the individual right, and this requires periodic examination of the balancing process, as an engineer checks the pressure gauges on his boilers.

What are the dominant characteristics of our system of criminal justice today?

First, it is a system in which there are many checks and reviews of the acts and decisions of any one person or tribunal.

Second, it is a system which reduces to a minimum the risk that we will convict an innocent person.

Third, it is a system which provides the utmost respect for the dignity of the human personality without regard to the gravity of the crime charged.

There are exceptions to these generalities in some states and in some courts, but I think this is a fair appraisal of the plus side of our system of criminal justice....

Many people tend to think of the administration of justice in terms of the criminal trial alone, because this is the part of the process which occurs in the local community, but more than that because it is charged with the human element; it is exciting, colorful and dramatic. This is why the movies and TV have given so much time to criminal trials.

But this is not the whole of the administration of justice. The total process is a deadly serious business that begins with an arrest, proceeds through a trial, and is followed by a judgment and a sentence to a term of confinement in a prison or other institution.

The administration of justice in any civilized country must embrace the idea of rehabilitation of the guilty person as well as the protection of society. In recent years, we have been trying to change our thinking in order to deemphasize punishment and emphasize education and correction.

I have suggested that our system of trials to determine guilt is the most complicated, the most refined, and perhaps the most expensive in the world. We now supply a lawyer for any person who is without means and it is the lawyer's duty to exercise all of his skill to make use of the large numbers of protective devices available to every defendant. But where do we stand in the second stage of the administration of criminal justice—the treatment and disposition of those who are found guilty? We can gain some light by a comparison of our entire system with the countries of north Europe.

To begin with, we find that, in Norway, Sweden, Denmark and Holland, for example, there is much less crime generally than in the United States.

In Sweden, with 8 million people, there are about 20 murders each year, and crimes of other kinds are appreciably at a lower rate than in this country. Washington, D.C., with about 800,000 population, has 160 to 170 murders each year.

I assume that no one will take issue with me when I say that these north Europe countries are as enlightened as the United States in the value they place on the individual and on human dignity. . . .

Here in our comparison we encounter an interesting paradox. The swift and efficient justice in north Europe is followed by a humane and compassionate disposition and treatment of the offender. The whole process from the moment of arrest to the beginning of sentence is free from the kind of prolonged conflict which characterizes our administration of criminal justice, in which we have glorified and idealized the adversary system with its clash and contest of advocates.

I recently made comparisons of specific cases in Holland, Denmark and in the United States.

A typical case in Denmark, for example, is disposed of in about six weeks, and the first offender is almost always placed on probation under close supervision, and free to return to a gainful occupation and normal family life. It is not unusual, as I have said, for an American case to have two or three trials and two or three appeals over a period of from three to six years. When the American defendant is finally sentenced after this prolonged process, he has been engaged in a bitter warfare with society for years.

Even after the American is committed to a prison, we afford him almost unlimited procedures to attack his conviction or seek reduction of his sentence, and as a result American courts are flooded with petitions from prisoners, and the warfare continues. Under our system the "jailhouse lawyer" has become an institution. In short, while the correction system struggles to help the man reconcile his conflict with society, the statutes and judicial decisions encourage him to continue the warfare.

If the prisoner is like most human beings, his battle with authority and in the courts develops a complex of hostilities long before he goes to prison. These hostilities are directed toward the police who caught him, the witnesses who accused him, the district attorney who prosecuted him, the jurors who judged him, and the judge who sentenced him—and, finally, even the free public defender who failed to win his case.

I doubt that any defendant can conduct prolonged warfare with society and not have his hostilities deepened and his chance of rehabilitation damaged or destroyed. To encourage the continuance of this warfare with society after he reaches the prison hardly seems a sound part of rehabilitation, nor is it likely to contribute to restoring him to good citizenship.

Let me pursue our paradox: When we in America have lavished three or five or even ten years of the complex and refined procedural devices of trials, appeals, hearings and reviews on our defendant, our acute concern seems to exhaust itself.

Having found the accused guilty—as 80 to 90 per cent of all accused persons are found—we seem to lose our collective interest in him. In all but a few states we imprison this defendant in places where he will be a poorer human being when he comes out than when he went in—a person with little or no concern for law or for his fellow men and very often with a fixed hatred of all authority and order, and he is mindlessly and aggressively determined to live by plundering and looting.

In referring to the north Europe countries, I do not intend to suggest that they have completely solved all these problems, but only that they seem to deal with them more intelligently and less emotionally. They do so by recognizing that for the most part people who commit crimes are out of adjustment with society and that confusion and personality problems have something to do with this. They do not find that any useful social purpose is served by giving him two or three trials and two or three appeals and drawing out the warfare with society.

When they finally make the decision to deprive a guilty person of his liberty, they look ahead to the day when he will be free. They probe deeply for the causes of his behavior and, to do this, they place behavior scientists in the prisons.

We do this, but only in a token sense.

In the Federal prison system, which is far better than most of the states, there is a ratio of approximately 1 psychiatrist or psychologist for each 1,500 inmates.

In the state prisons the ratio of psychiatrists to prisoners is far less—as little as 1 psychiatrist for each 5,000 inmates; some states in the United States have none. And remember, we are talking about maladjusted people confined by society with a purpose of healing them.

Yet in tiny Denmark the ratio is roughly 1 psychiatrist for each 100 prisoners and, in the maximum-security prisons, where the dangerous and incorrigible prisoners are confined, the ratio is 1 psychiatrist for each 50 prisoners.

The vocational and educational programs available in our best prisons are a help, but the rate of return of prior offenders shows that something is not working. With few exceptions in the more enlightened states, the basic attitude of legislatures is that criminals are bad people who do not deserve more. Wisconsin happens to be among the most advanced of the states, and this is not surprising when we remember that most of those who populate this state derive from the enlightened countries of north Europe.

In part, the terrible price we are paying in crime is because we have tended—once the drama of the trial is over—to regard all criminals as human rubbish. It would make more sense, from a coldly logical viewpoint, to put all this "rubbish" into a vast incinerator than simply to store it in warehouses for a period of time, only to have most of the subjects come out of prison and return to their old ways.

Some of this must be due to our failure to try—in a really significant way—to change these men while they are confined. The experience of Holland, Sweden and Denmark and the other countries I mentioned suggests two things: that swift determination of guilt, and comprehensive study of each human being involved in extensive rehabilitation, education and training may be the way. This, and programs to identify the young offenders at a stage early enough to change them offer the best hope anyone has suggested.

In all of these countries there is also a more wholesome attitude toward the prisoner after he is released.

The churches and the government cooperate in maintaining what are called "after-care societies" which have existed for hundreds of years. Through these societies, each released prisoner has an experienced and friendly counselor and adviser to assist him with his problems. These people are volunteers who might be compared with citizens in this country who take part in the VISTA [Volunteers in Service to America] program or the Big Brother movement. . . .

We lawyers and judges sometimes tend to fall in love with procedures and techniques and formalism. But as war is too important to be left to generals, justice is far too important to be left exclusively to the technicians of the law.

The imbalance in our system of criminal justice must be corrected so that we give at least as much attention to the defendant after he is found guilty as before. We must examine into the causes and consequences of the protracted warfare our system of justice fosters.

Whether we find it palatable or not, we must proceed, even in the face of bitter contrary experiences, in the belief that every human being has a spark somewhere hidden in him that will make it possible for redemption and rehabilitation. If we accept the idea that each human, however "bad," is a child of God, we must look for that spark.

Should you come to the conclusion, as you watch our system of justice work, that we lawyers have built up a process that is inadequate or archaic or which is too cumbersome or too complex, or if you think we have carried our basic principle too far, or if for any reason you think the system does not meet the tests of social utility and fairness, you have a remedy. You have the right and the ultimate power to change it.

Neither the laws nor the Constitution are too sacred to change—we have changed the Constitution many times—and the decisions of judges are not holy writ.

These things are a means to an end, not an end in themselves. They are tools to serve you, not masters to enslave you.

THE PURPOSES OF IMPRISONMENT [4]

Historically there have been many successive objectives in the state's actions in dealing with criminals. All of these objectives still are with us and any realistic approach should take each into account. However, there has been a shift in emphasis from four earlier to two more modern penal interests. Let us consider the traditional objectives first, then examine recent concerns.

The original and still prominent interest of many people in reacting to crime is simply *revenge*. Governments initially became involved in dealing with criminals as a means of reducing the anarchy caused by private feuds between criminals and their victims, in which friends and families became involved until all were committing crimes against others. The government still is pressured to satisfy the public's sympathy for the victim and anger at the offender whenever a very revolting crime occurs. However, the public is less insistent on this demand now than formerly, particularly when it interferes with other objectives.

A second major public concern, related to the first, has simply been the *incapacitation* of criminals as long as they

[4] From "Crime and Its Control in the United States," by Professor Daniel Glaser, head of the Department of Sociology, University of Illinois. *Forensic Quarterly*. 41:355-65. Ag. '67. Reprinted by permission.

are considered dangerous. That is why we have prisons, just as it is the reason for security units in mental hospitals for that small proportion of the mentally ill who are considered dangerous to society. Since deprivation of liberty imposes suffering, incapacitation may often satisfy those interested in revenge, but modern penal officials deny that criminals are confined simply to make them suffer.

The third objective, related to the preceding two, is what the lawyers call *"general* deterrence." It is concerned not with the apprehended criminal so much as with deterring others who might contemplate crime if they thought they could succeed in it. While we presume that many are deterred from crime by the prospect of punishment, it is well established that the certainty of apprehension and punishment is much more related to general deterrence than is the severity of punishment, beyond some minimum effective penalty. This probably is why use or nonuse of the death penalty has had little relationship to the crime rate. Thus, murders in the United States declined from 10 per 100,000 population in 1930 to 5 per 100,000 in 1966, while executions in this period dropped from 200 to only 1 during 1966. . . . Apparently, other factors than general deterrence by capital punishment determine the murder rate.

The fourth traditional objective in government action toward criminals is what the lawyers call *"individual* deterrence." This is intended to discourage convicted criminals from returning to crime, rather than to prevent others from becoming criminals, although the same penalty may serve both individual and general deterrence objectives. Extensive research in the psychology of punishment shows:

(a) Punishment does not stop a person from repeating behavior that has been rewarding to him nearly as much as does reward for alternative behavior.

(b) Punishment of a person for pursuing highly gratifying behavior only promotes emotional disturbance in him if he does not have any other way of satisfying the need which the punished behavior served.

(c) The most effective way to change behavior is to make alternative behavior accessible and rewarding, while preventing the prohibited behavior from being rewarding. Important rewards here are not just material gain, but also social approval and a favorable conception of oneself.

The Goal of Treatment

The fifth objective in government action towards criminals is that which we call *treatment*. This, viewed broadly, includes all measures to increase the criminal's capacity to satisfy his needs by legitimate means. Deficiencies in education and vocational training are the most obvious handicaps in most offenders. Less than 5 per cent of prison inmates have completed high school, and a large proportion have had no sustained and successful job experience. This partially reflects the young age of most felons. Half the persons arrested for major crimes in the United States have not yet reached their nineteenth birthday. . . .

Almost everyone growing up in our society engages in a certain amount of delinquency. However, for most of us a combination of action by the family, the school, the church, or other agencies, or simply a fright from the prospect of apprehension or from punishment, moves us to curtail or terminate our delinquent pursuits. However, the typical major offender has gotten into a vicious circle in which his early delinquent activities handicap him in school or in seeking work, so that he is progressively more retarded in his studies and limited in employment prospects. Disproportionately, such youth also lack family ties capable of competing successfully with the influence of delinquent associates. The treatment task, therefore, is much more than a need to supply opportunities for education and work. Effective treatment also requires psychotherapeutic programs for persons whose emotional disturbance contributes to their crime or impairs their success in legitimate pursuits. Most crucial for

effective treatment, however, are measures to change the social circles from which offenders get their standards and support in delinquent and criminal behavior.

Social Reintegration

This brings us to a sixth objective in government policy
for dealing with criminals, one that has become increasingly
prominent during the 1960's. This objective is the *social
reintegration* of offenders. It has become increasingly evident
that merely correcting the vocational handicaps of delinquents and criminals is not likely to alter their behavior, if
they achieve friendship, approval, and even admiration in
delinquent or criminal circles and are alienated and un-
comfortable in the company of anticriminal persons. Essentially, the over-all task of correcting criminals might be summarized as one of increasing their "stake in conformity," in
terms of both the material and social awards they anticipate
from a law-abiding way of life, and decreasing their "stake
in criminality," by reducing their social dependence on delinquent associates. The ramifications of concern with this
social integration objective are manifold.

In the prison, recognition of the importance of a social
reintegration objective has meant a change from a repressive
relationship between staff and inmates to one of increased
communication between them. In progressive prisons efforts
are made to involve staff with inmates in collaborative relationships in the institution work places, schools, and recreation activities. . . .

These concerns also foster a reduction of mass treatment
of inmates in institutions; instead of handling them in large
groups, in a formal fashion, individual and informal procedures have been preferred. Thus, even in many maximum
security Federal prisons, and in some states, there has been
disappearance in recent years of long lines of men marching
under rules of silence and sitting at long narrow tables facing
in one direction in order to eat. Instead they move informally

and eat at four-man restaurant-type tables, sitting wherever they prefer, as the public does in a restaurant. In summary, the atmosphere of many prisons has been made much more like that in which the inmate will have to live if he is to succeed as a member of the general population in the free community. In addition, prisons have been made more permeable from the outside, with an increase in visitors and correspondence for prisoners, as well as the involvement of many volunteers from the community in prison recreation, study, hobby, and counseling groups.

Parole was initially introduced to defer decision on the optimum time for a prisoner's release until he could be observed in the institution, as well as to permit government employees to assist and control him somewhat after his release. One of the most dramatic developments in corrections has been the extent to which traditional parole programs have been supplemented by methods of temporary release of prisoners, and of making their complete release a much more gradual process. Temporary release on one or more occasions before the final parole date can include a furlough for a few days at a time, or to look for jobs, or simply for social adjustment. Those states which have used furloughs most extensively with adult offenders, Michigan and Mississippi, report less than 1 per cent failing to return.

Even more dramatic has been the rapid growth of work-release programs in prisons, whereby inmates may be employed at jobs in the community near the prisons, returning to the institution only at night and on weekends. Thousands of prisoners now are experiencing this realistic kind of employment while serving their sentences, in contrast to the traditionally limited prison work. They also thereby help to pay for their support and for that of their families, in addition to saving funds for post-release needs.

A still more graduated transition from incarceration to freedom occurs in the Federal prison system and in a few states where prerelease guidance centers have been established in those large cities from which most prisoners come and to which they return. These centers are places to which men, still legally prisoners, may be assigned a few months before their date of formal parole or discharge from sentence to prison. The men in these centers wear civilian clothes and leave the centers daily to seek jobs and to work at such jobs when they procure them. They return at night to the center where they can be counseled on their outside experiences. As their release date approaches they increasingly are given additional leaves from the centers to visit their prospective homes and for recreational purposes; some may even be permitted to move to their homes before their actual date of parole begins, returning to the center only for counseling sessions. . . .

An additional type of innovation in prison and parole which seems likely to increase is the very early release of offenders to highly intensive parole supervision. In California experiments a random half of youth correctional institution inmates were paroled within a month after their commitment, to case loads of only eight to twelve per parole officer. These officers were augmented by tutoring and counseling specialists at a community treatment center to which the parolees had to report daily. Different styles of parole supervision were specified for different types of offenders, ranging from highly supportive psychological counseling for the immature and inadequate to firmer controls for the more confirmed and manipulative delinquents. Results have been dramatically successful for most types of offenders with markedly fewer infractions on parole than occurred for those in a control group released after an average of eight months institutionalization to regular parole services. The cost of supervision in the community, even with these intensive staff services and small case loads, was still only about one third of the cost of institutional confinement.

WHY WE NEED A GUN CONTROL LAW [5]

There can be no more valid domestic concern today than the increasing growth, the increasing sweep, and the increasing violence of crime. Crime is increasing in the cities. It is increasing in rural areas. It is increasing, most rapidly of all, in the suburbs.

The national crime rate has doubled since 1940. Just since 1958, it has increased at a rate five times faster than the rate of population growth and just between 1963 and 1964, the FBI's Uniform Crime Statistics inform us, serious crimes increased by 250,000—a jump of 13 per cent.

These are figures which hardly require elaboration. The physical and fiscal toll of crime is learned anew each day in every city and community. What does require elaboration, however—what requires our most urgent and responsible attention is what we—the Federal Government and the Congress of the United States—are going to do about it. . . .

The subcommittee has received evidence disclosing that in 1963 alone, some 1 million "dangerous weapons" were sold by mail order.

It has also been disclosed that over a three-year period in Chicago, 4,000 persons bought weapons from only two mail-order dealers and that of these, fully one fourth had criminal records.

Almost every edition of every major newspaper carries stories reporting crimes involving guns. Most often we read of hand guns. But it remains a fact that fully 30 per cent of all murders committed by firearms involve rifles and shotguns.

These are facts of which we are rapidly becoming more urgently aware. There is a gathering momentum of sorrow,

[5] Excerpts from testimony of Nicholas deB. Katzenbach, former United States Attorney General and presently Under Secretary of State, May 19, 1965. United States. Congress. Senate. Committee on the Judiciary. Subcommittee to Investigate Juvenile Delinquency. *Federal Firearms Act; Hearings Pursuant to S. Res. 52.* 89th Congress, 1st Session. Supt. of Docs. Washington, D.C. 20402. '65. p 33-57.

outrage, and commonsense concerning the deadly uses to which firearms are put.

In a country in which more than half the 9,300 murders in 1964 were committed with firearms, many of them assuredly obtained by mail, congressional action is called for now.

In a country in which half the 20,000 suicides of 1963 were committed with firearms, many of them assuredly obtained by mail, congressional action is called for now.

In a country in which 26,000 aggravated assaults and the vast majority of 64,000 armed robberies were committed last year with firearms, congressional action is called for now.

In a country in which 216 law enforcement officers have been murdered with firearms in the past five years, compared with only 9 by other means, congressional action is called for now.

And in a country which has lost four Presidents to assassins' bullets, including the wrenching shock of November 22, 1963, congressional action is called for now.

As long as I live, I can never forget that it was a mail-order rifle—sent to a post office box that had been rented under an assumed name by a man with an established record of defection and mental instability—that killed President Kennedy.

I might add that it was a mail-order pistol that the same man used to commit murder upon a police officer.

It is for these compelling reasons of public interest and public safety that the Administration has proposed and most vigorously supports S. 1592, to control the mail-order sale of guns.

This measure is not intended to curtail the ownership of guns among those legally entitled to own them. It is not intended to deprive people of guns used either for sport or for self-protection. It is not intended to force regulation on unwilling states.

The purpose of this measure is simple: It is, merely, to help states protect themselves against the unchecked flood of mail-order weapons to residents whose purposes might not be responsible, or even lawful. S. 1592 would provide such assistance to the extent that the states and the people of the states want it.

First, the central provision of this measure is one which prohibits unlicensed persons from transporting, shipping, or receiving firearms in interstate or foreign commerce. It is this provision which eliminates the unarguable evils of mail-order traffic in weapons.

Sportsmen could continue to take their shotguns or rifles across state lines. Pistols could continue to be carried in conformity with present state laws. But no longer could hundreds and thousands of persons with criminal records buy weapons interstate from mail-order dealers—nor could the dealers sell to them. Sales would be made by local dealers and thus be subjects of local record-keeping.

These records would then have new meaning: they would not be rendered futile by a flow of mail-order guns. I think it is safe to say that this result alone would earn the committee and the Congress the gratitude of law enforcement officers in all parts of the country.

Second, a retail gun dealer would be required to limit his sales of hand guns to persons who are residents of his state and to limit all sales of weapons to those eligible by age and state and local law to own them. The age minimum established is twenty-one years, except for rifles and shotguns for which the age is eighteen.

Third, the bill would raise the annual license fees from the present token $1 for a dealer and $25 for a manufacturer to realistic figures, calculated to discourage applications from persons not genuinely in the firearms business. This provision is designed to bring about a higher level of responsibility in the firearms trade.

Fourth, another strengthening amendment would give the Secretary of the Treasury reasonable discretion as to who should be licensed to manufacture, import or deal in the deadly weapons with which the Federal Firearms Act is concerned.

GUNS DON'T CAUSE CRIME—PEOPLE DO [6]

As a member of Congress, a former prosecuting attorney, and an ardent conservationist, I am vitally concerned that the public interest be protected in the matter of laws governing the sale and distribution of firearms.

This should go without saying. Unfortunately, however, certain editorial proponents of this proposed legislation have been guilty of greatly oversimplifying the issue of Government regulation of firearms. As a result, many citizens opposed to S. 1592, such as myself and other Members of Congress—sincerely believing its enactment not in the public interest—have been the targets of editorial misrepresentation and unfair attack. . . .

The question is asked: Why should anyone object to a Federal law, the purpose of which is to place added legal controls on the sale and distribution of firearms to criminals?

Indeed, no one argues against this ostensible purpose of S. 1592. But those of us opposed to this bill respond with the question: If enacted, will S. 1592 accomplish this purpose, or will it—like so many nobly intended laws before it—merely compound the very social problem it seeks to remedy?

Consider the fact that we now have on the lawbooks of this nation over 20,000 laws governing the sale, distribution, and use of firearms. Contrary to what some of the more zealous antifirearms editorial writers would have us believe, the situation in the United States is certainly not one of unrestricted and unregulated firearms sale and usage.

S. 1592 is directed at keeping firearms out of the hands of the criminally irresponsible. Yet, despite 20,000-odd laws which, one way or another, are directed toward the same purpose, a rising national crime rate gives alarming evidence that the criminal element does not want for weapons with which to wage war against our law-abiding citizenry.

* Excerpts from testimony of Representative John D. Dingell (Democrat, Michigan), June 3, 1965. United States. Congress. Senate. Committee on the Judiciary. Subcommittee to Investigate Juvenile Delinquency. *Federal Firearms Act; Hearings Pursuant to S. Res 52.* 89th Congress, 1st Session. Supt. of Docs. Washington, D.C. 20402. '65. p 374-90.

Consider the fact that in the one state where the manufacture and sale of handguns is absolutely prohibited—the state of South Carolina—the rate of homicides and assaults by firearms is among the highest in the country. This is further evidence that while restrictive firearms laws may succeed in disarming the law abiding, they are ineffective in dealing with the lawbreaker.

Consider the fact that in New York, where the stringent Sullivan Act is aimed at disarming the individual, a soaring rate of violent crimes has made city streets unsafe for the unarmed, law-abiding citizen.

Not long back a young woman was assaulted by an individual, and in defense of herself pulled a switchblade knife. It was rather promptly reported in the papers. And as a result of this, in defense of her virtue and chastity, having exercised what I regard as the common and ordinary right of self-defense, she was threatened with prosecution, and indeed was actually brought into the criminal procedures for prosecution by the authorities of that state—while she was seeking solely to defend her person as a law-abiding citizen.

Theoretically, and according to the records, only 17,000 of New York City's 8 million inhabitants can lawfully possess handguns.

But daily we read in the papers of persons assaulted by slings and billies, knives and switchblades, zip guns, with literally no right to protect and defend themselves against these.

Although the law-abiding citizen cannot acquire a license for a handgun without searching police scrutiny, the criminal element is not the least bit hampered by the Sullivan Act.

S. 1592 is but another theoretical approach to a real problem—and it is doomed to fail in its purpose of disarming the criminally irresponsible.

Even if S. 1592 had been in effect on that tragic day in November of 1963, President Kennedy still could have been assassinated by the same person with the same or better weapon at the same time and place. The fact that it is illegal to discharge a firearm within the city limits of Dallas, and that murder is a capital offense in Texas, did not prevent this heinous crime.

If we are really interested in passing legislation to outlaw the assassination of our Presidents, we might give serious thought to pushing through legislation of the type which I have joined in sponsorship, and that is to make it a crime, punishable by death, to assassinate the President or the Vice President of the United States.

The same or better weapon could have been procured from a police auction, as a war trophy, from a hardware or sporting goods store, from loan by a friend or neighbor, by theft, or by inheritance.

The threat to our society today is not the weaponry of crime, but crime itself. Lawbreakers are no more apt to abide by laws governing possession of deadly weapons than they are to abide by general criminal laws.

Most latter-day legislation aimed at restricting firearms sale, distribution and usage has the effect of unilaterally disarming the law-abiding in the face of increasing crime rates.

Indeed, I would go so far as to say that it insures the criminal that his proposed victim will be unarmed while he has the advantage both of stealth, choice of time and place for the attack, and also the privilege of having a weapon which would be denied to the law-abiding citizen.

Specifically applied to one section of S. 1592, that part dealing with mail-order shipment of firearms, it should be kept in mind that the overwhelming majority of these purchases are made by law-abiding citizens. The criminal, as we have shown, will acquire or even handmold his weaponry in some way.

CRIME IN THE CITIES: AN UNNECESSARY CRISIS [7]

Without achieving a millennial abolition of human misery, some cities in the United States have managed to reduce

[7] From article by William Bowen, a member of the board of editors. *Fortune* 72:140-5+. D. '65. Courtesy of *Fortune* Magazine, December 1965.

their crime rates. While interim FBI reports showed a continuing nationwide increase in crime during 1965, several large cities, including Cincinnati, Oklahoma City, Rochester, Atlanta, and Chicago, reported substantial *decreases* during the first six or nine months of 1965. Atlanta, for example, recorded 13 per cent fewer "index crimes" during the first nine months of 1965 than during the corresponding period of 1964. Index crimes are the offenses that make up the FBI crime index: murder, nonnegligent manslaughter, forcible rape, robbery, aggravated assault, burglary, larceny ($50 or more), and auto theft. Starting earlier, Chicago recorded successive statistical decreases in crime in 1962, 1963, and 1964, years in which the nationwide crime index climbed precipitously. For the first nine months of this year Chicago reported a 15 per cent decline in index offenses from the same period of 1964.

Atlanta and Chicago have something to tell other cities about how to combat crime. But their most valuable and encouraging lesson is that it can be done—that it is possible to reduce the incidence of crime without waiting for the realization of a society in which nobody is poor, disgruntled, stunted, or warped. Atlanta and Chicago, it need hardly be said, have not abolished poverty, brought about a moral renaissance, or eliminated human misery, perversity, and folly. The nonsecret of the cities' success—relative success, that is, measured against the general failure elsewhere—is energetic, intelligent law enforcement, adequately supported by the political structure and by public opinion.

"Law enforcement," says Clinton Chafin, superintendent of detectives in the Atlanta police department, "is normally not going to be much better than the public wants it to be." When the mayor, civic leaders, and public opinion want better law enforcement, better law enforcement follows: the police department gets more money; police morale improves; the departmental managers think harder; patrolmen and detectives work harder; it becomes less difficult to recruit competent young men for the police force; citizens report crimes or suspicious goings-on more readily, and are more willing to appear as witnesses. The first step toward reducing crime rates, in short, is to want to reduce crime rates. . . .

The Force of Deterrence

In any city at any time, the police can reduce the incidence of crime within a limited area by increasing the number of man-hours of patrol in that area. But cities cannot afford to station a policeman on every block. To prevent crimes, society has to rely to a great extent upon deterrence —prevention when no policeman is in sight. In most communities in the United States over the past several years, deterrence has weakened. Society's never total capacity to assure that punishment follows crime has deteriorated, and that deterioration accounts in part for the increasing incidence of crime.

The force of deterrence in any community depends upon several interacting factors. One of these, of course, is the performance of the police—how quickly they respond to calls for assistance, how effectively they solve crimes and apprehend criminals. This performance is affected by the quantity and quality of police manpower, equipment, training, and morale.

Authorized manpower strengths of police departments have kept up with population growth, but the man-hours devoted to law enforcement, after traffic control and other police chores are taken care of, have not kept up with crime rates. In many cities the police department cannot even attract enough recruits to get up to authorized strength; not enough young men want to be policemen any more. Over most of the United States, police pay has not kept up with rising levels of civilian affluence during the postwar years: a bottom-rung patrolman gets $586 a month in New York, $496 in Philadelphia, $441 in Indianapolis, $390 in Miami. In many cities even a captain's starting pay is not much to look forward to: $591 a month in Indianapolis, for example, $681 in Philadelphia, $696 in Miami (in New York it's a relatively high $1,051). . . .

Police officials who believe that cities have skimped excessively on funds for law enforcement have a sturdy ally in James Vorenberg, Harvard Law School professor on leave as executive secretary of President Johnson's Commission on Law Enforcement and the Administration of Justice. "The policeman's job," Vorenberg says, "ought to be made more attractive in every way—in terms of what he does, what he's paid, and how he's respected in the community. We have no right to go on griping that the police aren't doing their jobs, and at the same time go on underpaying them and failing to provide them with the resources they need to do their jobs."

More is needed, however, than increases in police-department budgets, for the force of deterrence depends only in part upon the effectiveness of the police. Says Thomas J. Cahill, police chief of San Francisco (and the only policeman member of the President's commission): "The police alone cannot cope with crime. What we do is devoid of real results if what happens afterward is not conducted effectively—the work of prosecutors, judges, prison administrations, parole boards." Atlanta's chief of police, Herbert T. Jenkins, makes the same point: "The police, the courts, and the penal system are links in a chain. Law enforcement is no stronger than the weakest of the three." . . .

In Atlanta

In Atlanta, with the help of the newspapers and civic leaders, Mayor Ivan Allen, Jr., last year rallied public opinion behind a campaign to combat crime. He increased police pay and established a blue-ribbon crime commission. Prodded by the mayor and encouraged by the new public mood, the police department began thinking and working harder.

The department put more patrolmen and detectives on duty at times when, and places where, crimes were most likely to occur. In any big city crime tends to follow patterns of time and place. For example, more robberies and assaults occur on Friday (payday) and Saturday than on other days —people go out more, drink more, have more money in their pockets. The detective division organized an intelligence unit, the Fugitive Squad, and its original function of searching for wanted persons was expanded to include keeping track of people with felony records, whether wanted or not. "We try to know where they are and what they're up to," says Clinton Chafin, superintendent of detectives.

Atlanta's campaign against crime pushed beyond the boundaries of the city. The police department persuaded other agencies to cooperate in organizing a State Auto Police Squad to look for and recover stolen cars. Atlanta and the seven surrounding counties set up a joint police organization, Metropol, to cooperate in apprehending criminals who crossed city or county lines. "We're solving more of the crimes that occur," says Police Chief Herbert T. Jenkins. "Also, I have a feeling the courts have become more vigorous in their handling of criminal cases. All this helps to deter crime. The certainty of punishment is the greatest deterrent there is."

In Chicago

In Chicago, deterrence is working too. Chicago's success in coping with crime is largely traceable to one man, Orlando W. Wilson, sixty-five, superintendent of police since 1960. [He retired in August 1967.—Ed.] But Wilson would not have been able to achieve that success without the sturdy political and budgetary support he has received from Mayor Richard Daley.

Wilson, formerly dean of the School of Criminology at the University of California, has applied thought, rational administration, and modern technology to police work. The police department uses a computer to obtain almost instantaneous access to stored information about wanted persons and stolen automobiles. The administration of detective work has been completely restructured so that each felony is assigned to a particular detective who is responsible for solving it. This pinpointing of responsibility largely accounts for the improvement in the percentages of crimes solved.

Wilson's central contribution to the theory and practice of big-city police work is the emphasis he puts upon "aggressive preventive patrol." The core function of the police, as he sees it, is not to arrest criminals but to prevent crimes. A criminal act, he wrote in his textbook on police administration, "results from the coexistence of the desire to commit the misdeed and the belief that the opportunity to do so exists. . . . The elimination of the actual opportunity, or the belief in the opportunity, for successful misconduct is the basic purpose of patrol." Patrol, says Wilson, should be "frequent and conspicuous," and in Chicago it is. Since 1960 the number of police automobiles has increased from about 650 to 1,500. Patrol cars, black in pre-Wilson days, are now blue and white and are topped by a blue revolving light that in emergencies pierces spectacularly into the night. In Chicago you know the police are around.

To get maximum effectiveness out of its patrol force, a police department needs swift communications, and Chicago now has the most advanced police communication system in the United States, or the world. Much of the equipment was custom designed. The city is divided into eight zones, each with its own radio frequency and its own group of dispatch desks, called "consoles," at the communication center. But there is a single police-assistance number for the entire city, PO 5-1313. Under a unique arrangement with the Illinois Bell Telephone Company, the consoles are wired up with the telephone system in such a way that when somebody dials PO 5-1313 from anywhere in Chicago, the call is automatically directed to a console for the particular zone from which the caller is telephoning. By glancing at a map above the console, the dispatcher can swiftly tell what patrol car can be sent to the scene.

The average elapsed time between telephone call to dispatcher and radio message to patrol car is less than four minutes. In urgent situations the time can be reduced to less than one minute—the dispatcher tells the caller to hold on, radios the patrol car, sends it on its way, then proceeds to get additional information from the caller. It frequently happens that the patrol car arrives while the caller is still talking to the dispatcher.

COMBATING CRIME: SEVEN STEPS [8]

Despite the seriousness of the problem today and the increasing challenge in the years ahead, the central conclusion of the Commission [President's Commission on Law Enforcement and the Administration of Justice] is that a significant reduction in crime is possible if the following objectives are vigorously pursued:

First, society must seek to prevent crime before it happens by assuring all Americans a stake in the benefits and responsibilities of American life, by strengthening law enforcement, and by reducing criminal opportunities.

Second, society's aim of reducing crime would be better served if the system of criminal justice developed a far broader range of techniques with which to deal with individual offenders.

Third, the system of criminal justice must eliminate existing injustices if it is to achieve its ideals and gain the respect and cooperation of all citizens.

Fourth, the system of criminal justice must obtain more people and better people—police, prosecutors, judges, defense attorneys, probation and parole officers, and corrections officials with more knowledge, experience, initiative, and integrity.

Fifth, there must be much more . . . research into the problems of crime and criminal administration, by those both within and without the system of criminal justice.

[8] From the report of the President's Commission on Law Enforcement and Administration of Justice. *Challenge of Crime in a Free Society*. Supt. of Docs. Washington, D.C. 20402. '67. Summary, p v-xi.

Sixth, the police, courts, and correctional agencies must be given substantially greater amounts of money if they are to improve their ability to control crime.

Seventh, individual citizens, civic and business organizations, religious institutions, and all levels of government must take responsibility for planning and implementing the changes that must be made in the criminal justice system if crime is to be reduced.

In terms of specific recommendations, what do these seven objectives mean?

1. Preventing Crime

The prevention of crime covers a wide range of activities: Eliminating social conditions closely associated with crime; improving the ability of the criminal justice system to detect, apprehend, judge, and reintegrate into their communities those who commit crimes; and reducing the situations in which crimes are most likely to be committed.

Every effort must be made to strengthen the family, now often shattered by the grinding pressures of urban slums.

Slum schools must be given enough resources to make them as good as schools elsewhere and to enable them to compensate for the various handicaps suffered by the slum child—to rescue him from his environment.

Present efforts to combat school segregation, and the housing segregation that underlies it, must be continued and expanded.

Employment opportunities must be enlarged and young people provided with more effective vocational training and individual job counseling. Programs to create new kinds of jobs—such as probation aides, medical assistants, and teacher helpers—seem particularly promising and should be expanded.

The problem of increasing the ability of the police to detect and apprehend criminals is complicated. In one effort to find out how this objective could be achieved, the Commission conducted an analysis of 1,905 crimes reported to the Los Angeles Police Department during a recent month. The study showed the importance of identifying the perpetrator at the scene of the crime. Eighty-six per cent of the crimes with named suspects were solved, but only 12 per cent of the unnamed-suspect crimes were solved. Another finding of the study was that there is a relationship between the speed of response and certainty of apprehension. On the average, response to emergency calls resulting in arrests was 50 per cent faster than response to emergency calls not resulting in arrests. On the basis of this finding, and a cost effectiveness study to discover the best means to reduce response time, the Commission recommends an experimental program to develop computer-aided command-and-control systems for large police departments.

To insure the maximum use of such a system, headquarters must have a direct link with every on-duty police officer. Because large-scale production would result in a substantial reduction of the cost of miniature two-way radios, the Commission recommends that the Federal Government assume leadership in initiating a development program for such equipment and that it consider guaranteeing the sale of the first production lot of perhaps twenty thousand units.

Two other steps to reduce police response time are recommended:

> Police callboxes, which are locked and inconspicuous in most cities, should be left open, brightly marked and designated "public emergency callboxes."
> The telephone company should develop a single police number for each metropolitan area, and eventually for the entire United States.

Improving the effectiveness of law enforcement, however, is much more than just improving police response time. For example, a study in Washington, D.C., found that courtroom time for a felony defendant who pleads guilty probably totals less than one hour, while the median time from his initial appearance to his disposition is four months.

In an effort to discover how courts can best speed the process of criminal justice, the known facts about felony cases in Washington were placed in a computer and the operation of the system was simulated. After a number of possible solutions to the problem of delay were tested, it appeared that the addition of a second grand jury—which, with supporting personnel, would cost less than $50,000 a year—would result in a 25 per cent reduction in the time required for the typical felony case to move from initial appearance to trial.

The application of such analysis—when combined with the Commission's recommended timetable laying out time-spans for each step in the criminal process—should help court systems to ascertain their procedural bottlenecks and develop ways to eliminate them.

Another way to prevent crime is to reduce the opportunity to commit it. Many crimes would not be committed, indeed many criminal careers would not begin, if there were fewer opportunities for crime.

Auto theft is a good example. According to FBI statistics, the key had been left in the ignition or the ignition had been left unlocked in 42 per cent of all stolen cars. Even in those cars taken when the ignition was locked, at least 20 per cent were stolen simply by shorting the ignition with such simple devices as paper clips or tinfoil. In one city, the elimination of the unlocked "off" position on the 1965 Chevrolet resulted in 50 per cent fewer of those models being stolen in 1965 than were stolen in 1964.

On the basis of these findings, it appears that an important reduction in auto theft could be achieved simply by installing an ignition system that automatically ejects the key when the engine is turned off.

A major reason that it is important to reduce auto theft is that stealing a car is very often the criminal act that starts a boy on a course of lawbreaking.

Stricter gun controls also would reduce some kinds of crime. Here, the Commission recommends a strengthening of the Federal law governing the interstate shipment of fire-arms and enactment of state laws requiring the registration of all handguns, rifles, and shotguns, and prohibiting the sale or ownership of firearms by certain categories of persons —dangerous criminals, habitual drunkards, and drug addicts. After five years, the Commission recommends that Congress pass a Federal registration law applying to those states that have not passed their own registration laws.

2. New Ways of Dealing With Offenders

The Commission's second objective—the development of a far broader range of alternatives for dealing with offenders —is based on the belief that, while there are some who must be completely segregated from society, there are many instances in which segregation does more harm than good. Furthermore, by concentrating the resources of the police, the courts, and correctional agencies on the smaller number of offenders who really need them, it should be possible to give all offenders more effective treatment.

A specific and important example of this principle is the Commission's recommendation that every community consider establishing a Youth Services Bureau, a community-based center to which juveniles could be referred by the police, the courts, parents, schools, and social agencies for counseling, education, work, or recreation programs and job placement.

The Youth Services Bureau—an agency to handle many troubled and troublesome young people outside the criminal system—is needed in part because society has failed to give the juvenile court the resources that would allow it to function as its founders hoped it would. In a recent survey of juvenile court judges, for example, 83 per cent said no psychologist or psychiatrist was available to their courts on a regular basis and one third said they did not have probation officers or social workers. Even where there are probation officers, the Commission found, the average officer supervises seventy-six probationers, more than double the recommended caseload.

The California Youth Authority for the last five years has been conducting a controlled experiment to determine the effectiveness of another kind of alternative treatment program for juveniles. There, after initial screening, convicted juvenile delinquents are assigned on a random basis to either an experimental group or a control group. Those in the experimental group are returned to the community and receive intensive individual counseling, group counseling, group therapy, and family counseling. Those in the control group are assigned to California's regular institutional treatment program. The findings so far: 28 per cent of the experimental group have had their paroles revoked, compared with 52 per cent in the control group. Furthermore, the community treatment program is less expensive than institutional treatment.

To make community-based treatment possible for both adults and juveniles, the Commission recommends the development of an entirely new kind of correctional institution: located close to population centers; maintaining close relations with schools, employers, and universities; housing as few as fifty inmates; serving as a classification center, as the center for various kinds of community programs and as a port of reentry to the community for those difficult and dangerous offenders who have required treatment in facilities with tighter custody.

Such institutions would be useful in the operation of programs—strongly recommended by the Commission—that permit selected inmates to work or study in the community during the day and return to control at night, and programs that permit long-term inmates to become adjusted to society gradually rather than being discharged directly from maximum security institutions to the streets.

Another aspect of the Commission's conviction that different offenders with different problems should be treated in different ways, is its recommendation about the handling of public drunkenness, which, in 1965, accounted for one out of every three arrests in America. The great number of these arrests—some 2 million—burdens the police, clogs the lower courts and crowds the penal institutions. The Commission therefore recommends that communities develop civil detoxification units and comprehensive aftercare programs, and that with the development of such programs, drunkenness not accompanied by other unlawful conduct, should not be a criminal offense.

Similarly, the Commission recommends the expanded use of civil commitment for drug addicts.

3. Eliminating Unfairness

The third objective is to eliminate injustices so that the system of criminal justice can win the respect and cooperation of all citizens. Our society must give the police, the courts, and correctional agencies the resources and the mandate to provide fair and dignified treatment for all.

The Commission found overwhelming evidence of institutional shortcomings in almost every part of the United States.

A survey of the lower court operations in a number of large American cities found cramped and noisy courtrooms, undignified and perfunctory procedures, badly trained personnel overwhelmed by enormous caseloads. In short, the Commission found assembly line justice.

The Commission found that in at least three states, justices of the peace are paid only if they convict and collect a fee from the defendant, a practice held unconstitutional by the Supreme Court forty years ago.

The Commission found that approximately one fourth of the 400,000 children detained in 1965—for a variety of causes but including truancy, smoking, and running away from home—were held in adult jails and lockups, often with hardened criminals.

In addition to the creation of new kinds of institutions—such as the Youth Services Bureau and the small, community-based correctional centers—the Commission recommends several important procedural changes. It recommends counsel at various points in the criminal process.

For juveniles, the Commission recommends providing counsel whenever coercive action is a possibility.

For adults, the Commission recommends providing counsel to any criminal defendant who faces a significant penalty —excluding traffic and similar petty charges—if he cannot afford to provide counsel for himself.

In connection with this recommendation, the Commission asks each state to finance regular, statewide assigned counsel and defender systems for the indigent.

Counsel also should be provided in parole and probation revocation hearings. . . .

4. Personnel

The fourth objective is that higher levels of knowledge, expertise, initiative, and integrity be achieved by police, judges, prosecutors, defense attorneys, and correctional authorities so that the system of criminal justice can improve its ability to control crime.

The Commission found one obstacle to recruiting better police officers was the standard requirement that all candidates—regardless of qualifications—begin their careers at the lowest level and normally remain at this level from two to five years before being eligible for promotion. Thus, a college graduate must enter a department at the same rank and pay and perform the same tasks as a person who enters with only a high school diploma or less.

The Commission recommends that police departments give up single entry and establish three levels at which candidates may begin their police careers. The Commission calls these three levels the "community service officer," the "police officer," and the "police agent."

This division, in addition to providing an entry place for the better educated, also would permit police departments to tap the special knowledge, skills, and understanding of those brought up in the slums.

The community service officer would be a uniformed but unarmed member of the police department. Two of his major responsibilities would be to maintain close relations with juveniles in the area where he works and to be especially alert to crime-breeding conditions that other city agencies had not dealt with. Typically, the CSO might be under twenty-one, might not be required to meet conventional education requirements, and might work out of a store-front office. Serving as an apprentice policeman—a substitute for the police cadet—the CSO would work as a member of a team with the police officer and police agent.

The police officer would respond to calls for service, per form routine patrol, render emergency services, make preliminary investigations, and enforce traffic regulations. In order to qualify as a police officer at the present time, a candidate should possess a high school diploma and should demonstrate a capacity for college work.

The police agent would do whatever police jobs were most complicated, most sensitive, and most demanding. He might be a specialist in police-community relations or juvenile delinquency. He might be in uniform patrolling a high-crime neighborhood. He might have staff duties. To become a police agent would require at least two years of college work and preferably a baccalaureate degree in the liberal arts or social sciences.

As an ultimate goal, the Commission recommends that all police personnel with general enforcement powers have baccalaureate degrees. . . .

5. Research

The fifth objective is that every segment of the system of criminal justice devote a significant part of its resources for research to insure the development of new and effective methods of controlling crime.

The Commission found that little research is being conducted into such matters as the economic impact of crime; the effects on crime of increasing or decreasing criminal sanctions; possible methods for improving the effectiveness of various procedures of the police, courts, and correctional agencies.

Organized crime is another area in which almost no research has been conducted. The Commission found that the only group with any significant knowledge about this problem was law enforcement officials. Those in other disciplines —social scientists, economists and lawyers, for example—have not until recently considered the possibility of research projects on organized crime.

A small fraction of 1 per cent of the criminal justice system's total budget is spent on research. This figure could be multiplied many times without approaching the 3 per cent industry spends on research, much less the 15 per cent the Defense Department spends. The Commission believes it should be multiplied many times.

That research is a powerful force for change in the field of criminal justice perhaps can best be documented by the history of the Vera Institute in New York City. Here the research of a small, nongovernment agency has in a very short time led to major changes in the bail procedures of approximately one hundred cities, several states, and the Federal Government.

Because of the importance of research, the Commission recommends that major criminal justice agencies—such as state court and correctional systems and big-city police departments—organize operational research units as integral parts of their structures. . . .

6. Money

Sixth, the police, the courts, and correctional agencies will require substantially more money if they are to control crime better. . . .

Almost all of the specific recommendations made by the Commission will involve increased budgets. Substantially higher salaries must be offered to attract top-flight candidates to the system of criminal justice. For example, the median annual salary for a patrolman in a large city today is $5,300. Typically, the maximum salary is something less than $1,000 above the starting salary. The Commission believes the most important change that can be made in police salary scales is to increase maximums sharply. An FBI agent, for example, starts at $8,421 a year and if he serves long and well enough can reach $16,905 a year without being promoted to a supervisory position. The Commission is aware that reaching such figures immediately is not possible in many cities, but it believes that there should be a large range from minimum to maximum everywhere.

7. Responsibility for Change

Seventh, individual citizens, social-service agencies, universities, religious institutions, civic and business groups, and all kinds of governmental agencies at all levels must become involved in planning and executing changes in the criminal justice system.

The Commission is convinced that the financial and technical assistance program it proposes can and should be only a small part of the national effort to develop a more effective and fair response to crime.

In March of 1966, President Johnson asked the Attorney General to invite each governor to form a state committee on criminal administration. The response to this request has been encouraging; more than two thirds of the states already have such committees or have indicated they intend to form them.

The Commission recommends that in every state and city there should be an agency, or one or more officials, with specific responsibility for planning improvements in criminal administration and encouraging their implementation.

Planning agencies, among other functions, play a key role in helping state legislatures and city councils decide where additional funds and manpower are most needed, what new programs should be adopted, and where and how existing agencies might pool their resources on either a metropolitan or regional basis.

The planning agencies should include both officials from the system of criminal justice and citizens from other professions. Plans to improve criminal administration will be impossible to put into effect unless those responsible for criminal administration help make them. On the other hand, crime prevention must be the task of the community as a whole.

While this report has concentrated on recommendations for action by governments, the Commission is convinced that governmental actions will not be enough. Crime is a social problem that is interwoven with almost every aspect of American life. Controlling it involves improving the quality of family life, the way schools are run, the way cities are planned, the way workers are hired. Controlling crime is the business of every American institution. Controlling crime is the business of every American.

Universities should increase their research on the problems of crime; private social welfare organizations and religious institutions should continue to experiment with advanced techniques of helping slum children overcome their environment; labor unions and businesses can enlarge their programs to provide prisoners with vocational training; professional and community organizations can help probation and parole workers with their work.

The responsibility of the individual citizen runs far deeper than cooperating with the police or accepting jury duty or insuring the safety of his family by installing adequate locks—important as they are. He must respect the law, refuse to cut corners, reject the cynical argument that "anything goes as long as you don't get caught."

Most important of all, he must, on his own and through the organizations he belongs to, interest himself in the problems of crime and criminal justice, seek information, express his views, use his vote wisely, get involved.

In sum, the Commission is sure that the nation can control crime if it will.

BIBLIOGRAPHY

An asterisk (*) preceding a reference indicates that the article or a part of it has been reprinted in this book.

Books, Pamphlets, and Documents

Abraham, H. J. Freedom and the court; civil rights and liberties in the United States. Oxford University Press. New York. '67.

Abrahamsen, David. Psychology of crime. Columbia University Press. New York. '60.

Allen, F. A. Borderland of criminal justice; essays in law and criminology. University of Chicago Press. Chicago. '64.

American Bar Association. Commission on Organized Crime. Organized crime and law enforcement; ed. by Morris Ploscowe. Grosby Press. New York. '52-'53.

American Bar Association. Standing Committee on Public Relations. Law and courts in the news. The Association. Chicago. '60.

American Law Institute. Model code of pre-arraignment procedure; tentative draft no 1. The Institute. Philadelphia. '66.

Amos, W. E. and Wellford, C. F. eds. Delinquency prevention: theory and practice. Prentice-Hall, Inc. Englewood Cliffs, N.J. '67.

Association of the Bar of the City of New York. Special Committee on Radio, Television and the Administration of Justice. Freedom of the press and fair trial; Harold R. Medina, chairman. Columbia University Press. New York. '67.

Ausubel, D. P. Drug addiction: physiological, psychological, and sociological aspects. Random House. New York. '58.

Bakal, Carl. The right to bear arms. McGraw. New York. '66.

Barth, Alan. The fundamentals of freedom: what are they? where did they come from? what do they do for us and we for them? Center for Information on America. Washington, Conn. 06793. '62.

Barth, Alan. Law enforcement versus the law. Collier Books. New York. '63.
    Same with title Price of liberty. Viking. New York. '61.

Bedau, H. A. ed. Death penalty in America; an anthology. rev. ed. Doubleday. New York. '67.

Bell, Daniel. The end of ideology; on the exhaustion of political ideas in the fifties. Collier Books. New York. '61.

Bittle, W. E. and Geis, Gilbert. Longest way home; Chief Alfred C. Sam's back-to-Africa movement. Wayne State University Press. Detroit. '64.

Bloch, H. A. and Geis, Gilbert. Man, crime and society: the forms of criminal behavior. Random House. New York. '62.

Brenton, Myron. The privacy invaders. Coward-McCann. New York. '64.

Bromberg, Walter. Crime and the mind. rev. ed. Macmillan. New York. '65.

Bromberg, Walter and Bellamy, F. R. How to keep out of jail. F. Watts. New York. '66.

Cahn, E. N. ed. The great rights. Macmillan. New York. '63.

Caldwell, R. G. Criminology. Ronald. New York. '65.

Capote, Truman. In cold blood. Random House. New York. '66.

Carter, T. S. Crime prevention; notes for the guidance of police officers and security officers. Police Review Publishing Co. London. '65.

Cavan, R. S. Criminology. 3d ed. Crowell. New York. '62.

Cavan, R. S. Juvenile delinquency: development, treatment, control. Lippincott. Philadelphia. '62.

*Cipes, R. M. The crime war. New American Library. New York. '68.

> *Reprinted in this book:* Controlling crime news [excerpts from chapter 5]. Atlantic. 220:47-53. Ag. '67.

Cloward, R. A. and Ohlin, L. E. Delinquency and opportunity—a theory of delinquent gangs. Free Press. New York. '60.

Conrad, J. P. Crime and its correction; an international survey of attitudes and practices. University of California Press. Berkeley. '65.

Cook, F. J. Secret rulers: criminal syndicates and how they control the U.S. underworld. Duell. New York. '66.

Cray, Ed. The big blue line; police power vs. human rights. Coward-McCann. New York. '67.

Dash, Samuel and others. The eavesdroppers. Rutgers University Press. New Brunswick, N.J. '59.

Davis, F. J. and others. Society and the law. Free Press. New York. '62.

Endleman, Shalom, ed. Violence in the streets. Quadrangle. Chicago. '68.

Erikson, E. H. Childhood and society. Norton. New York. '50.

Fellman, David. Defendant's rights. Rinehart. New York. '58.

Felsher, Howard and Rosen, Michael. Justice U.S.A.? Macmillan. New York. '67.

Felsher, Howard and Rosen, Michael. Press in the jury box. Macmillan. New York. '66.

Friendly, Alfred and Goldfarb, R. L. Crime and publicity. Twentieth Century Fund. New York. '67.

Geis, Gilbert, ed. White-collar criminal. Atherton. New York. '68.

Gibbons, D. C. Changing the lawbreaker: the treatment of delinquents and criminals. Prentice-Hall. Englewood Cliffs, N.J. '65.

Glaser, Daniel. Effectiveness of a prison and parole system. Bobbs. Indianapolis. '64.

Glueck, Sheldon, ed. Problem of delinquency. Houghton. Boston. '59.

Glueck, Sheldon, and Glueck, E. T. Predicting delinquency and crime. Harvard University Press. Cambridge, Mass. '59.

Glueck, Sheldon, and Glueck, E. T. Ventures in criminology. Harvard University Press. Cambridge, Mass. '64.

Hoover, J. E. Crime in the United States; the uniform crime report, 1963. Beacon Press. Boston. '65.

Houts, Marshall. From evidence to proof. C. C. Thomas. Springfield, Ill. '56.

Jones, Howard. Crime in a changing society. Penguin. Baltimore. n.d.

Kamisar, Yale and others. Criminal justice in our time. University Press of Virginia. Charlottesville. '65.

Kaufmann, U. G. How to avoid burglary, housebreaking, and other crimes. Crown. New York. '67.

LaFave, W. R. Arrest: the decision to take a suspect into custody. Little. Boston. '65.

Lewis, Anthony. Gideon's trumpet. Random House. New York. '64.

Lewis, Oscar. La vida; a Puerto Rican family in the culture of poverty—San Juan and New York. Random House. New York. '66.

Library of Congress. Legislative Reference Section. Should law enforcement agencies in the United States be given greater freedom in the investigation and prosecution of crime? Selected excerpts and references relating to the national debate proposition for American colleges and universities, 1965-1966 . . . comp. by the American law division. 89th Congress, 1st session. (House Document no 304) Supt. of Docs. Washington, D.C. 20402. '65.

Loth, D. G. Crime in the suburbs. Morrow. New York. '67.

Mayers, Lewis. American legal system. rev. ed. Harper. New York. '64.

Messick, Hank. Silent syndicate. Macmillan. New York. '67.

Mills, James. Panic in Needle Park. Farrar. New York. '66.

National Council on Crime and Delinquency. Council of Judges. Guides for juvenile court judges on news media relations. The Council. 44 E. 23d St. New York 10010. '65.

*Ostermann, Robert. Crime in America. (Newsbook) National Observer. Silver Spring, Md. '66.

Packard, V. O. Naked society. McKay. New York. '64.

Paulsen, M. G. Equal justice for the poor man. (Pamphlet no 367) Public Affairs Committee. 381 Park Ave. S. New York 10016. '64.

Peterson, V. W. Gambling: should it be legalized? C. C. Thomas. Springfield, Ill. '51.

Redston, George and Crossen, K. F. Conspiracy of death. Bobbs. Indianapolis. '66.

Ringel, W. E. Arrests, searches, confessions. Gould Publications. Jamaica, N.Y. '66.

Roche, J. P. Courts and rights. 2d ed. Random House. New York. '66.

Savitz, L. D. Dilemmas in criminology. McGraw. New York. '67.

Sobel, N. R. New confessions standards: Miranda v. Arizona. Gould Publications. Jamaica, N.Y. '66.

Sokolow, M. and Louria, Donald. Nightmare drugs. Simon & Schuster. New York. '66.

Sykes, G. M. Crime and society. 2d ed. Random House. New York. '67.

Sykes, G. M. Society of captives; a study of a maximum security prison. Princeton University Press. Princeton, N.J. '58.

Taft, D. R. and England, R. W. Jr. Criminology. 4th ed. Macmillan. New York. '64.

Tiffany, L. P. and others. Detection of crime. Little. Boston. '67.

Tully, Andrew. FBI's most famous cases. Morrow. New York. '65.

Tyler, Gus, ed. Organized crime in America. University of Michigan Press. Ann Arbor. '62.

United States. Congress. House. Committee on the Judiciary. Law enforcement assistance; hearings before Subcommittee no. 3, May 20, 1965. 89th Congress, 1st session. Supt. of Docs. Washington, D.C. 20402. '65.

United States. Congress. Senate. Committee on Commerce. Interstate shipment of firearms; hearings on proposed bills S. 1975 and S.2345, amendments to the Federal Firearms Act. 88th Congress, 1st and 2d sessions. Supt. of Docs. Washington, D.C. 20402. '64.

United States. Congress. Senate. Committee on the Judiciary. Sub-
    committee on Criminal Laws and Procedures. Criminal laws
    and procedures; hearings held March 22-May 11, 1966 pursuant
    to bills S2187, S2188, S2189, S2190, and S2191, and 2578, re-
    lating to crime syndicates, obstruction of investigation, wire-
    tapping, immunity, narcotic drug addiction, and admissibility
    in evidence of confessions. 89th Congress, 2d session. Supt.
    of Docs. Washington, D.C. 20402. '66.

*United States. Congress. Senate. Committee on the Judiciary. Sub-
    committee to Investigate Juvenile Delinquency. Federal fire-
    arms act; hearings, pursuant to S. Res. 52. 89th Congress, 1st
    session. Supt. of Docs. Washington, D.C. 20402. '65.
        Reprinted in this book: Excerpts from testimony of Nicholas deB.
    Katzenbach. p 33-57; Excerpts from testimony of John D. Dingell. p 374-90.

United States. Department of Health, Education, and Welfare.
    National Institute of Mental Health. National Clearinghouse
    for Mental Health Information. Current projects in the pre-
    vention, control, and treatment of crime and delinquency.
    Supt. of Docs. Washington, D.C. 20402.
        Semiannual.

United States. Department of Health, Education, and Welfare.
    National Institute of Mental Health. National Clearinghouse
    for Mental Health Information. International bibliography on
    crime and delinquency. Supt. of Docs. Washington, D.C. 20402.
        Bimonthly

United States. President's Advisory Commission on Narcotic and
    Drug Abuse. Final report. Supt. of Docs. Washington, D.C.
    20402. '63.

*United States. President's Commission on Law Enforcement and
    Administration of Justice. Challenge of crime in a free society;
    a report. Supt. of Docs. Washington, D.C. 20402. '67.

*United States. Supreme Court. United States Reports. 384 U.S.
    436 (1966). Miranda *v.* Arizona. Supt. of Docs. Washington,
    D.C. 20402. '67.

Williams, E. B. One man's freedom. Atheneum. New York. '62.

Wolfgang, M. E. and others, eds. Sociology of crime and delin-
    quency. Wiley. New York. '62.

Yablonsky, Lewis. Tunnel back: Synanon. Macmillan. New York.
    '65.

Periodicals

America. 113:238-40. S. 4, '65. Crisis in crime control. G. R. Blakey.

America. 117:32-4. Jl. 8, '67. Crime, confessions and the Supreme Court. G. L. Chamberlain.

American Bar Association Journal. 51:534-8. Je. '65. Right to a fair trial. L. F. Powell, Jr.

American Bar Association Journal. 52:431-3. My. '66. New standards for criminal justice. J. E. Lumbard.

American Bar Association Journal. 52:443-7. My. '66. Reconciling the Fifth Amendment with the need for more effective law enforcement. R. A. Givens.

American City. 81:130+. Je. '66. Safest large city.

American City. 82:87-9+. F; 107-9. Mr. '67. Riot control. G. M. Chamberlain.

American Mercury. 84:54-60. Ap. '57. Should you own a gun? Karl Hess.

Annals of the American Academy of Political and Social Science. 339:1-10. Ja. '62. American penal system: spirit and technique. L. B. Schwartz.

Annals of the American Academy of Political and Social Science. 339:90-110. Ja. '62. Police authority and practices. R. C. Donnelly.

Annals of the American Academy of Political and Social Science. 339:111-24. Ja. '62. Procedures before trial. F. W. Miller and F. J. Remington.

Annals of the American Academy of Political and Social Science. 339:142-56. Ja. '62. Sentence and treatment of offenders. J. V. Bennett.

Annals of the American Academy of Political and Social Science. 339:157-70. Ja. '62. Juvenile delinquents and their treatment. P. W. Tappan and Ivan Nicolle.

*Annals of the American Academy of Political and Social Science. 347:51-7. My. '63. New York: criminal infiltration of the securities industry. L. J. Lefkowitz.

*Annals of the American Academy of Political and Social Science. 347:74-81. My. '63. New approach to the control of organized crime. Morris Ploscowe.

Annals of the American Academy of Political and Social Science. 347:82-92. My. '63. Local and state action against organized crime. E. H. Lumbard.

Annals of the American Academy of Political and Social Science. 347:93-103. My. '63. Federal viewpoint on combating organized crime. H. J. Miller, Jr.

Annals of the American Academy of Political and Social Science. 364:86-95. Mr. '66. Violence and organized crime. Gilbert Geis.

Annals of the American Academy of Political and Social Science. 371:104-26. My. '67. National goals and indicators for the reduction of crime and delinquency. Daniel Glaser.

Annals of the American Academy of Political and Social Science. 374:1-15. N. '67. On exploring the dark figure of crime. A. D. Biderman and A. J. Reiss, Jr.

Annals of the American Academy of Political and Social Science. 374:47-57. N. '67. Interrogation and the criminal process. A. J. Reiss, Jr. and D. J. Black.

Annals of the American Academy of Political and Social Science. 374:58-69. N. '67. Role of the police. B. J. Terris.

Annals of the American Academy of Political and Social Science. 374:82-91. N. '67. Community-based correctional treatment: rationale and problems. E. K. Nelson, Jr.

*Annals of the American Academy of Political and Social Science. 374:113-22. N. '67. Why organized crime thrives. H. S. Ruth, Jr.

Atlantic. 215:61-7. Ja. '65. Uncertain criminal law: rights, wrongs, and doubts. I. R. Kaufman.

Atlantic. 217:52-7. Ja. '66. Who goes to prison: caste and careerism in crime. Bruce Jackson.

Changing Times. 21:54-5. Jl. '67. Science vs. crime: new twists in an old war.

Christian Century. 80:955. Jl. 31, '63. Justice and the death penalty. D. R. Gordon.

Christian Century. 84:523-4. Ap. 26, '67. Only half-civilized.

Columbia Law Review. 65:848-66. My. '65. Police power to stop, frisk, and question suspicious persons.

Commonweal. 85:281. D. 9, '66. Crime in the streets.

Commonweal. 87:9-10. O. 6, '67. Great juggling act. John Leo.

Congressional Digest. 44:225-56. O. '65. Should law enforcement agencies be given more freedom in crime investigation and prosecution? pro & con.

Congressional Digest. 45:289-314. D. '66. Question of enacting proposed Federal "gun control" legislation; pro & con.

*Congressional Digest. 46:193-224. Ag.-S. '67. Congress and the national crime problem; pro & con.

Cornell Law Quarterly. 39:195-212. Winter '54. Public security and wire tapping. Herbert Brownell, Jr.

Crime and Delinquency. 12:165-9. Ap. '66. Lawyer and his juvenile court client. J. L. Allison.

Current. p 41-7. F. '67. How to safeguard privacy. Alan Westin.

Current History. 52:321-6. Je. '67. Genesis of crime. R. K. Woetzel.

Current History. 52:327-33. Je. '67. Organized crime in the United States. G. R. Blakey.

Current History. 52:334-40+. Je. '67. Independent offender. R. W. England, Jr.

*Current History. 52:349-53+. Je. '67. Drug addiction and crime. Charles Winick.

Current History. 53:8-14+. Jl. '67. Local and state law enforcement today. V. W. Peterson.

Current History. 53:65-9+. Ag. '67. U.S. courts and criminal justice. W. M. Beaney.

Current History. 53:88-93+. Ag. '67. Prisons and prison reform. J. P. Conrad.

Current History. 53:102-6+. Ag. '67. Criminal and the community. Gus Tyler.

Editorial Research Reports. 2 no 11:685-700. S. 22, '65. Compensation for victims of crime. R. L. Worsnop.

Editorial Research Reports. 1 no 13:243-60. Ap. 5, '67. Wiretapping and bugging. Jeanne Kuebler.

Esquire. 65:59-67+. Mr. '66. Logistics of junk. David Lyle.

Esquire. 65:96-7+. My. '66. Bugging the bedroom. Nicholas Pileggi.

Esquire. 65:102-3. My. '66. You ought to be left alone. E. V. Long.

Field & Stream. 68:12+. Ap. '64. Anti-gun extremists are at it again. Richard Starnes.

Forensic Quarterly. 41:171-7. My. '67. Crime and the ghetto. W. M. Young, Jr.

Forensic Quarterly. 41:195-206. My. '67. "Hue and cry" for a modern era. J. E. Hoover.

Forensic Quarterly. 41:233-42. My. '67. Gun control legislation: a question of extent. F. L. Orth.

*Forensic Quarterly. 41:355-65. Ag. '67. Crime and its control in the U.S. Daniel Glaser.

Forensic Quarterly. 41:453-66. N. '67. Combating crime through improved police-community relations. A. S. Trebach and J. H. Stein.

Forensic Quarterly. 41:477-84. N. '67. Fact and fable about wire tapping and bugging. E. S. Silver.

Forensic Quarterly. 41:495-8. N. '67. Oregon work release program. G. W. Randall.

*Fortune. 72:140-5+. D. '65. Crime in the cities: an unnecessary crisis. William Bowen.

Harper's Magazine. 224:46-50+. Mr. '62. Great narcotics muddle. B. H. De Mott.

Harper's Magazine. 228:121-36+. Ap. '64. Special supplement on crime and punishment; symposium.

Harper's Magazine. 229:62-8. D. '64. Traffic in guns: a forgotten lesson of the assassination. Carl Bakal.

*Harper's Magazine. 234:50-4. F. '67. Big city thieves. John Bowers.

Journal of Criminal Law, Criminology and Police Science. 57:123-9. Je. '66. Police in a changing society [Great Britain; address]. P. A. Devlin.
    Reprinted from Police Journal, London, February 1966.

Journal of Criminal Law, Criminology and Police Science. 57:265-70. S. '66. Democratic restraints upon the police. F. E. Inbau.

Journal of Criminal Law, Criminology and Police Science. 57:271-82. S. '66. Supreme Court and the police: a police viewpoint. V. L. Broderick.

Journal of Criminal Law, Criminology and Police Science. 57:291-300. S. '66. Crime, the courts, and the police. O. W. Wilson.

Journal of Criminal Law, Criminology and Police Science. 57:305-11. S. '66. To police the judges—not just judge the police. D. W. Craig.

Ladies' Home Journal. 82:74-5+. Mr. '65. Mail-order guns. T. J. Dodd.

Law and Contemporary Problems. 31:253-71. Spring '66. Right to privacy and American law. W. M. Beaney.

Law and Contemporary Problems. 31:281-306. Spring '66. Privacy: its constitution and vicissitudes. Edward Shils.

Life. 58:105-18. Mr. 5, '65. Realities we must face but won't. James Mills.

Life. 63:94-7. S. 8, '67. Carlos Marcello: king thug of Louisiana.

Life. 63:98-102+. S. 8, '67. Mobsters in the marketplace: money, muscle, murder. Sandy Smith.

Life. 64:44-51. Ja. 5, '68. Mob: a classic case history of how the Mafia finds a pigeon and penetrates respectable segments of our society. Sandy Smith and William Lambert.

Look. 29:23-4. N. 30, '65. New hope for drug addicts. R. H. Berg.

Look. 30:20-7. My. 31, '66. Suburbs: made to order for crime. J. R. Moskin.

Look. 31:101-4+. Mr. 7, '67. Chairman of the national crime commission answers some tough questions about crime. N. deB. Katzenbach.

Look. 32:14-21. F. 6, '68. Police in crisis: white cop and black rebel. Fletcher Knebel.

McCall's. 92:92-3+. Mr. '65. Climate of crime. Samuel Grafton.

McCall's. 92:112-13+. Ap. '65. Our new drug addicts. Samuel Grafton.

McCall's. 92:110-11+. My. '65. What do we want from our policemen? Samuel Grafton.

*McCall's. 92:73+. Je. '65. Of crime and punishment. Samuel Grafton.

McCall's. 94:93+. F. '67. Trial by headline. Louis Nizer.

McCall's. 95:58-9+. F. '68. Privacy. A. F. Westin.

Nation. 196:49-52. Ja. 19, '63. Addiction: beginnings of wisdom. A. R. Lindesmith.

Nation. 201:527-9. D. 27, '65. Cops, guns, and homicides. Sol Rubin.

Nation. 203:693. D. 26, '66. High cost of imprisonment.

Nation. 204:307-8. Mr. 6, '67. Crime & affluence: case of the culpable victim. Michael Fooner.

Nation. 205:115-16. Ag. 14, '67. Crime and politics. Gilbert Geis.

Nation. 205:360-5. O. 16, '67. Hooked on law enforcement. E. Z. Friedenberg.

*National Observer. p 1. F. 12, '68. How organized crime expands and prospers. M. R. Arnold.

National Review. 18:362-4. Ap. 19, '66. Has the Fifth Amendment become a menace to human rights? Park Chamberlain.

National Review. 18:606-8. Je. 28, '66. Don't say a word, Mac; Supreme Court decision.

Nation's Business. 55:84-6. O. '67. Bitter world of the policeman.

New Republic. 154:14-16. F. 12, '66. After the arrest: interrogation and the right to counsel. A. M. Bickel.

New Republic. 155:19-22. Jl. 30, '66. Lawless lawmen. Alan Barth.

New Republic. 155:16-22. D. 24, '66. Wiretap war. R. M. Cipes.

*New Republic. 156:16-20. Mr. 18, '67. Cops, courts, and Congress. J. O. Newman.

New York Times. p 31. S. 27, '67. Nixon links crime to legal system. R. B. Semple, Jr.

New York Times. p 69. O. 22, '67. Organized crime called "bugaboo." S. E. Zion.

New York Times. p 1+. N. 4, '67. Johnson predicts a revolt by public against crime. R. B. Semple, Jr.

New York Times. p 35+. N. 4, '67. 20th precinct: violence and misery. Maurice Carroll.

New York Times. p 18. N. 6, '67. Sweden is trying a "family prison." S. R. Conn.

New York Times. p 52. N. 26, '67. Eavesdropping curbed on coast.

New York Times. p 7. D. 20, '67. New tack in bugging. Fred Graham.

New York Times. p 27. D. 31, '67. Lucchese "family" active in Florida. Edward Ranzal.

New York Times. p 30. Ja. 12, '68. Drug scene: nation's illegal traffic is valued at up to $400-million annually. Martin Waldron.

New York Times. p 1. Ja. 25, '68. Wall Street found infiltrated by organized crime rings. Maurice Carroll.

New York Times. p 1+. Ja. 29, '68. Six precincts in slums produce third of city's violent crimes. David Burnham.

New York Times. p 1. F. 8, '68. President urges concerted drive to combat crime. Max Frankel.

New York Times. p 41. F. 12, '68. City courts facing a growing crisis. E. C. Burks.

New York Times. p 41. Mr. 8, '68. Underworld is plaguing Mafia with abductions. Richard Severo.

New York Times. p 38. Mr. 14, '68. U.S. legal system called a failure. S. E. Zion.

New York Times. p 1+. Mr. 28, '68. Arkansas prisons: a grisly record. Walter Rugaber.

New York Times. p 46. Ap. 10, '68. Senate's own riot [editorial].

New York Times. p 52+. My. 20, '68. Fear of muggers looms large in public concern over crime. David Burnham.

New York Times. p 1+. Je. 6, '68. Johnson appoints panel on violence. Max Frankel.

New York Times. p 1+. Je. 7, '68. President prods Congress as House votes crime bill. Max Frankel.

*New York Times. p 34. Je. 11, '68. Johnson statement on violence.

New York Times. p 1+. Je. 13, '68. Senators predict strict gun curbs as pressure rises. J. W. Finney.

New York Times. p 20. Je. 13, '68. Strict gun control practiced abroad. Albin Krebs.

New York Times. p 1+. Je. 15, '68. Rifle group mounts drive against gun controls. J. W. Finney.

New York Times. p 1+. Je. 16, '68. Top arms makers back ban on sale of rifles by mail. J. W. Finney.

New York Times. p 1+. Je. 20, '68. President signs broad crime bill with objections. Max Frankel.
  Transcript of President's statement on signing crime and safety bill. p 23.

New York Times. p 1+. Je. 25, '68. President calls for registering of all firearms. Max Frankel.
  Text of President's message to Congress. p 24.

New York Times Magazine. p 15+. O. 13, '63. Robert Kennedy defines the menace. R. F. Kennedy.

New York Times Magazine. p 23+. S. 20, '64. Walls do have ears. Vance Packard.

New York Times Magazine. p 36+. N. 29, '64. Criminal gets the breaks. Daniel Gutman.

New York Times Magazine. p 34-5+. N. 7, '65. When the cops were not "handcuffed." Yale Kamisar.

New York Times Magazine. p 27+. N. 21, '65. We ask the wrong questions about crime. W. M. McCord.

New York Times Magazine. p 36-7+. O. 2, '66. Confession debate continues. I. R. Kaufman.

New York Times Magazine. p 36-7+. N. 6, '66. Judges go back to school. Gertrude Samuels.

New York Times Magazine. p 8-9+. Je. 18, '67. Normal week for crime. Robert Rice.

New York Times Magazine. p 44-5+. D. 10, '67. Cops' right (?) to stop and frisk. F. P. Graham.

*New York Times Magazine. p 19+. Ja. 28, '68. Just call "the doctor" for a loan. F. J. Cook.

New York Times Magazine. p 23-5+. My. 19, '68. Why we are having a wave of violence. J. Q. Wilson.

Newsweek. 69:65. Je. 5, '67. Crime and publicity.

Newsweek. 70:24. Jl. 31, '67. Crime in the suburbs.

Newsweek. 71:75. F. 5, '68. Two sides of the story: police-press cooperation.

PTA Magazine. 61:2-3. Ap. '67. Crime in our communities. Jennelle Moorhead.

*Reader's Digest. 89:53-60. D. '66. Let's have justice for non-criminals, too! E. H. Methvin.

Reader's Digest. 89:127-9. D. '66. Are we a nation of hoods? Patty Johnson.

Reader's Digest. 92:75-80. Ja. '68. Our alarming police shortage. William Schulz.

Reader's Digest. 92:129-31. F. '68. Wanted: police weapons that do not kill. Arnold Sagalyn and Joseph Coates.

Redbook. 128:76-7+. F. '67. Police. Sam Blum.

Reporter. 31:33-5. O. 8; 8. N. 5, '64. Gun law that didn't go off E. B. Drew.

Reporter. 36:43-5. Ja. 12, '67. Corpus Christi's squad car lawyer. James Biery.

Reporter. 37:37-41. D. 14, '67. Justice of sorts. C. P. Crow.

*Reporter. 38:30-1. F. 8, '68. Pros and cons of stop and frisk. R. H. Kuh.

Saturday Evening Post. 237:68-70. Je. 6, '64. Big brother is listening. B. H. Bagdikian.

Saturday Evening Post. 239:12+. Jl. 30, '66. Speaking out: give drugs to addicts so we can be safe. J. J. Goldstein.

Saturday Evening Post. 239:74-8. Ag. 13, '66. Britain's Rx for our drug addicts. John Kobler.

Saturday Evening Post. 240:25-7+. F. 11, '67. Criminal and the law. Martin Mayer.
Adapted from the author's book: The lawyers. Harper. New York. '67.

*Saturday Evening Post. 240:28-9. F. 11, '67. Plan of action. E. M. Kennedy.

*Saturday Evening Post. 240:38-47. Ap. 22, '67. Arrested by detectives Valesares and Sullivan—Charge: murder. B. J. Friedman.

Saturday Evening Post. 240:27-31. N. 18, '67. Mafia: how it bleeds New England. Bill Davidson.

Saturday Review. 47:18. Ag. 1, '64. Case for registering guns. Tom Batman.

Saturday Review. 49:25+. Ja. 29, '66. Justice in the courtroom: can the poor get it? Gertrude Samuels.

Saturday Review. 49:79-80. D. 10, '66. Four-letter word called news; objections to American Bar Association's proposals to safeguard criminal cases against prejudicial publicity. R. L. Tobin.

Saturday Review. 50:48. Jl. 1, '67. Humane policing. E. F. Fennesy, Jr. and others.

Science. 153:1080-3. S. 2, '66. Victim-induced criminality. Michael Fooner.

Science. 156:1579-82. Je. 23, '67. Crime control: task force urges use of science and technology. J. Anderson.

Science Digest. 62:38-40. D. '67. Chromosomes and crime. J. A. M. Graham.

Science News. 90:305-6. O. 15, '66. Rethinking crime. P. McBroom.

Science News. 91:11. Ja. 7, '67. Does law make crime?

Senior Scholastic. 88:6-10. Mr. 18, '66. Rising storm over crime and the courts [with comments].

Senior Scholastic. 90:7-10+. F. 17, '67. Crime and the lawbreaking mentality.

Senior Scholastic. 90:11-12. F. 17, '67. Is the U.S. coddling criminals? [pro and con discussion]

*Senior Scholastic. 90:10-13. Ap. 14, '67. Electronic eavesdropping; is ours a bugged society?

*Senior Scholastic. 91:18-20. N. 30, '67. Courts: pyramid of U.S. justice.

*Senior Scholastic. 92:4-9. F. 15, '68. Crime and lawlessness: who's to blame, the police or the public?

Time. 87:40. Mr. 25, '66. Code for cops & confessions.

Time. 88:96+. O. 7, '66. Free press & fair trial: silencing the bar and the police; American Bar Association's report.

Time. 89:20-1. Mr. 24, '67. Crime & the great society: findings of the President's Commission on Law Enforcement and Administration of Justice.

Time. 89:38+. Je. 23, '67. Crusading in Indianapolis.

*Time. 90:18-19. Jl. 28, '67. Violence in America.

Time. 90:51. N. 3, '67. When defendants testify.

Trial. 4:9-11. D. '67-Ja. '68. New discipline: judicial administration. Earl Warren.

U.S. News & World Report. 56:69-72. Ap. 20, '64. There is a tendency to tolerate crime; interview. W. H. Parker.

U.S. News & World Report. 57:89-90. N. 9, '64. An answer to the rise in crime and violence; excerpts from address, September 8, 1964. G. B. McClellan.

*U.S. News & World Report. 58:56-60+. Ap. 26, '65. Warning to parents: why young people go bad; interview. Sheldon Glueck and E. T. Glueck.

U.S. News & World Report. 59:60-3. Jl. 5, '65. Lawlessness in U.S. —warning from a top jurist; address, June 17, 1965. C. E. Whittaker.

U.S. News & World Report. 59:67. Ag. 9, '65. We mollycoddle criminals. J. E. Hoover.

U.S. News & World Report. 59:68-9. Ag. 9, '65. Are courts to blame? or police? or society? interview. W. H. Parker.

U.S. News & World Report. 60:102-4. Ap. 18, '66. FBI's war on organized crime. J. E. Hoover.

*U.S. News & World Report. 61:51-2. Ag. 1, '66. Policeman looks at crime; interview. O. W. Wilson.

U.S. News & World Report. 62:86. F. 6, '67. What the British are doing to crack down on crime; interview. R. H. Jenkins.

*U.S. News & World Report. 63:70-3. Ag. 7, '67. What to do about crime in U.S.; excerpts from address delivered at Ripon College, Ripon, Wisconsin, March 25, 1967. W. E. Burger.

U.S. News & World Report. 63:12. Ag. 21, '67. New evidence of the terrific spurt of crime in America.

U.S. News & World Report. 63:41-3. S. 25, '67. Era of growing strife in U.S.

U.S. News & World Report. 64:49-51. F. 5, '68. Crime problem: why it's not solved.

University of Pennsylvania Law Review. 103:157-67. N. '54. On current proposals to legalize wiretapping. L. B. Schwartz.

Vital Speeches of the Day. 32:351-2. Mr. 15, '66. Crime reporting: need for professionals; address, February 14, 1966. N. deB. Katzenbach.

Vital Speeches of the Day. 34:22-4. O. 15, '67. Crime in the city: can it be controlled? address, June 5, 1967. H. R. Leary.

Vital Speeches of the Day. 34:114-16. D. 1, '67. Crime: a contemporary responsibility; address, October 16, 1967. H. C. Donnelly.

*Wall Street Journal. p 1. Ja. 18, '68. Crime and labor: mobsters grab power in 16 teamster locals in the New York area. Nicholas Gage.

Washington Post Potomac Magazine. p 20-7. Ja. 28, '67. How people stay off juries. Harriet Douty.